Two Rotors: One Planet

Peter Wilson

Printed in the United Kingdom
First printing, 2020

ISBN: 978-1-8380443-0-5 (paperback)
ISBN: 978-1-8380443-1-2 (eBook)

TJR Publishing
threejourneysround@btinternet.com

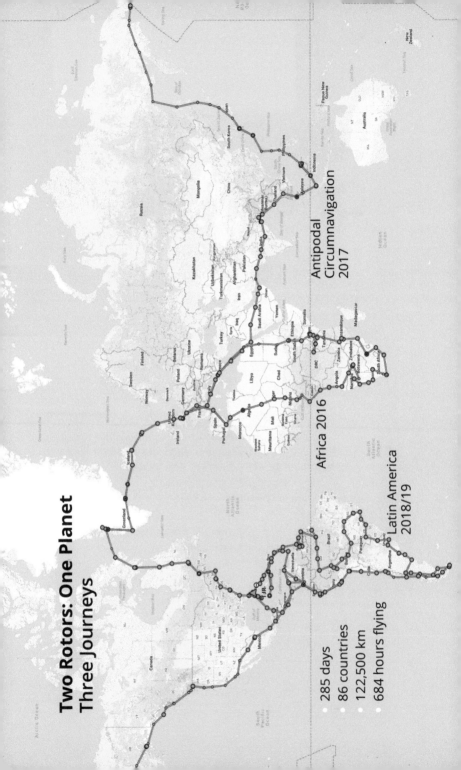

Two Rotors: One Planet
Three Journeys

Antipodal
Circumnavigation
2017

Africa 2016

Latin America
2018/19

- 285 days
- 86 countries
- 122,500 km
- 684 hours flying

"An astonishing and inspiring view of our rapidly changing world"

Dr Nigel Winser FRGS
Life Scientist and former
Executive Vice President of Earthwatch

———————

"An absolutely stunning achievement"

Jennifer Murray
Businesswoman, artist, mother of three and
first woman to fly a helicopter solo around the world

———————

"Peter visited some of the best locations in the biosphere"

Gérard Moss, MBE **& Margi Moss**
Pilot, public speaker, environmentalist, explorer and
first person to fly a motor glider solo around the world

———————

"The lecture, delivered in front of royalty here in Oman, was inspiring, and revealed an extraordinary attention to detail not only in the form of complex expedition logistics, but also social messaging"

Mark Evans MBE, FRGS
Explorer, Executive Director Outward Bound Oman

———————

"An inspirational geographical essay of our world and our time"

Steve Brooks
Entrepreneur, aviator, explorer and
first person to fly a helicopter from the North pole
to the South pole

———

Acknowledgements

To see the world from the platform of the helicopter I was flying has fulfilled the dream of a lifetime and I count myself extremely fortunate. I thank my late father, Professor James Wilson, for my passion for earth sciences and my wife, Lavinia, for my introduction to flying helicopters.

The genesis of my long-range flying adventure has been a convergence of countless things and I have learnt a lot from many influencers in my life. In particular, Jim Murray OBE, Professor Emeritus at Heriot-Watt University, encouraged me as a young engineer to set my sights high. My friend, Martin Grieder, also set a great example for me with his dedication to both work and extreme sports.

I thank Cissy Walker for her pivotal introductions, which kicked off the Africa journey; Dame Frances Moore for her introduction to *Save the Children*; and David Constantine of *Motivation International*. I thank Nigel Winser most sincerely for his steadfast mentorship to my project and meaningful introductions; my *Three Journeys Round* (TJR) venture would not have unfolded without his guidance.

For steering my sustainable development visits, I thank Louise Leakey, Andrew Mitchell, Marcelo de Andrade, Claudio Hirsch and Jose Koechlin. For supporting my route development and backing me while on the journeys, I thank Keith Ketchum, John Pattinson, David Brown, Craig Siepman, Jean Kichenbrand, Evgeny Kabanov, Steve Brooks, Felipe Nascimento, Martin Bruno and Melvyn Becerra. I thank Peter Drissell for so crucially unlocking my passage through India.

Acknowledgements

For their kind hospitality en route, I thank Duncan and Tanya Brown, Brent Mudde, Dr Laurie Marker, David Brown, Ali and Mark Flatt, Sue Roberts, Kip Ole Polos, Mark Evans, Valerie Taylor, Siva (pilot) and Rani, James Greaves, No. 7 Flight of the Army Air Corps, Robert DeLaurentis, Dean Grieder, Betsey Sanpere, Ninian and Anna, Wille Tufro, Edelio Mella, Óscar Muñoz and Sergio Nuño.

For their support and hospitality in Brazil, I especially thank Gérard and Margi Moss. For introducing me to the wonders of Greenland, I thank Jørgen Søndergård and Mikael Strandberg.

For encouraging me, I thank Charles McCann, Charles Stewart, Quentin Smith, David Monks *(Helicopter Club of Great Britain)*, Sam Rutherford, Steve Jones, Jennifer Murray, Mikhail Farikh (RIP) and Tim Tucker.

A special thanks goes to the team who helped me prepare and who were my constant, 'virtual' companions every day of every journey: Michelle Hilsdon (fuel logistics), David Cross (aircraft preparation and maintenance), and Eddie and Ahmed of *G.A.S.E.* (handling, permits, accommodation, social media and flight following), all of whom went above and beyond the call of duty. *TJR* couldn't have been completed without the trusty red helicopter and for that, I thank Leon Smith and Ruth Downey of *Helicopter Services* most sincerely for their substantial support, advice, trust and friendship.

Neither could *TJR* have been achieved without the generous support and hospitality of the *Robinson Helicopter Company* (RHC) dealers, all of whom are identified in this book. A particular thank you goes to Marco Audi *(HBR)* and Kurt Robinson (CEO of *RHC*), who got me out of a bind in São Paulo.

I thank my crew members, Matthew Gallagher *(RTW)* and Robin Doten *(LATAM),* for contributing so spiritedly, achieving something special together and for putting up with me!

Flying-wise, I owe everything to Leon Smith who taught me.

He has helped me develop my flying over the years and I have heeded his advice for different conditions, which has kept me safe. Leon is indeed a special friend.

Finally, I have met and made friends with literally thousands of people in the course of the last five years of my *TJR* project. I thank my sponsors whose support made this project possible; my family – Lavinia, Hannah and Fraser; my sister Shelagh; and my friends and colleagues for their understanding, encouragement, help and kindness at every step.

Peter Wilson
Fellow of the Royal Geographical Society
International Member of The Explorers Club, NY
Fellow of the Institution of Mechanical Engineers
Helicopter Pilot
BSc (Hons), MSc, CEng, CPL(H), FI(H)

Foreword
by the world's busiest adventurer

Peter Wilson set out to undertake three remarkable journeys by helicopter: Round Africa 2016, Round the World 2017 and Round Latin America 2018/2019. The ultimate purpose of these journeys was to raise the profile of a better planet through sustainable development. He had the privilege to witness much of the world's stunning geography at first hand, visiting locations that few people will ever see.

From an early age, I wanted to discover the world with its infinite diversity and beauty, and explore my own limits. My first expedition at the age of fifteen was rowing across the Sea of Azov. I have always craved adventure and looked to my relationship with Nature and people to develop a way through the beauty of life.

I have had the privilege of circumnavigating the globe six times, including a balloon flight and crossing the Atlantic Ocean 15 times by various means. I have completed the Adventure Grand Slam by reaching Five Extreme Poles on earth: The North Pole, the South Pole, the Pole of Inaccessibility in the Arctic Ocean (northernmost point farthest away from any land mass), Everest and sailing around Cape Horn, the southernmost tip of South America. You gain most when you set yourself a goal and achieve it. Accepting challenges is the breath of life. Now in my sixties, I have completed more than 70 unique expeditions, authored 22 books and more than 3,000 paintings.

All of my expeditions have required immense organisation and meticulous logistical planning. Having set the fastest round the world, non-stop, solo hot-air balloon record, I appreciate the massive challenge of aerial circumnavigation: the organisation, pilot skills, technical detail, teamwork, navigational and meteorological knowledge required. My future solar-powered endeavours to fly around the world and sail across the oceans will further illustrate the innovation, teamwork and technology required to live on earth sustainably.

Peter's pioneering world journeys, compelling and courageous in equal measure, have set new records and are of considerable interest to explorers and geographers worldwide. His book highlights how living well and within the means of Nature is not out of our reach. Our world is a truly extraordinary place, but it needs a helping hand in order to save us.

Fedor Konyukhov
Survivalist, adventurer, explorer, artist, author and priest
www.konyukhov.ru

Track my journey
while you read!

While reading this book, you may want to follow my satellite track on the internet, using Google maps to learn more about my journey, height and speed.

Go to **www.threejourneysround.com** and click on the blue circle at the bottom of any page.

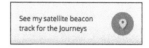

This will open a window with the *'Explore'* map, and first click *'Clear Filters.'*

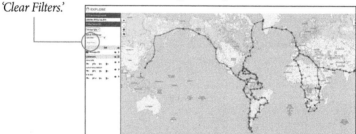

You can switch individual journeys on/off, zoom in/out and change the view. For *Africa*, I recorded points every 10 minutes and for *Round the World* and *Latin America*, I recorded points every two minutes. The distance travelled between recorded points would depend on my speed.

There are one or two gaps in transmission in Africa (Ethiopia to Sudan and into Stellenbosch, RSA) and the Caribbean (from Cayman to Havana) when the *InReach* device stopped working briefly, which was beyond my control.

You may also peruse the gallery of pictures in the book by going to the 'BOOK' tab on my website at: **www.threejourneysround.com**.

Enjoy the journey!

#threejourneysround | #sdgs | #rgs | #climatechange
#forests | #biodiversity | #earthday
#savethechildren | #mymotivationwheelchair
#r66 | #adventure | #explore | #leadership

Contents

Chapter 1	Brownout	13
Chapter 2	Worked hard, retired harder	17
Chapter 3	Interminable logistics	26
Chapter 4	Solo across the Sahara	45
Chapter 5	Only cheetahs purr	57
Chapter 6	The Cape of Good Hope	82
Chapter 7	The world's most dangerous national park	104
Chapter 8	Focus	130
Chapter 9	Arabia, 300 people per km² and Asia	148
Chapter 10	Beauty, diversity and destruction	173
Chapter 11	Provideniya	194
Chapter 12	Claustrophobic emotions	220
Chapter 13	Antipode #2	235
Chapter 14	The most beautiful place on earth	254
Chapter 15	Plenty of time	271
Chapter 16	20% of our oxygen from the Amazon rainforest	295
Chapter 17	Llanos de Moxos	321
Chapter 18	The Patagonia Steppe	346
Chapter 19	The longest country in the world	364
Chapter 20	Earthquake alarm call	382

1

Brownout

The distances across inhospitable terrain were vast and the corresponding views spectacular. The Sahara Desert is simply stunning with its emptiness; its beautiful forms and colours of sand and rock; its haze and dust; its dry heat, which is like an oven and yet, there were tiny green oases here and there. I had never seen any desert this close up and, since crossing from Granada in Spain to Oran in Algeria, I had already spent about 8½ hours flying south across the Sahara to Tamanrasset.

Algiers control wanted me to fly at Flight Level 75 (FL075), which is about 7,500 feet above sea level. So, this was the sum of my experience of flying an unstable helicopter so high above visual ground references. It was stressful enough just maintaining straight and level and the helicopter was only equipped to fly with visual references.

My other challenge was getting accurate weather forecasts between airports. There was no forecasting provision because nobody lived out there. On my flight into Tamanrasset, I had experienced some harsh up and down draughts as I skirted the Ahaggar Mountains. But now here I was, messaging my wife, Lavinia, from my air-conditioned hotel room. I told her it was a cool 28°C at FL075 but on the ground, it was about 40°C and my quick-drying, hand washable clothes were only taking two minutes to dry on the balcony. I was all set for my flight south to Agadez in Niger the following day and ready to face the gaggle of different officials who would surround the helicopter on the airfield in the midday sun. Lavinia wished me luck.

Leaving the protected hotel compound the next morning, I had the usual Algerian police escort truck with three policemen leading the way, along with the most engaging taxi driver who had also taken me to the hotel the previous night. Once again, we had a right old laugh. It was a bit like a sketch from *The Two Ronnies* as he anticipated my poor French and I, his poor English. We 'talked' and joked in a series of phrases and one-word responses about the economy, the police and security. His laugh was infectious. Everybody I had met was friendly, fascinating and open. I had slept well and was now pumping with adrenalin for this flight to Agadez in Niger.

After passing through Security, to my surprise, I was left to my own devices on the large, empty tarmac apron where the helicopter stood alone. There was a breeze rippling the smaller sand particles along and it was a dazzling, clear-blue sky, already hot at 8am. I took off, fully loaded, and climbed slowly en route to FL075 as instructed. Tamanrasset Tower wanted me to change to Algiers control but as usual, I couldn't get hold of them, so I went back and forth trying to establish two-way communications until eventually Tamanrasset Tower said goodbye and left me to keep trying on my own. I could of course hear Speedbird (British Airways) and other big jets flying at about FL340 (about 34,000 feet above sea level), talking to Algiers control. Eventually I did get hold of Algiers and went through all the usual "Negative HF, distance from Tamanrasset, estimate at this waypoint and ETA for Agadez" and so on, before promptly losing contact again.

Now get your head around this: I was flying at about 115 miles per hour across 400 miles of hot, sandy nothing. About an hour into the flight, I noticed that the haze was getting thicker below and my horizon wasn't as crisp. I was still confidently taking pictures and selfies and the time-lapse video camera was always running. About 15 minutes later, I could swear that the haze was getting thicker and rising, but it was still a gorgeous blue sky above me. It was hard to tell, but the contrast looking down seemed like it had gone but then again, I thought maybe flying at 7,500 feet above sea level with the ground dropping its altitude could have been a factor. However quite suddenly, I was inside the haze with sandy-coloured sky up, down, around and below – a complete 'brownout'!

It was hard enough to fly this helicopter high above ground references and it would be even harder not being able to see the ground. I'd been told that it was near impossible to fly in 'Instrument Meteorological Conditions' (IMC: weather conditions that require pilots to fly by instruments), without the vital instruments. I now had all of these problems happening at once. I was shocked, frightened and my heart was racing. All of a sudden, it felt really hot again. I told myself to calm down, the helicopter could fly and she didn't know that she couldn't see – that was just in my head. I tightened the resolution of both my electronic maps and included them in my scan of the artificial horizon and air speed indicator. It wasn't pretty: my speed and heading control were erratic but I was determined to stay right side up. Sweat was annoyingly running into my eyes. I thought, "What a mess! How would my children and Lavinia feel if I crashed and burned out here?" I didn't have much brain capacity left for any more morbid thoughts. The solution was entirely in my hands.

I established a controlled descent to 3,000 feet, not sure of the ground profile below. My heading and speed control were still erratic though I was succeeding. I kept telling myself to stay calm, keep the wings level, scan the gauges and make small adjustments. At 3,000 feet, it felt hotter than ever at 35°C and unfortunately, visibility wasn't any better there. I definitely couldn't contact Algiers control at this altitude. I made three relays calls through high-flying jets and was finally comforted by the fact that Algiers knew what I was doing and helped by giving me a safe clearance altitude to maintain above ground level, following my flight planned route.

I crossed into Niger without radio contact, frantically searching every electronic device I had to try and find another frequency. I picked up Niamey control via another Speedbird jet relay who informed me that Agadez was clear. After 90 agonisingly slow minutes, the brownout gradually lightened up and the ground included more rock with dark features, which I could see by looking down. Thank goodness. I began to relax a little as the visibility and contrast slowly but surely improved. Niamey passed me to Agadez Information about 100 nautical miles out and I picked up the cheerful controller immediately. He talked to me all the way into the airport, where I landed in near-perfect meteorological conditions. "Did that just happen?" I thought. The helicopter and I were covered in dust and that was possibly the only evidence left of my harrowing experience. I was thankful to be alive!

2

Worked hard, retired harder

I grew up in Zimbabwe spending the first 19 years of my life there. I was born the son of a geologist in 1957 and was able to rub shoulders with my father's contemporaries, including physicists and palaeontologists, by carrying his bags on field trips. Geology was physical work on the ground, drilling core samples, and there wasn't any access to satellite measurements or computer models yet. I was young but I was listening, and this experience seeded my passion for earth sciences, which has been fed by a lifelong subscription to *National Geographic*. The world population was about three billion in 1960.

I graduated in 1982 and worked as a Mechanical Engineer in Scotland. I was fascinated with why people resist change, how they cope with it and how they reconcile what it means for them to change. I founded *The Change Works* in 1992, co-founded *The Health Works* in 2004 and sold the combined businesses to *GE Healthcare* in 2014. I gained valuable experiences of team building, project management and implementing change in many business sectors, which paid my bills. Throughout my life, I had always been a traveller, meeting people to engineer better solutions. This engrained in me a passion for geography and human migration. The world population was about seven billion by 2010.

I came to helicopter flying quite late in life when my

wife, Lavinia, bought me a trial lesson in a Robinson R22 at Wycombe Air Park, with Leon Smith. In an instant, I was absolutely hooked! After gaining my private pilot licence, I went on to complete my commercial and instructor ratings at *Helicopter Services Limited* based at Wycombe Air Park. Over the years, I learned everything I know about flying from Leon and his team, and we developed a great friendship.

I was a weekend instructor for much of my flying in the Robinson R22 and some in the Robinson R44. In my limited private flying, I progressed to making slightly longer journeys. I flew over to Paris to complete the Heli-lanes, into Wales to fly in the mountains and around the UK and Ireland. I was also rubbing shoulders with friends who were doing crazy things like climbing Mount Everest. One of my best friends, Martin Grieder, achieved that on 18th May 2013 and also summited Lhotse within 24 hours, becoming one of only a few people to have achieved the feat at the time.

When I was able to sell my businesses, I started working out my last year and for the first time, I could actually think about a good answer to the "What are you going to do when you retire?" question. As an engineer, I had always wanted to build a house and I involved myself in learning the ropes, dabbling in a bit of property development with my brother-in-law, Geoff, and his son-in-law, who was already renovating houses. I was also thinking ahead to a flying project. I started researching my particular interests of climate change, sustainable development and poverty, using my engineering background to understand the available science. I had never really had the luxury of time before. We had added about four billion people to Earth between 1960 and 2010. My father was clear that this rapid population growth wasn't evolution anymore: it was an explosion in resource consumption and waste production that would break the Earth's existing systems. Sustainable development would mean that we need to live within Earth's means.

Charles McCann, of *Executive Benefit Services*, who I had known since 2000 through my business dealings, was also a helicopter pilot. We often compared war stories at our annual meetings. He had flown a Robinson R44 helicopter from California across North America, Greenland, Iceland and into Scotland where he lived. More recently, he designed a project called the *Three Capes Heli Challenge*, flying an R44 to Cape Wrath (northwest of Scotland), Cap Nord (top of Norway) and down to Cape Town (South Africa), which had unfortunately ended in an accident in Nairobi. In June 2014, Charles introduced me to Charles Stewart and Brian Johnson who had both been involved as co-pilots on his *Three Capes* project. My discussions with the three of them took on new meaning as I grilled them about how they had done it – the aircraft, the logistics, the paperwork, the insurances, the navigation, the weather – it was all new to me and practical, exciting stuff. I found myself learning about the challenges that I might face, and I was already making and keeping notes.

In the middle of the summer 2014, I jumped at the chance to join Charles Stewart when he flew from Wycombe to the Isle of Man for business, in a Robinson R66 Turbine, a relatively new type of helicopter to the UK at that time. Charles owned *SIPS Industries*, producing structural panels and building houses with exceptionally green credentials. He was an expert at house-building and passionate about adventure travel in trucks, autogyros and now, helicopters.

He was a big, smiley man with a gregarious personality and a southern African work ethic, always madly busy, juggling multiple projects. I liked him and we had much to talk about, in both the house-building and flying project departments.

Helicopter Services maintained some of their helicopters at *HQ Aviation* in Denham. There, Quentin Smith also had some exciting flying stories that seeped out from time to time. In 1996, Jennifer Murray, flying with Quentin, had become the first female pilot to fly around the world in a Robinson R44. In 2000, Jennifer flew around the world again, this time solo. She was accompanied by Colin Bodill in a microlight, another R44, flown by Quentin and a Caravan chase plane. A few others were also circumnavigating in turbine helicopters in 2013; two Russian Robinson R66 Turbine helicopters circumnavigated by crossing Russia, the largest country in the world. The first helicopter was piloted by Mikhail Farikh and Alexander Kurylev and the second by Dmitriy Rakitskiy and Vadim Melnikov. Quentin knew all of these pilots and was gifted at recounting fabulous stories and imparting his considerable flying knowledge. The tales of adventure and the video footage were thrilling, the geography stunning, the places remote, the conurbations huge, the world's weather a challenge and the logistics complicated.

In August 2014, I decided to get the Robinson R66 on my pilot's licence and get to grips with the aircraft's characteristics myself. Working for *Helicopter Services*, I produced their type rating course for the R66 and, while *Helicopter Services* borrowed R66s from *HQ Aviation*, we were able to type rate pilots now interested in this new helicopter. In November, François Mias bought an R66 in the UK. I conducted his type rating using his own machine for *Helicopter Services* and then François and I delivered it to his hangar in Darois near Dijon in early December. My experience with and attraction to the R66 was growing and François, who was an instrument rated pilot, taught me a lot as we experienced bad weather on the way.

In October, Charles McCann had arranged a meeting for us with Mark Beaumont up in Scotland. Mark was a record-breaking, long-distance cyclist, adventurer, broadcaster, documentary maker and author. We were sounding out whether an expedition involving Mark would attract the backing of a documentary company. Mark was an affable character with a steely determination to succeed and our discussions were frank. His interest was piqued but his stark observation that I had no credible experience was true, and it hurt! After the meeting, I reflected that Mark made his living this way, but his comment only made me more determined. Anyway, Mark concentrated on setting more cycling world records in 2015 (Cairo to Cape Town) and 2017 (round the world). I stayed in contact and as my own plans developed, he graciously provided advice, introductions and a meaningful sounding board.

In November 2014, Geoff (my brother-in-law) and I went up to Scotland to join a *SIPS Industries* course on how to build your own house, delivered by Charles Stewart. By now, Charles and I were minded to join forces in some sort of long-range flying adventure – our working assumption was Africa. For me and Geoff, developing some property was also going to happen. Charles had already completed both projects and all I had for him was endless questions! He remained patient and helpful. For the flying project, Charles and I discussed where we would go, what logistics we would need, who in their right mind would rent us a helicopter, what preparation and documentation would be required, and so on.

My last day at work, on the project that had been my life for over 22 years, was 31st December 2015. I now had no accountability for the business I had started, I was retired and free to concentrate on my next exciting projects.

I was introduced to Sam Rutherford in early 2014, who organised trips for groups of adventure pilots. Sam ran a company called *Prepare2Go* (P2G), arranging the logistics for getting news teams into and out of interesting places. He was an ex-military helicopter pilot and a fixed wing pilot. He had a lot of experience and I had been in conversation with him as he offered me advice and answered my many and varied questions regarding a possible long-range flying project. In February 2015, I went to meet Sam and his team in Belgium to discuss a group helicopter trip to Moscow in the May – approximately 35 hours of flying. I was thinking that this would be a great way to have some fun, meet the Russian long-range pilots and learn the ropes. For me, there were so many potential what-if questions and dependencies, which I would understand much better by embarking on such a trip. Charles and I talked a lot on the phone while he multi-tasked his day job with *SIPS Industries*, which took him all over the UK. One thing was becoming clear to us: a turbine, rather than a piston, helicopter would be best for the job. Basically, a turbine performs better at altitude and the fuel is more readily available since it's what all commercial aircraft use worldwide. So, where and how would we access a turbine helicopter?

Quentin at *HQ Aviation* agreed to rent Charles and I a Robinson R44 for the trip to Russia with *P2G*. The R44 was familiar territory for us both. As we prepared our personal documentation, visas and aircraft documentation for permissions, as guided by *P2G*, our excitement grew.

Charles talked to me about how he might go about planning his own exit from *SIPS Industries*. He was happy to reach a balance between lifestyle and income, giving him time to pursue his travel expedition objectives – *if* the price for his business was right. I looked over his business operations and we could see growth opportunities that would need resourcing. Charles wanted to start our journey, knowing that he would be in a good position to leave the business for a few months. He had some interested parties and set about testing the water but he wasn't really giving himself a lot of time to prepare his business.

Charles and I were now thinking of three different journey options: flying from London around Africa, or the world or Latin America. We were assuming that our first journey would be Africa because we had the most experience for this continent; we had both lived there and Charles had already flown there. We decided that, although the weather would probably be ideal for leaving in April 2016, we would delay any start to our Africa journey until the middle of 2016. All I needed was that peg in the ground from which to work backwards.

In the meantime, *Helicopter Services* had been looking to purchase a Robinson R66 to service the type rating demand expected. *Helicopter Services* felt that an R66 would be a popular first turbine for many. Between January and May 2015, there weren't that many R66s in the UK yet, and even fewer for sale. However, there was one example that caught Leon's eye and it arrived at *Helicopter Services'* Wycombe base at the beginning of May. She was viper red and her tail number was G-DIGA – having previously belonged to a company selling excavators and diggers! If I could get G-DIGA ready and my documentation reprocessed for Russia in time, Leon said that I could use her for my Moscow trip. I was elated! Charles and I could experience an R66 on a proper trip and check her out. Charles would also be able to contrast her performance with the R44. Little did I know that DIGA, as she became known, and I would travel far and wide together.

On 8th May 2015, Charles and I joined six other helicopters to fly to Moscow. We were sponsored by *SIPS Industries*, *Helicopter Services* and *Airbox Industries* who supplied their *RunwayHD* navigation software with geo-referenced maps. We became the first unofficial, unescorted private group without Russian speakers on board to achieve this. It was a fabulous adventure and we met so many kind and interesting people on our nine-country journey.

An unexpected overnight in Gomel, Belarus became four nights, as our permit negotiations to enter Russia dragged out and we swapped sightseeing in Moscow for sightseeing in Gomel! We were all arrested on a Sunday morning when we became illegal immigrants for a day because our Belarussian visas had expired. Fortunately, Sergei, the local ex-KGB man, was also in charge of airport security and looked after us like we were his family. We finally said our goodbyes and departed to Moscow with a FL075 clearance.

We were warmly welcomed in Moscow by Mikhail Farikh himself. He was a private helicopter pilot and the first Russian to fly around the world by helicopter and to reach the North Pole. He held world records in helicopter competitions and helped popularise general aviation in Russia. It felt exciting to be joining the "Aviation Nation, Helicopter Tribe, Long

Range Section", to quote Mikhail. From Mikhail, I gained a very clear understanding of the flying administration, specifically in Russia, and the dynamic planning required to fly in the right weather. Flying a non-Russian-registered aircraft in Russia was a nightmare at that time. I now knew that we needed some sort of handling support to help us make any big flying project work. While we admired the enthusiasm of Sam, we couldn't afford the cost of *P2G's* operation for something big like Africa, so I added this research challenge to my list of problems to solve.

DIGA performed magnificently and Charles and I were lucky to have had access to her capacity, speed, range and fuel efficiency, especially at altitude. So, the choice of helicopter was agreed between us – it would be an R66 – all I had to do was persuade Leon to let me use DIGA again! The whole Russian experience cemented my determination to make our own long-range flying project happen and we committed to a journey around Africa. Logically, around the world was a second choice because we had people to speak to who had done it before, and Latin America became our last choice because of its more complicated logistics from London – and we had other problems to solve first! All of a sudden though, we had three potential, massive journeys. Charles and I continued to talk on the phone and meet up in Scotland and around his house-building projects in the south of England. My working title for the project became *Three Journeys Round*.

3

Interminable logistics

In June 2015, *HQ Aviation* organised a *Robinson Helicopter Company* (RHC) Safety Course at Denham. The course was delivered by Tim Tucker who I'd met earlier in my career on a safety course at the Robinson factory in California. Tim was a legend in *RHC*. He had been one of the original development pilots, had owned one of the very first R22s and had been giving safety courses all over the world at *RHC* dealers for years. He was well-known and well-liked by everybody and he had good connections. There wasn't much he didn't know or couldn't do with a Robinson helicopter. I attended the course at Denham with DIGA and asked Tim to fly with me. I explained about the *Three Journeys Round* project and unofficially, he offered to advise me as best he could. I couldn't have asked for more and he was true to his word.

Brian Paisley, another colleague who I'd met through *Helicopter Services*, flew DIGA to the *HQ Aviation* summer fly-in party at Denham. There, I met John Pattinson who ran *Aircovers*, a company making the most advanced covers to protect aircraft from all the elements, in desert, tropical and arctic conditions. He had heard of the *Three Journeys Round* project from Quentin and offered to protect DIGA and provide hanging pockets and other useful restraining Velcro attachments. I was happy and clearly, I would advertise *Aircover's* involvement.

In late September, Brian Paisley and I joined Quentin and a few other helicopters on an *HQ Aviation* long weekend trip to Scotland. This would mean more practice for me in DIGA, sharing the flying with Brian. Four helicopters proceeded to the Lake District and then two helicopters went on to Scotland: an R66 and an R44. At one point, we landed to talk to Cissy Walker, a friend of Quentin's. Cissy invited us to stay and join her other guests for dinner. Later that day, we landed on the lawn at Conaglen. Cissy's guests examined the helicopters and Quentin gave a few short flights.

Cissy was interested in the *Three Journeys Round* project, possibly because of our common Africa connection, which I discovered later. She quizzed me about my purpose – I had to have a purpose beyond the aviation adventure, she insisted. Cissy was a conservationist and, together with her husband David, lived part-time in Kenya and part-time in London. She was involved with the *Lewa Wildlife Conservancy* near Nanyuki.

The dinner was a splendid, gregarious affair. It was fantastic to share that little bit of Scotland with Cissy and an even greater pleasure to appreciate the company of her lovely friends that Sunday evening. Cissy seated me next to Dame Frances Moore, the ex-Director of *Save the Children* (STC) in the Middle East. Dame Frances recounted incredible stories of her exploits there and she also quizzed me on my project objectives, suggesting that it also needed a charitable element. She observed that DIGA was red, which perfectly matched the colours of *Save the Children*. Dame Frances said she would make the necessary *STC* introductions in London for me.

Events moved quickly from thereon. Cissy was back in London in a few days and on 6th October, she introduced me to her long-time friend and conservation contemporary, Nigel Winser, inviting us both to tea. Nigel was a life scientist who trained at Westminster University. He'd had a 40-year career supporting field research and conservation projects, principally in East Africa, Oman and Asia, with the *Royal Geographical Society* and the *Earthwatch Institute*. Nigel was working on projects in north Kenya, Oman and Sarawak (Borneo). This included the *Il Ngwesi Group Ranch Conservancy* in north Kenya and the *Trust for African Rock Art* based in Nairobi. Nigel and I made a good connection and we were convinced that he could help me to structure my purpose and research effectively. I was delighted when he offered to mentor my sustainable development research. He would introduce me to key planetary caretakers, once our route around Africa was confirmed.

Once again, I couldn't have asked for more support. My whole business career had depended on successful networking and so it would be too with the *Three Journeys Round* project. Nigel introduced me to David Constantine who was co-founder of *Motivation International*, a leading provider of mobility solutions for disabled people living in the developing world and in particular, Africa. Nigel suggested that supporting a smaller charity, as well as a larger one, would be a good idea.

Cissy and David would be in Kenya in two weeks' time, so Cissy suggested that I should go and spend a week with them, and she would make some more introductions locally. With our daughter, Hannah, safely at university and our son, Fraser, on a school trip to China, I had no trouble convincing my wife Lavinia that we were off to Kenya for the last week in October. After some frantic organisation, we flew to Nairobi to meet Cissy and David. Then we all flew from Nairobi Wilson to Lewa Downs.

Nigel Winser met us with staff from Il Ngwesi Eco-lodge and we took a game drive to meet Ian Craig for lunch at his house. Ian was a pioneering Kenyan conservationist. He had established what became the *Lewa Wildlife Conservancy*. His vision propelled *Lewa* to great success: it had grown to become a world-renowned catalyst and model for conservation that protected endangered species and promoted the development of neighbouring communities. Ian spearheaded the formation of the *Northern Rangelands Trust* (NRT), an umbrella body that supported community conservancies across northern and eastern Kenya. Today, the *NRT* has 33 member conservancies that work across 44,000 square kilometres of prime dryland wildlife territory. Together, they help to develop, support and fund thousands of people in hundreds of communities. I have forgotten what we ate for lunch – it was delicious – but I have never forgotten that encounter.

We continued the game drive to the world-famous Il Ngwesi Eco-lodge, which is owned and managed by the Maasai community and attracts thousands of international tourists. It generates funds for community development priorities including education, health and local livelihoods. We spent two gorgeous nights at Il Ngwesi, soaking up the African atmosphere with Nigel and James Kinyaga, a knowledgeable Maasai, as our guide. Sitting on the toilet, we could see the waterhole with a string of elephants, zebras, bucks, warthogs and birds arriving for a drink!

We left Nigel and relocated to Sirikoi Lodge, joining hosts Willie and Sue Roberts. Sirikoi is set in a peaceful glade surrounded by *Lewa Wildlife Conservancy*, which is a *UNESCO* World Heritage Site. Willie was also instrumental in founding the conservancy movement in Kenya. He set up the first wildlife conservancy in Kenya, saving the greater Mara from being carved up for farming. He laid down a clear path for success in community conservancies in Kenya and set an inspirational example for others to follow. He also introduced the white rhino to the area. Sirikoi has become an award-winning conservation lodge, built from the ground up by Willie and Sue. From the deck, we could see up to 20 species of big mammals at a time – it was as humbling as it was stunning. We had some great discussions and I felt confident that destinations for our journey around Africa would materialise.

Cissy, David, Lavinia and I flew back to Nairobi. Cissy had organised a whirlwind of important guests to come to her house and I had useful discussions with David Coulson, founder of the *Trust for African Rock Art* and Louise Leakey, a Kenyan palaeontologist and anthropologist. Louise conducted research and fieldwork on human fossils in Eastern Africa. David Coulson agreed to be involved in *Three Journeys Round* (TJR) and we thought that Africa's Rock Art heritage was something that could lead to sustainable development for communities who managed it. Louise had some great ideas involving the east of the Democratic Republic of Congo (DRC). She suggested that I investigate visiting Virunga National Park, the first and oldest national park in Africa. Louise also suggested that I land the helicopter at the *Turkana Basin Institute Research Centre* at Turkwel en route north through Kenya. She gave me contact details for Lawrence Martin, Director at the *Turkana Basin Institute* who was also Professor of

Anthropology and of Anatomical Sciences at *Stony Brook University*.

I also had the time to look up Ian of *Lady Lori Helicopters* at Wilson Nairobi Airport who I had met previously at *HQ Aviation* to discuss the flying conditions in East Africa. Getting local knowledge of conditions was key to staying safe. Cissy, David, Lavinia and I went out for a nice dinner at the Talisman at the end of our first Kenyan experience, before catching our late-night flight home. My head was buzzing with ideas.

Willie Roberts also put me in touch with his son, Jamie, of *Tropic Air Kenya*, who ran helicopters based at Nanyuki. Nigel introduced me to Kirstin Johnson, Director of *Il Ngwesi UK* and Kip Ole Polos, Chairman of *Il Ngwesi Group Range*. I had many people to follow-up and even more to thank.

By now, I was struck by the arguments for living within Earth's means and doing something to raise awareness of the *United Nations Sustainable Development Goals* (UN SDGs). It also made sense to fundraise for two charities that champion the rights and choices of children, women and the incapacitated who were often socially excluded. So, I decided to do something epic to raise the profile of the *UN SDGs*. The objective was to have an adventure by helicopter with a purpose. I discussed this with Charles, and it made sense to him too. We were both busy, although he wasn't as involved in the hospitality, visits and route planning as me, but we both understood that. Charles' news was that he had a contemporary in a parallel and non-competing business who was interested in buying *SIPS Industries* pretty much as it was. There were many synergies and Charles believed that he could now achieve his lifestyle objectives. I knew how hard it was to sell a business and this was great news for him. He continued to advise me on my property project, and I helped him by acting as a sounding board.

I needed to understand the *UN's* emerging *17 Sustainable Development Goals* and so I employed a Google search! In September 2015, all 193 of the *UN's* member states committed unanimously to *17 Global Goals* to achieve three extraordinary things in the next 15 years: end extreme poverty, fight inequality and injustice and finally, fix climate change. Talking to Nigel and thoroughly enjoying my research, my epiphany was recognising three game changers to permit 'development within Earth's means', which were:

1. Raising the living standards of the extremely poor, in an environmentally friendly way, would stabilise population growth at about nine billion people in 2050 (from the work of Hans Rosling at **www.gapminder.org**, which demonstrated that women who have a choice choose fewer children).

2. Respecting absolute planetary boundaries means that the biosphere could still support humanity beyond 2050 (from the work of Johan Rockström at the **www.stockholmresilience.org**. Scientists had calculated the parts per million of CO_2 equivalent that would cause humanity a problem).

3. Accounting for both Nature and people in order to make profit was the only way that humanity would enjoy sustainable growth on earth (from the work of Pavan Sukhdev on The Economics of Ecosystems & Biodiversity at **https://environment.yale.edu/TEEB**.

Basically, economists currently assume that Nature is free, and it most certainly is not. Capitalism needs to use Nature responsibly and pay for it).

Planning a big expedition from scratch is a huge undertaking that few people can really appreciate. Setting objectives, understanding the logistics that need to be put in place, raising sponsorship and configuring the right helicopter takes time and effort. I had the time to devote to it and, with the help of many kind people, I went about developing the *Three Journeys Round* project just like I had done with my own businesses. The platform would be a journey around Africa, a journey around the world and a final journey around Latin America. The idea was to meet individuals who are making a difference by living within Earth's means and asking them to tell their story.

Even with Dame Frances Moore's introduction to *STC*, it still took me until early April 2016 to get a contract to raise money for them, which permitted us to carry the *STC* logo and laid out a series of rules. It was a frustrating process and it seemed at times that all *STC* wanted to do was protect their brand name and take any money we could provide. I had to write a lot, call a lot and incessantly explain the project, then repeat myself to someone new who, by then, would have taken over the role of 'handling' me. I wanted to carry their logo and get some introductions to *STC* projects en route. *STC* operated in over 100 countries. I was prepared to follow the rules because they all made sense and I was used to such high standards of behaviour from my own corporate working life. *STC* in the UK was largely a money-raising entity: about a £350 million revenue business with staff costs of about £40 million. Their delivery was by a mixture of contracted third parties, managed by small, local *STC* footprints in the countries where they operated. I approached *UNICEF* too and found their contracting approach equally cumbersome. By the beginning of April, I had two contracts sitting in front of me. Following discussions with Charles Stewart, we chose to go with *STC*.

Charles McCann had raised money for *Motivation International* on his *Three Capes* project. I also found working with David Constantine helpful because he understood the idea of a helicopter journey and was able to make introductions to coordinate visits to see *Motivation's* work. Additionally, Charles McCann had also raised money for *Mission Aviation Fellowship* (MAF). For over 70 years, *MAF* had been flying light aircraft over jungles, mountains, swamps and deserts to enable over 2,000 organisations to bring medical care, emergency relief and long-term development to thousands of communities worldwide. Every four minutes, a *MAF* plane was taking off or landing somewhere. Charles Stewart introduced me to Keith Ketchum of *MAF International*, who was living in the UK and whose role was coordinating maintenance training for the aircraft fleet. Charles Stewart had saved Charles McCann's life in Nairobi by getting them both out of the burning wreckage after they crashed. They had lost everything, and *MAF* had provided support to both of them to get them home safely. As a result, *MAF* was not prepared to have its logo carried again. However, Keith Ketchum was able to support our route and visit planning, based on his vast flying experience of *MAF* pilots worldwide, which proved both comforting and invaluable. As I was learning again, being able to talk to someone who was flying locally was the best source of information and *MAF* were very experienced in almost every region that would matter to us.

To get sponsorship, I chased and chased every conceivable avenue, starting with my circle of friends and contacts. Charles threw in his ideas, but he was still very busy with *SIPS Industries* and so I knuckled down. I wrote email after email, then repeatedly called and followed up. I networked endlessly and ferreted around, however tenuous the lead. I wrote and rewrote briefs and taglines, trying to explain what I was doing, which helped me understand the project better, also discovering what people liked and disliked about it. Most people said that it wasn't for them or that I should have called last year because they were already committed to their next three-year strategy. I tried not to get downhearted, but I also had a huge workload regarding the journey logistics, project website and other practical problems to solve, plus the little property development project with Geoff that was also up and running.

I researched the *Corporate Responsibility Strategies* (CRSs) of hundreds of big companies, which was an eye-opener. In fact, towards the end of 2015, only a handful of companies were reflecting the *UN SDGs* in their *CRSs*. I found I could persuade aviation product companies to offer their product and conservation-minded companies to offer hospitality, but I failed to win a big-name financial backer for the project. Still, I ended up with a good number of crucially important supporters supplying products, services and good advice, but it was all exceptionally time-consuming.

By December 2015, Charles and I were still looking for someone to handle our flights. Sam Rutherford had introduced me to the company he used and, although I had spoken to them, I didn't get the feeling that they would help me plan my route. Since I wasn't sure of the best route, which would depend on a lot of information about point of entry/exit status, Immigration and Customs availability, opening times and fuel availability, I really needed someone who would help me through those iterations. I also needed to consider my choices of local visits and whether there would be impassable mountains and/or weather barriers. Charles had carried the burden of applying for permits for their *Three Capes* trip, which had proved numbingly bureaucratic and time-consuming, and had resulted in them having to talk and pay their way out of the inevitable problems en route. I wanted something less stressful, which could also help a schedule unfold so that we might keep to promised visit dates more closely. Lady Luck arrived and a telephone discussion with a pilot ferrying an aircraft in Africa led to an introduction to *General Aviation Support Egypt* (G.A.S.E.).

G.A.S.E. was started by a group of enthusiasts and professionals who wanted to foster general aviation in Egypt by offering assistance and services to visiting and transiting pilots of light aircraft. Now *G.A.S.E.* offered these same services to pilots wherever they were flying across the world, with its now global network of volunteers and enthusiasts. Specifically, I talked initially to Eddie at *G.A.S.E.* At the time, Eddie was a British ex-pat living within spitting distance of Cairo International Airport. He had a lifelong love of aviation and started working with aircraft after leaving school in 1970. He was also a pub quiz fanatic! Eddie's role at *G.A.S.E.* was planning routes with pilots, arranging hotels and accommodation, flight following and social media updates.

After that, I talked to Ahmed who was a younger man, Egyptian born and bred and who also had a lifelong love of aviation. He had worked for various Middle Eastern airlines as a flight dispatcher and also ran a number of online communities based around aviation hobbies. For *G.A.S.E.*, Ahmed was responsible for contacting handling agents, arranging fuel and was an expert at dealing with *Civil Aviation Authorities* (CAAs) for obtaining permissions and landing slots.

I explained the basic idea of the *Three Journeys Round* project and asked if *G.A.S.E.* could and would be the flight support agents for the project. Eddie sent me a simple document that described clearly how *G.A.S.E.* would support both my route planning and then the flying phases, including social media activity and inflight monitoring for *Search and Rescue* (SAR). He exampled equipment I would need for in-cockpit communications and how *G.A.S.E.* could book hotels en route once we were sure to arrive, thereby saving money. He explained that he and Ahmed knew a lot about Facebook, had constructed their own website and were totally computer-literate. He went on to describe all the navigation, flight planning and weather applications that they used to support flight planning and flying. I was bursting with excitement. Eddie was passionate and at the same time, his calm, unflustered response filled me with confidence that *G.A.S.E.* knew what they were doing and could be trusted to be part of the *TJR* team. Once again, I couldn't believe my good fortune at meeting Eddie and Ahmed who it turned out would become my significant and constant companions for all three journeys. Their support and friendship were truly magnificent.

After my visit to Kenya in October 2015, my work was mapped out. Charles and I had about eight months until take-off in mid 2016. I needed to develop our hospitality and visits; gain sponsorship; seek flying advice; arrange all of the logistics; sort the communications technology; manage the media, including creating a website and Facebook presence; arrange ship decals; make sure DIGA would be ready and have enough hours to fly to a maintenance stop; organise the safety equipment for desert, jungle and sea conditions; sort out necessary insurance; and arrange aircraft and personal documentation.

I made multiple lists and worked methodically, jumping from subject to subject and list to list. I enjoyed it, but it required stamina. This project was very important to me now, but not to everybody else, and I had to nudge politely to get things done. Most people were very interested in what I was trying to achieve but I came to realise that "Good luck" actually meant "You're mad!" I persevered, relying on my eagerness, determination (which others may call stubbornness) and supportive telephone conversations with Charles. I used my network and through various introductions, I found my way to people who could, would and wanted to help us, for which I was always grateful.

I followed up all the East African introductions from Cissy and Nigel. Nigel also introduced me to the Flatt family in Maun, Botswana and to Dr Laurie Marker of the *Cheetah Conservation Fund* (CCF) in Otjiwarongo, Namibia. *Helicopter Services* introduced me to *Jet 2*, who opened the door to *World Fuel Services*. At *World Fuel Services*, I met Michelle Hilsdon who agreed to support the contract fuelling arrangements, which was very important to reduce the amount of cash we would need to carry onboard. Along with *G.A.S.E.*, *World Fuel Services* became important planning and constant flying companions. *Helicopter Services* introduced me to *Pooleys* who opened the door to *Garmin* and *Jeppesen*. They also introduced me to Mike Mason who suggested that I approach *ClimateCare* who developed cost-efficient, high impact programmes to tackle poverty, improve health and protect the environment using a carbon offset programme. We offset our CO_2 footprint for the Africa journey with *ClimateCare*. *Airbox* agreed to supply navigation software and georeferenced maps again. I also approached *Rocket Route* who provided flight planning software and 24/7 operations support, and they agreed to help us.

Knocking on high street shop doors, I met Maraid who was managing a *Cotswold Outdoor* store. She persuaded *Cotswold Outdoor* to advise on suitable clothing and equipment for all weathers and the contents of a grab bag. Maraid took the lead in persuading other brands to supply clothing and camping equipment. John Pattinson from *Aircovers* introduced me to *Geotech* and *Starlite Aviation*. *Geotech* was the world-leading airborne geophysical survey company and flew helicopters in west Africa, down the west coast to South Africa. Craig Siepman and Jean Kichenbrand from *Geotech* provided me with one of the most comprehensive brain dumps of advice for my trip, and indeed any trip by helicopter, for which I was very grateful. *Starlite Aviation* also maintained helicopters and Durban looked like a great choice for maintaining DIGA halfway round – she would need a service every 100 hours. Talking to Keith Ketchum, their base in Angola operated by *MAF Canada* would be able to host me on the way south. John Pattinson also introduced me to a good friend and ex-RAF helicopter pilot with East African experience. Through his friend in the British High Commission in Malawi, I was introduced to Chris Badger who had set up *Central African*

Wilderness Safaris, providing specialist, eco-tourism-based safaris while protecting Malawi's areas of pristine wilderness. A charity they supported, called *Children in the Wilderness*, fitted well.

I worked with Eddie and Charles to plan our route from London to Cape Town and back. The presence of Ebola in West Africa meant that we would have to cross the Sahara and avoid the possibility of arriving in one West African country and not being permitted to go further because of a quarantine risk. While we didn't think there was much danger of infection to us, we didn't want to risk being stopped in our tracks. So, we agreed to route from Algeria to Niger and Nigeria – pretty much straight down. I produced a single spreadsheet with all the important information. We could quite easily change dates, the length of stays and assess the implications as we went along. Eddie supplied known airports and together we mapped out a route, which went through many iterations as visits matured and fuel and permissions were checked out. We planned doglegs to get into Botswana and the Democratic Republic of Congo. We shared the route with *World Fuel Services* for contract fuel and iterated some more. We tried to avoid expensive airports where smaller options existed. My basic principle with the helicopter was to fly directly to the point of interest and get fuel at an airport at either end of a flight thus maximising the convenience of being able to land right on the point of interest. It wasn't always permitted and didn't always work out that way, but that was the principle and was one significant benefit of a helicopter over any other form of transport.

Communications would be important. On the ground, we would use free Wi-Fi whenever we could and mobile networks if we had to, the cost of which would depend on our mobile contracts. This was for access to email, Facebook Messenger and WhatsApp. In the air, I wanted to set up a system to be able to communicate with *G.A.S.E.* inexpensively. Investigation showed that we could use the *Iridium* satellite network and the best of the beacons available was the *InReach* product. This was a small, personal beacon that could see the satellites and be Bluetoothed to an *iPad* or *iPhone* for text messaging. We chose a data package that provided frequent map chart plotting points and unlimited texting. This way, our track across a Google map could be live for all sorts of uses on our website, *G.A.S.E.* could follow us and get our speed and height telemetry and we could text each other as much as we wanted for exchanging weather, hotel or other information. Isn't technology wonderful! I was also able to Bluetooth my *iPhone* through the helicopter headsets, which meant that, subject to cell availability and costs, I could talk to people on the phone. Charles McCann's company, *EBS*, kindly sponsored a separate satellite phone and subscription to complete the safety communications arrangements.

I used *WIX* to build the *TJR* website because it was a 100% graphical interface and easy enough for me to understand and use. Eddie helped me set up my personal Facebook page and the *TJR* page from that. I worked with local companies on a logo design, embroidering logos on garments and getting ready to decal DIGA once we had all the sponsor logos to hand.

While playing around with Facebook, I found a school-time girlfriend from Zimbabwe, Michelle. I saw on Michelle's Facebook wall that she was involved in doing school makeovers in South Africa where she now lived. When she explained what she did, it led to a perfect introduction to David Brown of *Joint Aid Management* (JAM), an African-founded and headquartered, international humanitarian relief and development organisation. They operate sustainable aid programmes, supporting the most vulnerable people throughout the African continent. David was able to help me arrange visits to *JAM's* work in Angola, South Africa and Mozambique, which I factored into my route planning. I was also reaching out to other friends who might have found themselves in interesting locations, which included Roy Holden, my best friend at school. Roy's brother, Trevor, was working as a lodge manager and game guide in Tanzania and Trevor and I planned to hook up in Arusha.

David Cross, who was chief engineer at *HQ Aviation*, had over 20 years' experience with *Robinson* helicopters and had been servicing DIGA for *Helicopter Services*. I spoke to him about my plans and worked with him to understand what inspections and maintenance would be needed to keep the service in Durban to a simple inspection. The UK *CAA* insisted that we had a UK *CAA/EASA*-qualified engineer to perform the maintenance outside the UK! Planning and scheduling this with David Cross added to our challenge and costs. I was right to put my life in David's hands and, with his meticulous attention to detail, vast experience and intimate knowledge of DIGA's condition, he knew what I needed to do to fly her home safely. I know what it's like to make a parachute jump: the guy who has packed it taps you on the shoulder and says "Jump!" I needed to look after David and in turn, he would look after DIGA. As it turned out, the success of the *TJR* mission and my safety was in David's hands and that of the excellent team he had built at

HQ Aviation. We would go on to develop a good working relationship.

I was also trying to fit in some flying on top of the type ratings for *Helicopter Services*. I wanted to practice in DIGA at close to 'mission configuration' and to also fly in varied weather conditions. I managed windy and wet but couldn't simulate the desert to come. *Helicopter Services* let me use their flight simulator to develop my bad weather flying skills in the event that we might be exposed to marginal visual flight conditions. The thing about a helicopter is that you have to be able to see the horizon to keep the unstable flying machine the right way up. Obviously, even if you managed to stay right side up, it's easy to hit things in your way that stick up, especially flying close to the ground. I didn't have the instrument flying privileges, nor did DIGA have the instrument equipment to permit flying in Instrument Meteorological Conditions. DIGA was a relatively inexpensively-instrumented VFR helicopter. *Three Journeys Round* would be flown visually, keeping the ground in sight under visual flight rules (VRF) and visual meteorological conditions (VMC). Getting access to the Internet to look at the forecasts would be a crucial part of the daily regime. Charles and I would essentially be weathermen by the end of this project.

In the past, *Helicopter Services* had organised a helicopter ditching training course as a team-building exercise with *Andark Diving & Watersports*. Andy, who owned *Andark*, was also a helicopter pilot. I enquired, and Andy agreed to help us. Sharon of *Andark* was excellent at sorting our beacons, grab-bags, a life raft and immersion suits for the cold conditions. She knew everybody in the business and made all the introductions and connections to get other brands to help out.

I researched all the documents that were needed for DIGA; everything would have to be in good order to avoid any hiccups at airports. Insurance for both DIGA, Charles and I would also be key. *Hayward Aviation* insured *Helicopter Services'* helicopters and supported the project. Personal insurance for *Search and Rescue*, recovery and medical repatriation was the minimum we would accept. In the end, a company called *Dogtag* and another called *GEOS* provided the most suitable products. That wasn't the end of *SAR* requirements. All the 'red button' emergency devices needed to point to the same information and contacts and be registered with the *Falmouth Coastguard Distress Beacon Service*. This was very important paperwork that needed my full attention.

4

Solo across the Sahara

All of our fragmented plans were coming together with my endless chasing. It was getting harder to keep Charles up to date because of the rate of change of the *TJR* project and also because he was so busy. My own property development project was in a place where it could be concluded comfortably before our Africa journey without me in the country. I was also getting Mikhail Farikh's advice and all my practicing was coming together with some winter flying.

The end of February 2016 was the target for Charles completing his company sale. He was hard to get hold of, understandably, but something had happened, which I wasn't privy to. The bolt out of the blue came at the beginning of April when Charles contacted me and told me that, due to personal circumstances, he just could not commit to the Africa journey and most likely would have to drop out of the *TJR* project altogether! I was stunned and confused and didn't fully understand the reasons. I thought he might be persuaded but after about six weeks around mid-May, I accepted that I had lost a valuable and resourceful partner. He was clearly under pressure and I wished him well, but I was now on my own.

In April, Mikhail Farikh was on an Arctic expedition with three Russian R66s. Mikhail, Alexei Frolov and Oleg Prodan were all in one of the helicopters and while working, I was following Mikhail's Facebook updates and their *InReach* satellite beacon track at my desk. On 18th April 2016, the tracker stopped and sadly, it was confirmed that all three had perished in a crash during severe weather conditions. This was a huge shock to many, and a salutary reminder that flying in the right weather is so important for safety reasons. It made me think about what I was about to embark on. Mikhail had been so encouraging to me and the *TJR* project and he knew what he was talking about.

Bad things often come in threes, don't they? On 2nd May 2016, my father, Professor James Wilson, passed away after a few short days in hospital from the damage caused by a bleed to the brain. It was mercifully quick but totally unexpected. I cried hard and the process of grieving took time. Mum and dad had emigrated to the protectorate of Southern Rhodesia in 1953 and lived and worked a full life there. They only returned to the UK in 2004 after 50 years. Latterly, mum had suffered from dementia and, after fracturing her femur, was relocated to a new nursing home straight from hospital. Jim's health had deteriorated but his mind was all there; now on his own, he was just able to get about the centre of the village where he lived, using his Zimmer frame, unless it was windy or icy. He used his *iPad* to travel widely through both Google Earth and Street and kept up-to-date with family and friends via email and Facebook. I would share discussion time with him, and he would offer me books; one called *Snowball Earth* by Gabrielle Walker was a particularly good read. It was a story of great global catastrophe that spawned life on earth as we know it.

However, by early 2015, my sister, Shelagh, and I felt that dad was slipping away from us. He had deteriorated physically through the winter of 2014/15 and had lost his motivation to live. I had to respect his wishes but it was hard for me to accept. Throughout 2015, Shelagh and I persuaded him to try home help, which became three times a day, seven days a week and included food being delivered. The carers persuaded him to take on physiotherapy and basic exercise and slowly he regained his mobility, inch by inch. In April 2016, Dad took himself off to the barber's for a haircut and was feeling much fitter and ready to face the world again. He understood global warming better than I did and researched sustainable development. He liked our *Three Journeys Round* discussions from what he could read on the website. I showed him how he could literally follow a satellite beacon track of the journey and the Facebook posts on his *iPad*. He was motivated again and was looking forward to what his son would be serving up. Dad's funeral was on 22nd May and I cried again. I know I'm not the only one to lose a loved one but I now know how much it hurts.

I asked Leon about the prospect of finding another pilot to replace Charles at such short notice. We both knew that it wasn't going to happen and so I got his blessing to fly round Africa solo. The full consequences were dawning on me, G.A.S.E. and my family. I consulted Nigel Winser about it and told him I was planning to take off on 22nd July.

I sat in DIGA and engineered a better 'man-machine-interface' to give me access to all my extra communications gear, with my left or right hand, and to be able to feed and water myself while flying. *Aircovers* designed a series of hanging pockets for the left-hand seat where I could store provisions because I could only use what I could reach.

I was still nudging many items on my to do lists, such as how much cash would I need and where would I hide it because of the $10,000 limit; malaria tablet regime; visa requirements for Angola and DRC; cameras, video equipment and solo operation; memberships of *Aircraft Owners and Pilots Association* (AOPA) and the *Helicopter Club of GB*; paperwork for records that needed signing; vaccinations; website adjustments; sustainable development research; research of interesting facts for places I would visit; some spares and oils to be carrying; how to file flight plans; and what software would I use. It was like a marathon race but I was getting there. It was also summertime when everybody's spirits were up and so were mine.

In early June, I joined a group of helicopters who were flying to a small place called Hell near Trondheim in Norway to watch some motor racing. I decided to fly DIGA solo over the six days and see what the workload would be like. So off I went to Hell and back! While there, I met Matthew Gallagher, who was also flying an R66 and had set off late to join our group. One day, we teamed up and flew north just across the Arctic Circle. It was a memorable experience in beautiful weather conditions.

By July 2016, the *Three Journeys Round* project had been over three years in preparation. The previous nine months were much more like full-time for me, with the last three months becoming quite manic. However, after all the preparation, I was itching to go.

On Friday 22nd July, Lavinia and I arrived early at Wycombe Air Park. I checked the weather, filed my flight plan, went to prepare DIGA and then returned to the *Helicopter Services* office to wait. My daughter Hannah and son Fraser arrived, then Geoff, and we found more friends and the *Helicopter Service* folk all waiting expectantly. It was time. We all went off to DIGA for photographs and hugs. As

I popped on my life jacket, I had that naïve confidence you have before you fully understand what's happening! Leon rushed over and thrust Thingy into my hand and personally wished me good luck. Thingy was a small teddy bear that looked a bit like Piglet, the fictional character from A. A. Milne's Winnie-the-Pooh books. I climbed into DIGA, went through my routine checks, established the *InReach* communications with Eddie and after a few more waves and nods, I lifted and flew away. I was more excited than nervous.

I routed north around London to Le Touquet in France with my time-lapse video getting good footage. Le Touquet wasn't busy and I was soon on my second leg to Darois near Dijon to meet François Mias. At Chatillon-sur-Seine, about 40 nautical miles north, the fine weather had turned to light rain, low cloud and misty conditions, which triggered memories of December 2014 when François and I were forced to put down and wait a day while ferrying his helicopter to Darois. However, I landed safely, and it was wonderful to see François again and introduce him to DIGA and my 'flying *Three Journeys Round* office'. He looked after me that evening and it felt good to be getting the journey off to a positive start with the advice of someone who had useful experience of flying in France, Spain and Algeria.

The next day, I flew south to the coast and experienced the turbulence from Bezier to Perpignan that François had warned me about, as well as the severe turbulence coming off the Pyrenees after Perpignan. I had never seen anything like it before and was glad I had elected to stay low. Landing at Gerona, the *WFS* contract fuel worked efficiently and I sorted myself out at the airport hotel. On Sunday, I made a long and satisfying trip southwest to Granada. All my systems worked well, and I was rejigging equipment positions and developing a routine. The dry scenery of Spain and the blue sky were beautiful and the 40°C temperature a sign of things to come. My handler at Granada Airport had the patience of a saint dealing with the lethargic airport system and apathetic staff.

I arrived early morning at the airport to nudge my way through payments, flight planning, General Declarations, Security, Immigration and Customs, then began to prepare DIGA for my epic flight. I planned to coast out of Europe and coast into Africa, double hopping to a place called El Golea in Algeria. Nobody would advise the official route to Oran and so I picked a short two-hour flight directly across the sea! I lifted at 8am into a beautifully clear sky and flew southwest, skirting the Sierra Nevada Mountains. I found a frequency to take me to the international boundary and pass me to Oran who weren't happy, so they rerouted me via various official beacons including a 40 nautical mile approach to Oran Airport. I don't think the controllers had had much exposure to general aviation flying and treated me like a big jet, adding 50 minutes to my flight time.

Oran was hot and dry like Granada. *Air Algerie* would handle me all the way through Algeria and the turnaround at Oran was well managed. However, making payments and filing a flight plan took 1½ hours, then looking for a toilet, bottled water and money exchange took another ½ hour. It was now really hot back inside DIGA. I was asked to expedite a climb to FL075 and fly between restricted areas, while switching off all the navigation equipment and restarting it in the right sequence to establish the *InReach* communications with Eddie properly. However, once clear, I turned southwest and flew across the breathtaking desert scenes unfolding below, while concentrating hard because I was so high above my visual references. It was relatively bearable at 28°C. I descended to FL040 (about 3,000 feet above the ground) and 36°C, to get a closer look at the desert for the last 60 nautical miles into El Golea. Wow – it was an absolutely massive sandpit with undulating dunes for miles. I was learning to fly with my left hand on the cyclic stick, while taking photos with my right.

Formalities were efficient at this small airport and my hotel was frankly amazing for a tiny, remote desert oasis town but the Internet and wall plugs didn't work. I slept well with the air-conditioning shielding me from the dry 42°C heat outside. The next morning, I was collected from the secure hotel compound with a police escort. Back at the airport, I compared flying notes with a military pilot on the apron. He warned me of the difficulties of flying in the hazy desert conditions that I showed him in the photographs on my phone. I had a direct flight to In Salah to refuel in the middle of the day and then another immediately on to the southern town of Tamanrasset. After smiling goodbyes, photos and various interruptions, I took off slightly earlier than scheduled.

In Salah was another very small but perfectly formed airport building in the absolute middle of a 42°C hot nowhere! I landed with my back to the sun and put the front cover on DIGA to keep her cool. *Air Algerie* coordinated my turnaround by interested officials and police in less than 30 minutes. The tower controller came down to shake my hand and, after photographs, I lifted and climbed back to FL075, as requested.

Again, the unfolding desert landscape stretched to the horizon in all directions and I could once more see sections of the black tarmac of the Route Trans Saharienne below me, heading to Tamanrasset. I was wearing long sleeves and trousers to avoid sunburn and I was protecting my *iPad* with a small hand towel. As long as I kept it out of direct sunlight, it seemed to cope with the temperatures; I always had my *Garmin 795* programmed too. Approaching Tamanrasset, I could see the Ahaggar Mountains ranging from 4,000 to 8,000 feet just visible through the haze off to my left (east), a view that was accompanied by turbulence from the winds disturbed by the mountains. I secured DIGA as usual with both cabin and engine covers. I was the only person there and once again, I was escorted safely to a secure hotel compound by three policemen in their truck and a chatty taxi driver who tested what French I had left after leaving Paris in 1992.

The hotel Internet was Wi-Fi in the lobby only, or 'Lobby-Fi' as Eddie called it. The bandwidth was only good for messaging, not for uploading photographs. The staff were chatty and I was clearly a novelty! After a meal, I set about my evening hygiene regime and flying preparations for the following day. My plan was to cross into Niger: little did I know that this time tomorrow, I would be counting myself lucky to be alive, having survived my terrifying brownout experience.

However, I did make it to the international airport of Agadez in one piece! I landed on the small apron next to the ramshackle tower, with a modest arrival room, a couple of shacks and a military hangar. There was a half-finished, large concrete tower at the other end of a new, American-built runway.

Gado ran from the tower to welcome me and turned out to be the one-man band running the airport, performing almost every role. There were no formalities at all. Gado simply waved his hand and said it was all sorted. He was friendly, speaking both English and French perfectly. He handed me a hot tea in a shot glass and we talked for a while. It was stinking hot and the wind was calm. Looking at the dusty state of DIGA, Gado very kindly helped me wash her outside and hoover inside. By now, I had calmed down completely. There was no Wi-Fi to communicate with Eddie and he had no idea what had happened to me. With the help of some young military recruits, we pushed DIGA into the hangar, safe from the sun, possibly high winds later, swirling dust and sometimes hail, Gado informed me. "Really?!" I thought. Anyway, I left DIGA completely covered up for the soldiers to guard.

Gado drove me through town to the only hotel open, Hotel de la Paix, within its own guarded, secure compound. The room's air-conditioning worked for comfortable sleeping, thank goodness, but nowhere else; I had one working power socket, one light bulb and my headtorch. It was 100 USD a night for a dirty room, a bucket of water to flush the toilet and another to scoop water for a shower. The hotel was full of Chinese equipment, either broken down or fixed with exposed, dangling electric wires. Agadez is on the southern edge of the Sahara and it seemed dustier than the other sandy towns I had passed through. By 4pm, it was raining hard, really gusty with dust and rubbish being blown all over the streets and high into the air. On the bright side, the other hotel guests came and went from various parts of Niger and further afield and I got to chat with them while using the limited bandwidth of the Lobby-Fi. I could walk around the compound and, by climbing the water tower, I managed to capture some great photographs of the town and sunset. I then went to investigate dinner and was by now also getting the hang of eggs in their shell, yogurts, bread and strong coffee for breakfast – all safe enough.

I stayed in Agadez for two nights, which was a legacy of planning to see the African rock art at Dabous, called 'The Giraffe'. Those arrangements had unfortunately fallen through for security reasons, but permissions for flying between countries can only be delayed and not advanced. I spent some time organising ongoing logistics; WFS seemed to be having some problems with arranging fuel in Nigeria now and the weather for crossing the International Tropical Convergence Zone ahead was looking challenging.

Niger was an arid and impoverished but relatively stable country, surrounded by conflict zones where Islamist terrorist groups had taken root. Agadez itself was an ancient travel hub hosting thousands of migrants each year on one of the main routes across the desert. The US Nigerian Air Base 201 was sited close to the airport, hence the new runway.

I had a poignant conversation with a hotel employee who also spoke perfect English and French. He suffered from Type 1 diabetes in a country that couldn't care for him in the way that the British NHS does. He paid a large percentage of his salary for private medication, with the added anxieties of travelling to collect it. My thoughts turned to all those who lived outside the hotel compound in poverty.

On day 8, Friday 29th July, Gado drove me back along the dirt roads to the airport. The place was full of armed US Humvees and Gado told me that he had to sort out two arrivals before we could get DIGA out. Arrival one disembarked one passenger and the Humvees took off in a trail of dust towards the US Air Base. I chatted with the three American civilian crew of the plane who were based in Niamey and moved US staff about Niger, acting as casualty evacuation standby. I was interested in their local flying knowledge, and they in DIGA and the *Three Journeys Round* project. I noticed a model of the 'Giraffe of Dabous' and took a photo. Arrival two was a commercial flight. With the airport now free, everybody pitched in to get DIGA on the apron. We all said goodbye, I thanked and tipped the soldiers and Gado shouted permission to start-up as he ran to the tower. Over the radio, Gado instructed lift from current position direct to Kano and I climbed into the clear-blue sky.

Niamey control looked after me until the border when Kano control took over. The dusty, desert scenery changed slowly below with the addition of shrubs. I crossed vegetation indicating the path of dry riverbeds. Modest dwellings belonging to family groupings appeared and signs of human activity intensified, with visible animal tracks. By the time I got to Kano, the greenery had increased and almost all of the land below was demarked by fences and shrub borders. It was dry but the cloud build-up told of the water available and the conurbations of modest, tin-roofed houses were now all over the place. I was arriving into Kano, Nigeria with a population of about 3½ million and a country with a population of 140 million, with English as their first language.

Normally, I wouldn't leave DIGA until she was refuelled but, even with the resourceful help of my handler, Raphael, organised by *G.A.S.E.*, and the might of *WFS*, nobody would supply me fuel. Basically, the insurgent group, Boko Haram, based in northern Nigeria, had sought to recast the country as a state based on Islamic law since 2011 and they had recently disrupted supply to Kano. I retreated as night fell and as I taxied to my hotel, the heavens opened and the otherwise dusty, overpopulated roads were waterlogged, hiding all the deep potholes and making big, muddy splashes a serious hazard for the well-dressed pedestrians.

I did have a nudge and a wink that, once the 'fuel boss' had gone home, someone would call in the middle of the night and we would go and refuel DIGA for cash. That promise thankfully came to naught!

5

Only cheetahs purr

My Kano hotel was lovely, calm and everything worked, which was out of kilter with the mayhem around me. My taxi driver said that today was 'sanitation day' and everybody had to either stay off the streets or clean his or her patch of the city, which I thought was a good idea. However, back at the airport, Raphael reconfirmed my fuelling nightmare and the three jumbo jets ready for the Hajj pilgrimage were probably the refuelling priority.

Eventually, the airport's military officer suggested that I fly southwest to the domestic airport called Kaduna, which had fuel, and then continue south to Enugu. Luckily, I could make the one-hour flight with DIGA's remaining fuel. Everything was agreed and prepared at Kano for me. I was instructed to land at Kaduna, present my stamped papers, pay the agreed rate for fuel and leave. I wasn't supposed to be there but apparently, Kaduna would be none the wiser. It all went to plan, except when a C130 Hercules also landed and parked up right behind DIGA, with about 50 Nigerian troops milling around. "It'll be hard not to be noticed now," I thought, as the captain of the C130 came over for a selfie and wished me a safe flight!

The scenery from Kaduna to Enugu was pleasant, flying at about 3,500 feet above ground level under the cloud base: Nigeria understood visual flying rules. The scrub of Kano became the savannah of Kaduna and that gave way to forest and more significant hills and rivers. Abuja controlled me most of the way south until I lost contact.

Enugu was another frantic city with a population of more than three million. My handler, Godfrey, was a god-fearing gentleman and, with his help, we wrestled fuelling and formalities, visiting each department in turn, making payments and filling out forms in triplicate. Everybody wanted a piece of me and here, for the first time, I was openly asked for money to help speed up the process. Both Immigration and Customs were aggressive. "What can you do for us?" or "Make mine a happy day!" seemed to be the precursor to a bribe discussion. All of the offices were dark and dingy, with the TV blaring, but thankfully, there was air-conditioning. It was a wearing process in the humidity that took nearly four hours to complete from landing. Trying to find my hotel in the chaos of Enugu at night took another hour and I was glad of Godfrey's company.

Back at the airport in the morning, I retrieved my passport from two new immigration officers on shift who started with "Make mine a happy Sunday!" and this time, Godfrey successfully argued that I had paid the previous day!

Godfrey helped me prepare my flight plan southwest across the forest, past Mount Cameroon at 14,000 feet and into Douala. The weather would be tropical but I didn't have Wi-Fi to confirm a forecast. The commander of the military flight training school sought me out in Godfrey's office. He used R66s and had seen DIGA on the apron. I welcomed his advice on flying the local conditions and crucially, he had access to weather forecasts on his phone. He reckoned that I would be able to get through to Douala, skirting the low clouds here and there. We stood beside DIGA for a selfie and feeling more informed, I thanked Godfrey and took off.

I flew southwest at the base of a broken cumulous cloud layer over the thickening forests and full rivers. To the south, the bigger rivers of the Niger delta were all visible. I established contact with Calabar tower, the only airport directly en route. I flew through a bit of rain, had a much closer look at the dense forest canopy below and took some nice close-ups of the hills while flying very low. Out to my right (southwest), the delta ran to the sea, but there was also a military prohibited area to avoid, so I had a five-mile wide corridor to fly in.

I crossed into Cameroon, maintaining contact with Calabar. Inevitably, the misty microclimate from the forest rose to meet the descending cloud about 20 nautical miles inside Cameroon and it became impossible to proceed. I turned around and diverted to Calabar, about 30 minutes flying time away, and messaged Eddie.

I was marshalled by Eyo to a landing in the drizzle and he promised to look after me and became my trustworthy, unofficial handler. It was Sunday but Panshak, the Nigerian Air Force Intelligence Officer for the airport, interviewed me. He was very friendly and warned me about safety issues outside the airport and hotels. The airport 'formalities' from landing to hotel only took two instead of the typical four hours.

Eddie had arranged for me to stay at the Calabar Harbour Resort & Spa, which was certainly over-egging the location and amenities, but the food was edible, the staff were fun, and it had air-conditioning and Wi-Fi, unlike the airport. I met Eyo back at the airport early the next morning where the weather looked acceptable for another attempt to Douala. He chaperoned me round the same inefficient, manual systems, repeating everything to each department and meeting them on their terms in their pokey, air-conditioned offices, where the TV was blasting out a daily soap episode. It was a small airport complex and easy to navigate. I made friends with everyone on this shift and remained optimistic. Calabar's airport staff were friendly, Immigration and Customs were helpful and there wasn't any sign of corruption. Again, the tower didn't have a forecasting capability and I couldn't refuel here either because the underground refuelling system had been closed due to a quality control issue. I still had sufficient fuel in DIGA to reach Douala.

Unfortunately, I met the same unflyable weather and was forced to return to Calabar 20 minutes later! It was now 34°C and oppressively humid, at 95% relative humidity. Eyo met me again, smiling. I went through the familiar routine, handed my passport to Immigration and met the second shift of officials, showing them the pictures of the impenetrable clouds. I needed to get better forecasts and have some luck with the weather. Or possibly find a different route around, over the sea, and go further down the coast to Libreville, Gabon to get south of this messy International Tropical Convergence Zone (ITCZ). However, I would need to refuel and get the slow-to-materialise Gabon permit for that.

So, I settled into a daily routine with Eyo at the airport over the next three days, watching people and the weather, waiting and planning with *G.A.S.E.* The best weather looked like being Thursday, according to my forecasting and Mark I eyeball. Plan A was to conduct a short recce flight over the delta to gauge the weather for a sea crossing, return to Calabar for fuel and then fly across the sea, subject to permits for Libreville. Plan B would be to just go to Douala via the sea route, which would still be inside the ITCZ, using my last existing fuel. Panshak came to chat every day and turned out to be an important figure who helped me, as he promised.

The comings and goings in the humid airport lounge provided a welcome distraction. With weather-delayed flights, it was often full: Chinese contractors, one or two Europeans, well-dressed Nigerian men and colourfully dressed Nigerian women. The little food stall was doing a roaring trade. Chinese companies seemed to have projects all over Africa and Nigeria too, according to the lounge TV news. In discussions, everybody seemed to support a UK premiership football team! My customary dinner was usually rice or potatoes with some scrawny meat, while vegetables comprised completely boiled-to-death green beans. I had time to reflect that I hadn't washed off a single bug that had been squashed on DIGA's screen since entering Africa.

On Thursday 4th August, day 14, I flew my short recce flight south over the Niger Delta below a cloud base at 500 feet and confirmed a brighter-looking sea route. Back at Calabar, 200 litres of fuel appeared miraculously and, using the *InReach Iridium* messaging system, Ahmed confirmed that I still didn't have a permit for Gabon. So, I filed my flight plan for Douala and said goodbye to all the Calabar staff on my final round. Only Eyo accompanied me to DIGA and I was able to tip him discreetly and thanked him warmly for all his help. I lifted for the delta, lost communications as usual, then sneaked through the various airspace, avoiding prohibited areas, oil rigs in the mist and Equatorial Guinea airspace.

The weather improved briefly as I flew low-level up the river delta into Douala, where Gervais sorted me with a single invoice for his handling. I covered DIGA and tied down her blades against the expected stormy ITCZ weather to come, before Gervais drove me to my hotel, which for once took credit cards. With three people to a motorcycle with one holding the umbrella, the traffic and roadside street vendors made the journey an exotic experience. With a population of three million, Douala was a bubbling, albeit poor, urban economy, blessed with plenty of natural foods from the fertile conditions. Raphael, Eyo and Panshak all messaged me to check that I was there safely and wished me good luck.

The next day, Gervais escorted me airside to the weather station and flight planning office at the base of the tower. I still didn't have my permit for Gabon, but the weather was unflyable anyway and that was a good enough excuse. Douala was a big, international airport and it was going to be impossible to build relationships except with a few key people. Pascal, the weatherman, turned out to be a real gentleman and a significant help. He said that the weather would be poor over the weekend and he would help me the following day. It was raining heavily as we spoke and he kindly let me hook up to his phone data, which gave me communications.

I telephoned the director of the Gabon *CAA* who said that the minimum I must have to get my permit for a VFR flight was a portable HF radio or IFR capability for high flying above the weather, for the purpose of radio contact. He also confirmed that he would not accept my satellite phone as a solution, nor a VFR flight in combination with another HF capable aircraft. Damnit, why had it taken so long to reach this impasse?

Africa
The Journey

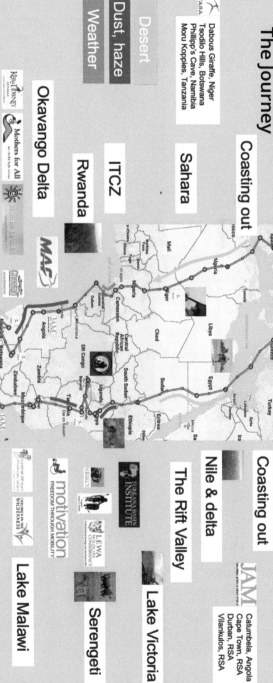

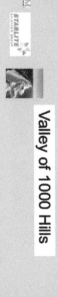

Dabous Giraffe, Niger
Tsodilo Hills, Botswana
Phillipp's Cave, Namibia
Moru Kopjies, Tanzania

Weather

Dust, haze

Desert

Coasting out

Sahara

ITCZ

Rwanda

Okavango Delta

Sossousvlei

The Cape - day 32

Coasting out

Nile & delta

The Rift Valley

Lake Victoria

Serengeti

Lake Malawi

Valley of 1000 Hills

Catumbela, Angola
Cape Town, RSA
Durban, RSA
Vilankulos, RSA

The Cheetah Conservation Fund, Otjiwarongo – Namibia

Masaai welcome at Il Ngwesi – Kenya

Desert brownout, Algeria – Niger border

ITCZ weather, Nigeria – Cameroon border

'Thingy' in Maun – Botswana

Me with JAM staff and kids, Durban – RSA

David Cross inspection, Durban – RSA

Gorilla from Rugendu family, Virunga National Park – DRC

Home visit with Motivation International,
Arusha – Tanzania

Drum refueling, Damazin – Sudan

Cheetah brothers at warthog kill, Lewa – Kenya

Eddie, Charlie Brown and me in Cairo – Egypt

Returning Thingy to
Leon, Wycombe Air
Park – UK

Crossing the Mediterranean at 8,000 feet

The airport's IT expert drove me to a technical IT shop in the city to check if a handheld HF solution for use in aircraft existed. By email, I begged the same question of Brad of *Pacific Avionics P/L*, an Australian company with experience in this field. By Monday, the short answer was 'no', the very expensive answer was 'maybe' and the general advice was to pick another route!

On Saturday, Gervais met and escorted me airside to meet Pascal. Since I was a pilot in transit using a General Declaration, I had been issued a 48-hour passport visa on Thursday when I'd arrived. For the moment, my weather delay was a satisfactory excuse to overstay and I hoped the lack of onward clearance through Gabon wouldn't become an immigration issue too.

Pascal had prepared detailed route forecasts for me and was also using a free website called OGIMET.com that gives a horizontal view of ground and clouds for the route, using *National Oceanic and Atmospheric Administration* (NOAA) data. This was brilliant. He skilfully explained how the ITCZ would shift over the next six weeks and informed me of the weather that I could expect for the rest of my journey. Pascal had about six years' experience of forecasting weather in Africa and he was a fantastic find.

I agreed to spend Sunday at my hotel, letting Gervais have time with his six children. I hadn't met anyone so far who had just two kids. The mentality seemed to be 'more is better'. Food-wise, I was now enjoying plantains cooked in a variety of ways, yam, pawpaw and loads of avocados, in addition to the tough and scrawny meat selections also available. Cameroon's climate provided plenty of fruit and vegetables.

On Monday, Pascal forecast the best weather window

for Tuesday or Wednesday. I hatched Plan B to fly across the sea to São Tomé via the Island of Principé, then fly on to Pointe Noire (Republic of the Congo) the following day, avoiding Gabon airspace altogether. Ahmed applied for both permits, which would take 48 hours, while Pascal forecast the route's weather.

That night, I had terrible cramps in so many different lower leg muscles and my hat was now white with sweat salt, even after only one day of wear. It showed how much water I was losing in the high humidity compared with the desert, so I started using the *Cotswold*-supplied rehydration tablets in my water bottle because I couldn't risk having a cramp while flying!

Back at the airport on Tuesday, Immigration was tut-tutting about me overstaying my 48-hour visa. I explained that flying visually (VFR) required that I wait for the right, safe weather. But the officer wanted 25 USD cash before he would stamp my flight plan to São Tomé for the next day. No receipt meant this was quite possibly an 'unofficial' commission to a small fish!

A *Geotech* helicopter had landed the previous day and Arnold, the pilot, had just left with his HF radio-equipped helicopter flying VFR. Getting away the following day would make me a total of nine days later than planned and delay all my downstream schedule. I needed to email all my hospitality contacts and rearrange my service logistics.

I was mightily relieved when my permits did arrive that evening. However, later on I was visited by another immigration airport official (a bigger fish) requesting that I give him 500 USD for the stamp on my flight plan. Standing in the hotel's public lobby, I convinced him to handle the matter more discreetly in the morning at the airport.

Gervais confirmed that this would be a bribe approach, for sure.

On Wednesday morning, Pascal confirmed that the current unflyable rain and low misty cloud would provide a narrow window of opportunity between 12pm and 2pm and then would deteriorate again. The weather en route was still forecast to be good. After that, I had time to negotiate with the 'bigger fish' and we settled on 200 USD, after which he wanted my *Three Journeys Round* business card to follow my journey, as if we were best mates!

Gervais wasn't convinced about the continuing, rainy low cloud, but I trusted Pascal. We said goodbye and I went and prepared DIGA alone. The weather gap opened up over the airport as expected at 12pm. I was just about to start DIGA when another 'official' appeared from the hangars opposite and requested my documents. I could smell a rat so instead, gave him Gervais' telephone number, which started an almighty shouting match between the two of them. I saw my chance and started DIGA. I did not need this distraction nor delay, and I lifted at 12:30pm into the heavy sky and out over the delta. The first 30 nautical miles south southeast from Douala to the coast provided atrocious low cloud to the treetops. This was marginal VFR, but I found a way to the coast where the weather was good enough to climb to 1,000 feet and continued the crossing to Principé, and on to São Tome.

Arriving at São Tome was a delight, with many friendly, smiling people. It was a tiny airport, with *WFS* fuel and one official for everything. Only a few people spoke any English; I couldn't speak Portuguese and so French became our common language. I walked 200 metres to my hotel and enjoyed a great fish meal with a view of the bay and ended up cleaning my teeth with beer because there wasn't any bottled water available. What a day! The elapsed time video showed how bad the weather was in the delta south of Douala. I'd vowed that I wouldn't fly in marginal VFR after the brownout in the Sahara, and here I was again.

From São Tomé, I flew direct southwest, half over water and half over the beach, to Pointe Noire. As I crossed the Equator over the sea, I was privy to the fabulous sight of breaching whales all around. DIGA also had a colony of tiny São Tome ants running around inside her, which I must have picked up drying the covers on the ground. On landing, I was able to stand on my shadow at midday!

Leaving for my hotel, the airport's Security Officer suggested that I pay 36 USD for 'protecting my helicopter' overnight. I thought to myself, "If the little guys in uniform are corrupt, imagine the example being set at the top?" 183 countries signed the '*UN Convention against Corruption*' adopted in 2003, as the only legally binding, universal anti-corruption instrument. If waste was a drip into a bucket, it is surprising how full the bucket gets in one hour. In turn, corruption was a full-on tap, stifling progress and defrauding many. I was annoyed.

The following morning was hazy with the light drizzle soon drying up as I lifted southwest to cross Cabinda, an enclave and province of Angola. I had a permit to overfly but Cabinda control doubted that, so I skirted inland over the forest, ignoring them politely and crossing the Democratic Republic of Congo into Angola. The forests gradually changed to a managed and deforested landscape, becoming quite barren and dry by Luanda.

I flew for about 10 nautical miles over the dusty roofs of the Luanda metropolis, past the stadium and city centre and was parked up next to another *Geotech* helicopter at this busy, commercial airport. Nzinga greeted me and all the formalities were handled quickly. She showed me to a small, boutique hotel that Eddie had arranged. The hotel sorted my laundry in a washing machine no less, the food was great and with good connectivity, my regime and communications needs were completed in time for a restful evening.

Nzinga and the formalities were so efficient that I lifted early to fly south to Catumbela Airport, on my birthday. The weather was now stable, dry and hazy due to the dust and the forests had given way to savannah. Flying low-level along the coast provided scenes of spectacular canyon features and fishing villages. Invisible power lines and radio masts were now a hazard. Catumbela was another big city, spreading down the coast, from the seaside to the hills. I crossed the Rio Catumbela and landed at the civilian end of the runway, which was parallel to the sea. It was gloriously hot and sunny now.

I was due to meet Duncan Brown, from *JAM*, at the airport. Duncan explained that *JAM* had three types of project, namely malnutrition clinics; providing water and sanitation; and feeding the kids at school as an incentive for them to attend. He said that about 38% of the population (biased to rural) in Angola lived in extreme poverty, they had five or six kids per woman and on average, one of them died. He was taking me to visit a malnutrition clinic.

Rural feeder clinics referred malnourished infants to the rehabilitation clinics and *JAM* supported the Angolan government with a programme of special formula milks, fed to the infants. The mum would stay with the infant and was also fed by the hospital. Even so, about 10% of infants would still die. The mothers seemed listless and trapped in this existence. This was what it was like to be living in extreme poverty on 1 USD per day.

Duncan and his wife, Tanya, entertained me on my birthday at their simple home with a braai and some birthday cake. They had wanted an African experience, and this was at the raw end, with two very young children. I had to admire their conviction and guts.

Duncan, Tanya and their two kids saw me off at the airport and I prepared DIGA in the glorious, fresh sunshine. I now had just Eddie for company, with no radio contact, and some awesome Angolan scenery unfolding beneath me. I climbed steadily towards Lubango, with the hills dotting the landscape becoming bigger and more numerous. I was only 1,000 feet above ground level so I could see clearly that the plains in-between had dried-up riverbeds. Isolated bomas appeared and became more numerous but I did not see any wildlife. Reaching 7,000 feet, I crested the hills from the north, looking south over Lubango. I was permitted to fly past the Cristo Rei statue on the cliff tops overlooking the city. *MAF* has been operating from Lubango for over 13 years. Both Brent Mudde and Nzinga from Luanda were waiting for me and formalities were streamlined.

Brent took me to the *MAF* compound to meet his wife, Helena, for lunch. Then we drove to see the Cristo Rei statue and on to another high city viewing point, talking about the horrors of the Angolan civil war. Three months into the dry season, Lubango was a powdery, dusty place. I was welcomed by Noortji and Marijn to their house in the *MAF* compound. Noortji was also a pilot and *MAF* used its aircraft to assist humanitarian support work.

Brent had invited round all the local expats for a good

old braai that night, in front of a raging campfire. For the first time for me it was chilly, 6,500 feet up, at 15°C. The whole climate and surrounds with blue gum trees reminded me of growing up in Salisbury, Rhodesia. The faith and resourcefulness of these people devoting their lives to support the Angolan people was humbling, and *MAF* did this worldwide. That night, I discovered the reason for there being no wild animals left: the 50,000 Cuban soldiers who supported the government during the civil war had shot and eaten them!

I slept soundly amongst friends and rose to freshly-made muffins and coffee with Noortji and Marijn. I felt relaxed in the hands of Brent and Nzinga, knowing that formalities were all sorted at the airport. It was pleasantly warm with low humidity. I flew low-level southwest across Angola to the Cubane River and then followed it for 100 nautical miles into Rundu, in the north of Namibia. I saw various signs of human activity along the riverbank: cattle, goats, people washing, farming, small industry and fishing. I was looking intently for my first sighting of wildlife in Africa, which finally came in the form of hippos in the river. I tried crocodile for dinner and soaked up the cool and dry climate, glorious sunset and night-time noises of Nature. I slept like a log under the mosquito net and woke to a dawn chorus, cooing doves and a glorious sunrise.

My flying from Rundu to Maun was to be in two parts. The first part was the familiar parched, flat savannah with dry riverbeds, signs of human activity from time to time and then the odd straight road in the middle of nowhere, going to nowhere, apparently. I overflew the Tsodilo Hills en route, a *UNESCO* World Heritage Site, consisting of rock art and caves. The second part was the Okavango delta. It started with the greening of trees at first, then swampy elements, then proper delta. There was all the megafauna that you would expect to see: elephants, zebras, buffalos, buck of various types and sizes and thousands of birds. I skimmed low at 500 feet above ground level all the way to Maun and felt privileged to do so.

Maun Airport was the busy hub for all the safari flights into the delta. I cleared Customs and said hello to staff from *Ker & Downey Botswana* (K&DB), run by Derek Flatt. They provide a quality safari experience, while preserving the environment and fostering economic and social development of the local communities and Botswana. *K&DB* supported *Bana Ba Letsatsi* (which means 'children of the sun'), a charity helping vulnerable, orphaned and at-risk children living in Maun, which I would visit the following day.

I flew back into the wonderful Okavango to the little runway servicing Kanana Lodge. OP, one of the guides, met me and I took a short game drive with Sethunya, another client from Botswana. We saw elephants, buck, birds and one giraffe, then enjoyed sundowners, while taking pictures of the most amazing sunset. Chatting around the campfire, listening to the evening chorus of chirping, clicking frogs and other nocturnal critters, was quite soporific.

I flew back to Maun and left DIGA ready for the next day's flight to Windhoek. Ali and Mark Flatt took me back to their house and I had just enough time to sort my flying administration, camera downloads, social media and flight planning – this had become a daily ritual, including writing my diary. In the afternoon I was going to visit two charities.

I met OP, my guide from Kanana, at *Bana Ba Letsatsi's* (BBL) modest facility. Oupha, who coordinated operations, showed us around. It had basic facilities for schooling kids, making meals, outdoor activities, a library, vegetable garden and chickens, but no residential accommodation. *BBL* helped orphaned or abused children between four and up to 15 years old to get back on their feet. The kids ideally went to school and then came here to get homework help, play and develop their confidence, receive counselling in a safe place. The staff engaged the 'parents' with social workers or the school in order to 'educate'. The problem is not uncommon, even in the UK. However, with the levels of poverty here, the different cultural views on the roles of women, in addition to the vices and temptation of alcohol and drugs, the lot doled out to these kids was dire.

Mothers for All (MfA), the second charity I visited, existed to provide income-generation projects and life skills training for the caregivers of children made vulnerable or orphaned by AIDS. It focused on women as the main primary caregivers. These women received money for the products they made. Some trained caregivers also became trainers for new recruits. Ali introduced me to Oretilé, who coordinated several groups, and we talked with one of them. Here, the women collected magazine paper and made jewellery products from it, sold in Maun through the small *MfA* organised infrastructure. The modest revenues gave the women disposable income and a small element of choice. Oretilé had trained the women how to grow vegetables sustainably, making compost and using water sparingly. This was for home use or for sale.

Back at the house, I wrote my visit reports, coordinated David Cross' arrival for DIGA's upcoming service and alerted the *Cheetah Conservation Fund* of my current position. I had a wonderful evening meal with Ali and Mark, chatting long into the night. Mark had been a fixed wing pilot all his life and we swapped respective stories. On the veranda, the orchestra of toads and reed frogs from the Thamalakane River was awesome. I slept very well again that night.

Mark, Ali and I had breakfast on the veranda overlooking the river, listening to the cooing doves and twittering birds. It again reminded me vividly of Rhodesia. I thanked my generous hosts for their hospitality and I was soon on my way heading southwest away from the Okavango at 1,000 feet above ground level.

For the first time, I had a 20-knot tailwind, which continued to blow and bump me about all the way to Eros Airport. I passed south of the international airport also serving Windhoek, climbed to clear the 7,500 feet hills south of Eros and enjoyed a white-knuckle ride in the turbulence, before landing at an elevation of 5,577 feet. I had to queue for the fuel truck behind three military aircraft but from there, it was an easy walk to my hotel, once formalities were over.

The Cheetah Conservation Fund (CCF) was the global leader in research and conservation of cheetahs. Established by Dr. Marker in 1990, it was based in Namibia at Otjiwarongo, a short flight north. I was looking forward to landing there the next day and meeting Dr. Marker in person. She had been recognised as a *Time* magazine 'Hero for the Planet'. The cheetah is the oldest of all the big cats but sadly, it is also Africa's most endangered big cat, with fewer than 7,100 left in the world.

I walked to the airport at 8:15am and was soon skimming the savannah low-level all the way to Otjiwarongo. We had the whole day and Laurie whisked me off to the impressive *CCF* International Field Research and Education Centre.

5 | Only cheetahs purr

After introductions, Tess conducted my orientation and Page introduced me to their Mendel dog-breeding programme and gorgeous puppies. Bruce, the General Manager, gave me a tour of the whole site by truck. The Mendel is a large Turkish dog breed, acclimatised to heat, conditioned to 'protect goats' and bred for the purpose of supply to the local farmers to reduce livestock predation. Cheetahs hunt during the day and so were visible scapegoats to blame for the dead goats. However, studies show that cheetahs only account for 3% of the livestock killings, with the rest carried out by more numerous, nocturnal predators like leopards. There are only 3,000 cheetahs left in Namibia.

A small number of orphaned baby cheetahs end up at the centre. Unfortunately, they can't learn survival skills in the wild from their mum, so they can never go back to the wild. However, at *CCF*, they are well looked after and exercised, fulfilling an ambassadorial role to let visitors, school trips and tourists see the cheetahs up close. That afternoon, with Laurie by my side, handlers introduced us to four hand-reared cheetahs. We were crouching inside the enclosure, being as quiet as possible. The cats were lying close by on the dusty floor, and one came over to Laurie and sat upright between us, within inches of my face, purring. Cheetahs are the only big cat to purr. It was a memorable moment! Laurie and I continued our conservation and sustainable development discussions with her guests over dinner.

6

The Cape of Good Hope

In the morning, Bruce organised all the staff for a farewell photograph with DIGA and Laurie, centre stage. I thanked them all for the experience and their resolve to save the cheetah.

I flew low, southwest across the same bush as before and saw baboons, ostriches, warthogs, ground birds and various buck. I was going from 5,000 feet to the coast. First, I flew to Phillipp's Cave where the numerous rock paintings in the Erongo Mountains were proof that, thousands of years ago, the ancestors of today's San Bushman had lived in the area. I picked my way through the hills, skimming ridges and flew through the rock formations. During the planning, I had failed to make Phillipp's Cave a stopover, so I continued on to Henties Bay with its beach-like terrain. I was soon on the coast, skirting around Swakopmund and past the area that NASA use as practice 'moon terrain', before arriving at Walvis Bay for refuelling.

I was advised to follow the coast south, inland to see Sossousflei, then back along the coast to Luderitz for the night. This represented about three hours of the most outstanding sand dune flying. The dunes of the first section rose from the narrow beach to about 500 feet high. There were incredible flamingo and seal colonies. The Sossousflei dunes were immense at 1,500 feet high, much redder and quite beautiful, unlike any dunes I had ever seen. Here it was a warm 24°C, while back on the coast, there was a line of fog at a chilly 11°C all the way to Luderitz, caused by the cool Benguela Current.

The sea breaking against the rocks outside my hotel room was restful to fall asleep and wake up to.

The following day was beautifully clear, fresh and windy, and I was soon on my way to Oranjemund to obtain *WFS* fuel. It was Sunday and in this conservative part of the world, I thought nothing of having to make a blind radio call and landing. A fireman came over and said I shouldn't be there without prior written permission and that the airport was only meant for employees of the diamond mining companies – ah, that explained all the security! My existing *WFS* fuel order provided credibility and, with a persuasive smile, I completed Immigration, phoned in my flight plan and left again.

I had finessed the time of the journey to enable a stop en route to meet up with Jannie and Desme Silver. Jannie had been helpful in suggesting a good route through Namibia. I landed at the GPS coordinates he had given me and we had 30 minutes for a cool drink together on the banks of the Orange River. Two hours later, flying east across the Northern Cape, I arrived at Upington Airport, South Africa where I was met by Jacques Venter. Jacques worked with *JAM* and he very kindly took me to visit the *RAF2000* autogyro factory, where I met the Mocke family. We then drove around the areas where Jacques was also helping to feed malnourished kids.

Jacques had already arranged a pass to access the apron with me so that he could help me prepare DIGA. He said a prayer for the good fortune of the trip and my next journeys. While I'm not religious, it was moving and I had a lump in my throat. Once again, determination and faith drove a person like Jacques to do great things for people less fortunate. It was wonderful to meet him.

I was attempting to fly all the way to Cape Town in one day. It was 8°C on the apron with a clear sky, however I had weather to negotiate ahead. Enjoying the scenery, I sneaked through gaps between hills and under the clouds, having to land for an hour to wait out the rain, and made it to a now-sunny Stellenbosch, via Cape Town International Airport for refuelling. The geology of the Cape area made for absolutely stunning viewing. In South Africa, it was easy to file and close flight plans on the phone and DIGA became well-known! Cheryldene and Ricky from *JAM* met and looked after me that evening.

I nipped out early to catch Sylvie from the *Stellenbosch Flying Club* and have my *Fédération Aéronautique Internationale* (FAI) certified, the necessary *World Air Sports Federation* paperwork for my world record application. Helius helped me with a coastal route from Stellenbosch, going around Cape Agulhas, the most southerly point of Africa, to Mossel Bay. My plan was then to route past Port Elizabeth and overnight in East London. There wasn't a cloud in the sky and it was crispy cold. When I filed my flight plans on the phone, they suggested that I fly low-level 'coastwise' all the way. So I did (you only live once!) and was rewarded with whale sightings and pods of dolphins.

Starlite Aviation, who would be hosting my service in Durban, had a Training Academy at Mossel Bay Airport. There, I was met by Cassie and all the other instructors and staff, who welcomed me (embarrassingly) like a hero; they'd been following my tracker. They had a good look at DIGA and refuelled her, while I was fed and advised. I would have loved to have spent longer there: the friendly welcome and interest in my journey was heart-warming and the time together too brief, but I only had two hours to spare. Too soon, I was flying low-level, coastwise to East London, along lovely beaches and past stunning scenery. It was enormously satisfying, stress-less flying. At East London, Les of the local flying club looked after DIGA for the night while Marie and Asekho from *JAM* kindly looked after me.

On Wednesday 24th August, I flew coastwise into Durban, managing to see a whale, more dolphin pods and even cattle on the beach! I was about 200 feet beyond the waves for ages and this would be the last time I would experience this in Africa. The last 10 miles into Durban took me along a built-up beach, past the harbour and then along the beachfront and into Virginia Airport and *Starlite Aviation*. David Cross from *HQ Aviation* had already arrived and was waiting for me. A lady called Jeanette, 10 lovely, noisy kids, plus staff and some partners from *JAM* were assembled for photographs with DIGA in a surprise welcome.

I was introduced to Emmanuel Mhungu who ran *Starlite's* maintenance operations, and Jeanette, who would look after us in the office. Then David got to grips with DIGA's 100-hour inspection with tools provided by *Starlite*, pulling off her covers and cleaning her dusty areas. By all accounts, DIGA was in good health. *Starlite* had fetched David from the airport and sorted our accommodation too, before we went out for an evening meal with Emmanuel, who hailed from Zimbabwe, where I was born.

With 18 partners, *JAM* helped to feed 26,000 children under six years old every day in the Durban area alone! On Thursday morning, Jeanette introduced me to Cathy from one partner organisation called *The Domino Foundation* and we travelled to see the activities at three separate crèches.

The first crèche was a modest business run by a lady looking after six young children in one room, with no running water. The toilet was an old paint tin outside. *JAM* funded *Domino* who provided porridge for breakfast and a rich soup for lunch on a daily basis. There wasn't much mental or physical stimulation for the kids but it was affordable for some working parents. The second crèche catered for 45 kids run by three teachers. There were two classrooms, teaching resources, a small yard and a kitchen and toilet. This was a more professional business, also supported by *JAM* and *Domino*, and the children seemed livelier. The final crèche was well-organised and had more space and resources than the others, with separate, seated toilets for boys and girls. The children were more confident and engaged me unilaterally with questions and cheeky remarks.

All of these children lived in extremely poor families but I could see that their life chances were improved dramatically with the food and crèche teaching activities provided. It was an inspiring example of how most parents, whatever their situation, strive to give their children a good start in life.

Lynn Ross from the Communications team arranged a group photo shoot for my departure. She made a touching farewell speech and I thanked *Starlite* for all the help they had given me and David.

Lifting from Durban was memorable: a steady climb over the built-up sprawl of Durban, towards the Valley of a Thousand Hills and the inclement weather coming down to meet me. The scenery was epic, with thousands of houses perched precariously on the hillside. I was given 'not above

6,000 feet' as I approached Johannesburg and I was only 400 feet above ground level! *Geotech's* helipad appeared right on the GPS button below and I let down for a gentle landing to meet up with Craig Siepman. Jean Kichenbrand, who had provided me with detailed advice via email before the trip, was unfortunately not around. I spent an hour with Craig discussing the journey and just nine minutes later, I landed at my final destination, Grand Central Airport, where I was going to spend the weekend with one of my father's former students, Dr John Orpen and his wife, Alison.

The weekend whizzed by as I caught up with outstanding actions and forward planning. I machine washed my clothes, introduced John to DIGA, topped up the oil and cleaned the sub-Saharan bugs off her windscreen. I improvised my budget sun visor with bungy cord, snoods and bulldog clips, replenished my USD cash and then relaxed on Saturday evening with John and Alison, fielding their questions.

David Brown of *JAM* lived in Johannesburg. On Sunday night, he invited my school friend, Michelle, and her husband, along with Martyn and his wife, to a nice evening meal out. Martyn had made my *JAM* visits work logistically in Catumbela, Stellenbosch, East London and Durban, with Vilanculos in Mozambique next. It was great to thank David personally and lovely to see Michelle again, albeit too briefly. In a lovely gesture, David gave me a red *JAM* feeding bowl, which was given to all the children they support. It was a good night out, but it was early to bed because I had to be up at 5:30am on Monday morning to get to Grand Central by 7am for a double hop.

John and Alison waved me off and I flew low-level over *Geotech* and out to the west. It was a clear 19°C with an inversion layer holding down the smog caused by the city and the coal-fired power stations. I flew eastwards over Witbank, past Nelspruit and into Kruger Airport, which was a beautiful, thatched building. The flying and easy administration in South Africa had been a joy. Lowveld Military controlled my crossing of Kruger National Park and I changed to Maputo control for the remainder of my flight north eastwards. It got really bumpy due to thermal turbulence at whatever height I tried and so I opted for low-level. Getting closer to Vilanculos, the ground was covered by trees and closer still, there was evidence of humans thinning the woods and using the land, but it was still very green. There were some big pools of water on the way in to Vilanculos and views of the rich-blue sea.

Nordino from *JAM* met me to explain the plans for an early start the next morning. We were to visit *JAM* farming and feeding activity at a rural settlement called Pambera about 20km away to the northeast. This gave me time to crack on with my daily regime, using the Lobby-Fi at the hotel while simultaneously slapping down the mosquitos trying to eat me. I had another wonderful night falling asleep and waking up to the sound of the waves in what was a holiday destination for South Africans.

Breakfast was spent overlooking the sea and talking to two people who worked in public health (HIV). We swapped stories before they moved on to their next assignment. Nordino picked me up at 8am and we drove through the rural scenery and dirt roads to a local school in Pambera. Louisa, the headmistress, showed me around, with Nordino translating.

This was how extremely poor people did their very best to educate their kids and I had already seen how dedicated teachers made the best of limited resources in other parts of Africa.

The school had 200 pupils – 100 girls and 100 boys – with one toilet for each gender. There were two shifts, with six hours of schooling per shift: 12 to 14-year olds in the morning and six to 11-year olds in the afternoon. *JAM* provided porridge, which was not only a source of nourishment but also a good incentive to come to school and receive possibly their best meal of the day. The girls were culturally under immense pressure to prove that they were fertile so they could be married off young. Louisa, a widow, had six children herself and managed the school during the day and her own family during the evening – a true superheroine.

At their demonstrator farm, *JAM* taught about 70 teachers and farm managers per year how to grow vegetables for their schools and manage their farms. There were demonstration crops of cabbage, spinach, lettuce and maize, along with water-efficient irrigation and simple mechanisation too. Nordino then took me to visit a farm nearby that had received help from *JAM*. About three years ago, in extreme drought, 34 families decided to collaborate and set up the *Agricultural Association of the Mothers of Pambera*.

The next day, I took off flying northwards to Malawi, leaving the delicious seafood (especially the prawns!) of Vilanculos behind me. I was able to overfly Pambera and took aerial photographs. It was sunny with increasing thermal turbulence and the scenery was delta-like and coastal. As I headed up to Beira, I saw sporadic settlements, mobile phone masts and what looked like natural gas stations from time to time. The ground was cut by the rivers meandering to the sea and with the rivers came the greener and sometimes irrigated fields.

I could tell that it was going to be hot flying north because the sun was ahead of me and it came directly in through the canopy all day. I crossed the Zambezi and then the border into Malawi; I could see that the inhabitants were taking full advantage of the water and cultivation because the population density increased markedly into Malawi.

After formalities at Blantyre had been completed, it was a quick skip northeast across flat country, a low-level flight to the Shire River and then, just like the Cubane River in Angola, I flew low up the river, over the bridge and into Mvuu Camp. The river was full of hippos and on the Liwonde National Park land to my right-hand side, there were elephants. I landed on the grass and was met by Matthews, a guide for *Central African Wilderness Safaris* (CAWS), and my hosts. I joined Matthews for a peaceful boat ride on the river until the sun set, watching hippos, crocs, waterbucks, impalas, warthogs, wagtails, cormorants, egrets and many more animals and birds.

CAWS provide eco-tourism-based safaris while protecting Malawi's natural heritage and the biodiversity it supports. *CAWS* also involve local communities by supporting *Children in the Wilderness*, a non-profit organisation that facilitates sustainable conservation through leadership development and education of rural children in Africa.

I set my alarm early to capture beautiful sunrise pictures and then went for an animal tracking lesson with Matthews. After breakfast, we crossed the river and rode bicycles for a few miles to Nanthomba School, housing a thousand children.

At the gate to the park, I met Patrick and Wello who had a 'roadside shop' full of spectacular carvings. They had swapped poaching for carving and the revenues allowed them to buy wood for more carving and to support their families. Their solar panel was charging a battery that was charging their phone and also powered three LEDs to provide light at home. Progress!

Edward and Donix met us at Nanthomba which took the lead for the eco-club supported by *CAWS* (and other donors). Matthews was a prime mover in setting up the eco-club and these teachers had made the club real for the kids who chose to participate. They taught the theory and used the vegetable garden and plant nursery as teaching resources, selling produce to Mvuu Lodge. Matthews came from the area, which was impoverished and had suffered from years of drought.

Edward ran a Q&A session, translating as Matthews and I talked with the eco-club volunteers. All the children already lived close to Nature and understood the essence of sustainable development because it was a matter of life and death to them. The questions were humbling. One lady, about 25 years old, with only two children, asked if it was possible to do what she wanted to do and not what was expected of her in society. This was a great example of how women and children can play such a critical role in eliminating extreme poverty and achieving sustainable development through education and choice. This wasn't like the extreme poverty I had seen in Angola where the women were listless; it was extreme poverty with a desire to change.

I had always recruited people into my businesses who showed desire and enthusiasm. With these intrinsic qualities, it was always possible to develop their capability and to provide an environment to enable their success. Teaching people to fish and having a fishing policy: I could see the parallels right here with the *UN Sustainable Development Goals*.

I woke up on Friday morning at 5am to the twittering of excited birds, the deep laughing of hippos in the Shire River and the barking, squealing and pitter-patter of baboon feet outside my lodge. Africa is a wonderful place to be when Nature wakes up. I planned to clear Immigration at Lilongwe and then fly the length of Lake Malawi into Mbeya, just inside the border of Tanzania. Then on Saturday, I was planning to get to Arusha in the north of Tanzania, stopping to refuel about halfway in Dodoma.

I was sad to be leaving the absolute tranquillity of Mvuu Lodge. I said goodbye to Matthews, who was preoccupied chasing away the greedy Vervet monkeys who were pinching bread off the breakfast tables, and I took a picture of DIGA, with a warthog minding its own business in the background. There were clouds but the weather was good as I hopped over to Lilongwe. There, I bumped into Jacques Venter who was passing through on a business trip. I filed a flight plan and flew northwest to join the western edge of Lake Malawi. The beach and lake were full of little fishing dugouts and fisherman had set up tables to dry out their catch. Lake Malawi was like an inland sea and flying up its shoreline was brilliant at low-level.

Ahmed of *G.A.S.E.* was now organising the refuelling at Mbeya, not *WFS* on this occasion. He messaged me and confusion developed over which of Mbeya's airports I was flying to and whether it had fuel. Apparently, a new airport had opened and the old one had closed within the last month but the flight planning office at Lilongwe hadn't mentioned this. Ahmed and I worked fast as a team since we only had 20 minutes until my Point of No Return (PONR) to

Lilongwe. I had to make a quick decision to divert to a new point of entry in Tanzania that had fuel available. Between us, we had to do all the weather, winds and fuel calculations for two options and pick the right one – or return!

I judged Dodoma to be the most attractive option due to winds and I anticipated it by turning to fly directly across Lake Malawi, while we still calculated furiously. I chose Dodoma but the decision was a bit hairy. When I climbed over the high ground to get across the hills in Tanzania, it played havoc with my *iPad* ETA calculations and that in turn played havoc with my head for a while! However, with Ahmed's help, I found the best winds for fuel efficient flying for endurance and landed with 30 minutes of fuel remaining.

The 24/7 hotel restaurant was extremely convenient to suit my timings for dinner and breakfast as I set off early the next day for Arusha. I made a lovely flight over some extremely dry terrain, thermally bumpy at times. I saw bomas scattered around with basic mud hut dwellings and a few scrawny-looking cows and goats. It looked like a tough existence down there. I was expecting to see Mount Meru (14,000 feet) and Kilimanjaro (19,000 feet), but the microclimate around the mountains obscured the landscape, except for the broad base of Mount Meru.

My host in Arusha was Rob Linck who was right there to greet me as I landed, dismounted and covered DIGA. He knew Kenya and Tanzania very well and confirmed that both were easy going with regard to general aviation. The Linck family kindly looked after me in their home for two nights, where I had the pleasure of also meeting Anita, Rob's wife, and two of his children.

The following morning, I met with Abdullah Munish,

Motivation International's technical co-ordinator in Tanzania. He had driven from a town called Moshi, at the foot of Kilimanjaro and, together with Emanuel, the *Motivation* co-ordinator in Arusha, we jumped into Abdullah's van to make some home visits. On the way, I learnt about Abdullah's car accident, Emanuel's accident while working in a tanzanite mine, the state of the economy, as well as gaining insight into the lives of the physically disabled in Tanzania. There were about four million people, out of a population of 45 million, with physical disabilities in Tanzania, caused mainly by road traffic accidents, violence and natural causes.

Abdullah had been in a car accident, 16 years ago. He had made his current wheelchair as a final year college project while on a *Motivation* and college-partnered course. Neither Emanuel nor Abdullah had insurance, nor was there any state assistance: they'd had to look after themselves. Now there was a growing self-help peer group of 30 members in Arusha, with about 200 in Moshi. Abdullah explained, "This was the chair that brought my life back." He was truly inspirational.

Motivation worked with the *Kilimanjaro Association for the Spinally Injured* (KASI) to provide direct support in four areas. They were mobility (providing the right wheelchair and training); survival (during recovery from an accident); empowerment (participating fully in the community with a disability); and inclusion (helping with child enrolment in schools with wheelchair access).

We were visiting the urban equivalent of rural poverty. There was electricity here but water was usually a tap outside the house and sanitation was basic. Small-scale farming couldn't sustain everyone and there wasn't enough industry to provide jobs – it was a vicious circle.

We met Julius and Judiathi and two of their four children. Judiathi had been pregnant at the time of Julius' car accident. He suffered a spinal injury high on his neck and so he couldn't help himself or even wheel his chair about. Judiathi was now the main breadwinner; she made bread, did small sewing jobs and bought and prepared vegetables for resale. The family struggled to make ends meet and prayed when they didn't have enough money to live on. There was no government support or insurance options, and family and friends had abandoned them after nine years. Their plight was desperate, although the children liked going to school and had aspirations of their own.

In the afternoon, I met up with Trevor Holden to plan a scenic route to Mwanza via the lodge that Trevor was managing. I redistributed the weight in DIGA to carry Trevor for the next two days. It was great to catch up with him after some 30 years. I had gone to school with his brother, Roy, in Rhodesia and Roy now lived in California.

The following morning was completely overcast for the first time and I agreed to meet Trevor at DIGA at 1pm, still allowing us plenty of time to get to Plantation Lodge. I said my goodbyes to the Linck family before Rob took me for a smoothie at the Arusha Coffee Lodge. Rob, who had also been chairman of the Aero Club at Nairobi Wilson Airport, gave me more contacts before we took our ritual selfies with Trevor and DIGA, with Mount Meru finally appearing as an eye-catching backdrop.

Trevor was excited about flying over his beloved Tanzanian home turf in a helicopter and we lifted from Arusha with great expectation of some good photos. Flying northwest to Lake Natron, the ground was bone dry as we passed the Monduli Hills on our left. We turned southwest, flying over Lake Natron, a sulphur lake with flamingos at its edge, before continuing towards a really big, active volcano, Oldoinyo Lengai (2,878 metres). The 'Mountain of God' in the Maasai language last erupted in 2006 and Trevor had climbed it twice since then! We flew over Empakai Crater with its lake that almost fills the entire crater floor, and on to a high plateau, which was a big Maasai area with cattle, goats and manyatta all around. We continued over the crater lip and into Ngorongoro Crater where we saw buffalos, wildebeest and giraffes. Leaving Ngorongoro, we descended to the lodge about five nautical miles to the south. Renate Marahrens, who owned Plantation Lodge, met us at DIGA with a fabulously friendly and relaxing welcome, leading to sundowners and dinner.

In the bar, Trevor phoned his mum who still lived in Zimbabwe and we had a few words, reminiscing about the 'good old days' of our childhood. Then he phoned his brother, Roy, in California, to update him on his day with the helicopter. I had grown up with Roy and he had experience in helicopters during the war in Rhodesia. This was the first time that Roy and I had talked since my university days when he came to Scotland, although we had kept in touch at Christmas time over the years.

I had a great night's sleep in an unbelievably luxurious lodge called Zanzibar, which Renata and Trevor had insisted I use. In the morning, Trevor showed me all of his handiwork and improvements at the lodge which had taken about 10 years. By midday, the weather was good to go, and we organised all the staff kids for a photo session and then surprised Renata with a quick spin in DIGA around her Plantation Lodge. Renata in turn surprised me with a gracious donation to *Save the Children* and *Motivation International*. Trevor climbed in and we set off to cross Ngorongoro Crater and then fly northwest across the length of the Serengeti National Park, before picking up the edge of Lake Victoria and flying clockwise round it to Mwanza.

We flew up the Oldupai Gorge, which was one of the most important paleoanthropological sites in the world; it had proven invaluable in furthering understanding of early human evolution. The British-Kenyan, paleoanthropologist-archaeologist team, Mary and Louis Leakey, established the excavation and research programmes at Oldupai Gorge, which achieved great advances of human knowledge. Still crossing the Serengeti, which means 'endless plains', we overflew Moru Koppies where there were a series of Maasai paintings. Soon enough, we were following the upper reaches of the Mbalageti River and flying westward down it to Lake Victoria. Along the green banks we saw the resident animals including elephants, topi, zebras, buffalos, wildebeest and loads of buck. Trevor said that the famous Serengeti migration was elsewhere, following the green grass and the rains, which hadn't reached here yet. The valley flattened out at about 4,000 feet above sea level and in the distance, we could see Lake Victoria. The lakeside was populated with some farming, industry and lots of little fishing boats.

Trevor kept the Mwanza officials busy while I prepared DIGA and sought advice on getting to Goma in the Democratic Republic of the Congo (DRC) the next day. Simon, who was a friend of Trevor's, whisked us off to his house where we were welcomed by his wife, Sia, and their two young children, Billy and Georgie. Simon and Trevor went way back and, while they had a lot to catch up on, I was also looking forward to the local restaurant's grub and a good natter with some new folks. We ate sudza (ugali) with our hands and the staff came around with a kettle and bowl to wash afterwards. We were seated outside in the relative darkness of a poorly lit veranda, beers on the table. Using the restaurant Wi-Fi, which was good, I was unfortunately preoccupied with getting my permit for entry to the DRC. Ahmed seemed to be struggling at this late hour and frustratingly, after such a wonderful day with Trevor, I was not permitted to fly the following day.

In the morning (Wednesday), Simon and Trevor departed, dropping the kids at school on the way, leaving me and Sia to unravel the unfolding permit story. After switching my mobile phone data on and off several times, I eventually blew my data budget! Each *Civil Aviation Authority* (CAA) had its own process and lead time for applying for a permit. *G.A.S.E.* were masters at understanding these requirements, making applications and satisfying requests from the documentation that they held for both DIGA and me.

I had originally wanted a permit to fly from Mwansa to Goma, then on to Entebbe in Uganda. However, due to the weather forecast over Lake Victoria and in discussion with Rob Linck, I had changed my permit request to fly from Mwansa to Goma to Mwansa but unbeknown to me, this change had been lost. I also believed that I could fly locally from Goma International Airport to Rumangabo in Virunga National Park where I had an official invitation to stay. This turned out not to be the case and in hindsight, I should have applied for a permit for Mwansa to Goma, to Rumangabo, to Goma, then back to Mwansa.

With limited communications, delays and time differences between Ahmed and the DRC authorities based in Kinshasa, it took a bit of time to decipher what was going on and make progress. Ahmed skilfully avoided paying a bribe to a brazen official in Kinshasa who said he could sort everything out for a 300 USD sum sent to his personal account!

Sia made lunch for the pair of us during the day and, when the kids came home, supper for us all. I helped Billy with a science experiment that was fun for both kids as well as for me! By 4:30pm, Ahmed had been successful and I had a permit for a flight on Thursday. I emailed Jean-Claude, my Virunga contact in Goma, who had been so patient and understanding during the day's challenges. I was relieved that I was only facing a one-day delay to my visit to Virunga National Park, which was a must see, ever since Louise Leakey had suggested it at our meeting in Nairobi in October 2015.

Virunga National Park is one of the most biologically diverse, protected areas on the planet. It is also a geological wonder containing two of the world's most active volcanoes and a *UNESCO* World Heritage Site (designated in 1979). However, for much of its history, the park had been threatened severely by armed conflict. However, thanks to the dedication of the park's rangers and wardens, Virunga has been able to survive. Born of a Congolese commitment to the protection of the park, the *Virunga Alliance* aims to foster peace and prosperity through the responsible economic development of natural resources for the four million people who live within a day's walk of the park's borders. The main sectors for development include energy, tourism, agro-industry, sustainable fisheries and infrastructure.

On Thursday morning, Sia and I dropped Georgia and

Billy at school, then I went on to Mwanza Airport. I called Jean-Claude and he said that Goma's weather was just a few isolated CBs (cumulonimbus: cloud forming a towering mass with a flat base at fairly low altitude and often a flat top, as in thunderstorms). I had some reservations because the hills were high but I lifted at 9am and set off for an amazing journey, after my permit nightmare the previous day. The flight westwards over the south of Lake Victoria was beautiful and the stretch leaving the lake was ridge after ridge at 5-6,000 feet. Then Rwanda was so beautiful, with rolling, green, high hills and lots of water up to 7,000 feet. It was actually called 'Mille Collines' meaning 'thousand hills' in French. I skimmed across the last, much higher hills at 7,200 feet with a tailwind and dropped down to Lake Kivu, which was also scenic, and could easily have passed for a Mediterranean coastline.

When I landed at Goma, I was expecting the usual refuel, Immigration and Customs routine and then to fly on the short 25 nautical miles to Rumangabo. But I was inundated with Kalashnikov-carrying security guards and officials! I had to wrestle for fuel, receive my 14-day visa stamp and was then hit with the bombshell that my permit was only valid for Mwanza to Goma to Entebbe and did not permit flying to Rumangabo. I explained that I thought there had been an error, but I was informed flatly that even so, I would have to reapply and obviously wait. By now, Jean Claude of *Virunga* had been permitted to join me and his French was much better than mine. We spoke to the director of the airport who said that he would normally be able to allow my local flight for a consideration but that the airport was currently under the watchful eye of a *CAA* inspector from Kinshasa who was conducting a three-day audit of all the operations. We spoke to the inspector directly and he said he would call Kinshasa and expedite my new application for the correct permit, which would have to be signed off by the Security Services in Kinshasa because of the local security situation. The inspector seemed to be honourable and I took him at his word, asking Ahmed to apply for the correct permit, which we should expect the next day.

Looking around, the Goma weather was indeed showing big CBs. It looked like it was building up to the rainy season. There was rain on the surrounding volcanoes and Nyiragongo had its own microclimate.

I fetched my bag from DIGA and covered her against the elements and prying eyes. This attracted an audience of airport staff who all wanted their picture taken with me and DIGA in turn. I was parked in front of the secure *United Nations'* facility and a local man called Kita, who spoke English well, became my handler. Kita was another of these unofficial individuals just hanging around the airside of the airport! An armed airport guard took it upon himself to watch the helicopter and he organised two young soldiers to sleep under DIGA at night. Obviously, I would tip them if they did a good job. Happy with the arrangements, Jean-Claude took me to the *Virunga* offices, which gave me a chance to get Wi-Fi and see what downtown Goma looked like. It was abject poverty but nonetheless a town full of all the services that people needed, just on an extremely low budget. But it wasn't the sort of place that I would want to walk around by myself.

That evening, I had a meal with Jean-Claude. While we discussed sustainable development and Virunga, my two-day delay would spoil any chance that I had to climb Nyiragongo (3,470 metres) and see the lava lake at night, but hopefully I would still see the gorillas. Jean-Claude gave me an interesting history lesson about Rwanda and the genocide. During colonial times, Belgium favoured the Tutsis over the Hutus. With independence, democratic voting saw the majority Hutus in power, and incredible tension and aggression built up between the two tribes. Someone killed the president (there are many conspiracy theories) and then the genocide that followed in 1994 took about a million lives in a few short months. The Tutsis, exiled in Uganda, returned and chased out the Hutus, many of whom fled to Goma.

After the Second Congo War was over in July 2003, confrontations between park personnel and rebel groups continued. 80 park staff were killed between 1996 and 2003, making a total of 152 since 1966, which had risen to 175 by April 2018 after my visit. Several armed rebel groups operated in the park, including the *FDLR* and *CNDP*, and clashes also occurred between park personnel and Mai-Mai militias in illegal settlements.

Forces Démocratiques de Libération du Rwanda (FDLR) was an ethnic Hutu group opposed to the ethnic Tutsi influence. *Congrès National pour la Défense du Peuple* (CNDP) was a political, armed militia established in the Kivu region of the DRC in December 2006. It controlled the Mikeno sector of Virunga National Park between December 2006 and January 2009. They generated income by levying fees from local people for protecting prohibited activities inside the park, like poaching and clandestine fishing, logging, producing and smuggling charcoal, but also through armed robberies and kidnapping. The term 'Mai-Mai' referred to any kind of community-based militia group active in the DRC, formed to defend their local territory against other armed groups. Most were formed to resist the invasion of Rwandan forces and Rwanda-affiliated Congolese rebel groups, but some also formed to exploit the war for their own advantage by looting, cattle rustling or banditry. In the course of increasing tensions, the park's chief warden, Emmanuel de Mérode, was shot and injured in April 2014 while travelling by road from Goma to Rumangabo, the location of *Virunga's* HQ.

7

The world's most dangerous national park

I breakfasted overlooking Lake Kivu and talked to a lady who was writing reports to obtain grants for a *Non-Governmental Organisation* (NGO). Jean-Claude drove me to the airport and I was able to take more videos of the bustling Goma streets. Kita met me and we wandered freely back and forth through all the security. The weather was warm but the light evening rain had not cleaned up the dusty haze that still existed. So far, East Africa seemed dustier than even the Sahara Desert, which was a more granular sand.

Kita and I retired to the airport shop to have a Fanta Orange and wait for my permit to be granted. I nudged the inspector as often as I dared, although he remained confident that it would be forthcoming. The airport was home to a big *UN* contingent with many white, liveried aircraft and Mi-8 helicopters supplied by different nations. There were also many different *NGOs* around with their own trucks and aeroplanes coming and going. At 3pm, the inspector finally told me that the Security Services in Kinshasa were disinclined to give me the new permit due to the security situation here and that would mean I only had my existing permit to leave Goma for Entebbe on Sunday. "Dammit!" I thought, and "Thank you very much for all your help," I said to the inspector. What a waste of time!

Jean-Claude implemented Plan B: an armed guard would accompany me in a Land Rover up to Rumangabo. While I was disappointed not to be flying DIGA up to their helipad, I was not going to miss out on seeing the Virunga gorillas. DIGA would be guarded again and Kita would meet me early Sunday on my return.

I enjoyed the ride up to Rumangabo; 75 bumpy minutes over character-building roads, trying to take photos of amazing scenery. There were volcanoes on either side, sharp volcanic rocks used for almost every kind of dwelling, cultivation up the side of every hill, lush vegetation, wretched people everywhere eking out a living and woman collecting water in yellow, plastic drums. All along the way there were miscellaneous, armed groups hanging about. We arrived safely and within 20 minutes, it was pitch dark. Julie and Anthony, the resident pilot who I'd been in touch with, welcomed me to an evening at Mikeno Lodge.

It felt great to be tucked up in bed as it thundered and rained hard that night. In the morning, I was driven to Bukima, close to the Mikeno Volcano, rising to 4,437 metres. Pierre would be my guide to see the gorillas, along with an AK47 for our protection. We had another man with a panga who cut a path for us through the jungle. Unbeknown to me at the time, there was another pair ahead of us who had followed the last known GPS position of the Rugendu family of gorillas. Pierre was in contact with them and we walked just outside the park across the cultivated fields, passing farmers and cows from time to time at an altitude of 7,200 feet. Then we crossed into the park and started our passage through the thick forest towards the gorillas.

All of a sudden, we were amidst the Rugendu family.

The gorillas were spread out over several small clearings and I was repositioned to see members of the whole family over about an hour. It was incredible to be so close to such immensely powerful and yet peaceful animals. The 250 kilo silverbacks had huge hands, biceps and leg muscles; they were incredibly strong and all they ate was the green foliage around them. We were right amongst them and they didn't seem to mind at all. Sometimes they would move quite quickly after a period of inactivity, before we had chance to get out of the way, so a baby gorilla would scuttle by really quite close to us. When the silverbacks did the same, there wasn't a lot of space at all!

Back at Mikeno Lodge, I waxed lyrical with other tourists about what I had seen. Anthony gave me some advice about routes back to Mwanza, taking in the lovely volcanoes around Rumangabo. We all felt the tremor of a magnitude 5.2 earthquake somewhere between Uganda and Tanzania, which wobbled and shook the furniture! My evening was spent around the main fire, updating my diary and listening to the various conversations in French, Dutch and English.

The following day was going to be a big flying day: Goma (DRC) to Mwanza (Tanzania) to Nairobi Wilson (Kenya) and finally into the *Aero Club of East Africa*. I was up at 5:15am again to settle up, say goodbye and catch the first Land Rover back to Goma Airport. At breakfast, I met Steffany Kisling, founder of *Sky Angels*, who trained flight attendants. We had time for a brief discussion about sustainable development. My timings worked like clockwork and Kita had everything under control at the airport. While everybody tried to get in on the act, I was able to discreetly tip Kita, the guard and the soldiers who had dutifully helped me, then I lifted at 9am. The irony of my routing was such that the 'incorrect DRC permit' said I could leave for Entebbe to the northwest, which routed me over Rumangabo! So, I happily filed for Entebbe, recorded my alternate airport as Mwanza and flew over Rumangabo. From there, I turned east, direct to Mwanza, flying north of Kigali. I already knew the weather was good because I had seen it with my own eyes on my drive to the airport! The volcanoes were awesome and I was flying over dense forest, once in Volcanoes National Park. I skimmed the ridge between the volcanoes left and right as I flew east into Rwanda. I got to 8,800 feet, 22°C, 1022 hectopascals, which equated to a density altitude of 12,750 feet. DIGA was working hard but doing fine. The vista that opened up as Rwanda appeared showed off the impressive beauty of this country. West Rwanda proudly showed off 7,000 feet rolling hills, cultivated vertically and well populated, with good roads.

Since I knew my way around, my refuelling stop at Mwanza was straightforward. My second flight of the day was northwest across Serengeti National Park. Again, the scenery was spectacular; there were animals including elephants, zebras, buffalos and wildebeest, and of course, cattle, goats and people on a grand scale. I crossed high ridges and rift valley features and I was up at 8,000 feet with some bumpy thermal activity. I had intermittent communications with Dar es Salam and Nairobi control and then finally, I was controlled into the very busy Nairobi Wilson Airport, landing at 5,500 feet above sea level.

I wanted to spend one night at the famous *Aero Club of East Africa*, absorbing the atmosphere and history as part of *TJR*. It was a bit tatty but the welcome was charming and the Wi-Fi brilliant, allowing me to catch up with my photographic uploads.

Day 53, Monday 12th September, was a rest day. I sorted DIGA and my subsequent flight plan and was looking forward to meeting Cissy Walker, who had influenced so much of *TJR* for me. Cissy, in the meantime, had sneaked through the Aero Club gate on to the airfield, airside. This turned out to be ill-advised because she got caught up in a "You shouldn't be here without permission/You may not take photos" spat with an official and we were escorted to the airfield security police to 'untangle ourselves'. We got away with a telling off but unfortunately, no photos of Cissy with DIGA, which was a shame.

At Cissy's house, I set the washing machine running and we went to the Talisman restaurant for lunch with Cissy's son, Nicholas. There, we bumped into Richard Leakey (Louise's dad) and Lawrence Martin from Stony Brook University, also out for lunch. I would be at the *Turkana Basin Institute* (TBI) –*Turkwel* in about five days' time and so it was a timely, chance encounter. Cissy, Nicholas and I stayed up far too late that night looking at my journey photographs, but it seemed a shame to waste the opportunity.

I rose early, ready to take a quick breakfast with David Coulson of *TARA* who lived close by. It was very nice to catch up with him again and go through the various sites I had flown over, showing him some pictures. *The Trust for African Rock Art* was an international, Nairobi-based organisation committed to recording the rich rock art heritage of the African continent and making this information widely accessible, while safeguarding those sites most threatened by humans and nature.

I hugged Cissy goodbye and joined the chock-a-block Nairobi traffic to the airport by taxi. After an administrative delay that only those who have used Wilson Nairobi Airport would understand, I was finally ready to take-off. At DIGA, I called the various telephone numbers I had been given by Jamie Roberts and Cissy to clear the way at Nanyuki and to understand the best approach to 'fly off the grid' to Sirikoi Lodge and Il Ngwesi. Then I lifted for Nanyuki. Wilson was a busy and well-controlled airport that understood helicopter movements. I took pictures of Kibera, the largest slum in Kenya, situated parallel to the airport.

I landed at Nanyuki Civil Airport on the equator, at an altitude of 6,400 feet above sea level. One of the *Tropic Air Kenya* pilots marshalled me down next to their helicopters. After refuelling, and with Mount Kenya on my right, I skimmed low-level over the lush, high ground via the 'country club', crested the hills and descended into the dry plain. Ahead of me, I picked out the trees protected by the electric fence and greenery denoting the river in front of *Sirikoi* that I remembered from my October visit with Lavinia in 2015. I assessed the wind and landed in a cloud of dust, flattening the rotor blades as quickly as possible.

Willie Roberts was there to meet me, with a big grin on his face, and we were soon having lunch with Sue Roberts and a guest. Our discussions quickly moved to sustainable development and conservation matters, all the while watching the zebras, elephants, giraffes, waterbuck, impalas and more animals meandering around the watery frontage to the raised deck, just a few metres away, behind the electric fence.

At 4:30pm, I was reunited with Legai, the Maasai guide who I'd met in 2015. The game drive was great viewing: we saw two lions, buffalos, giraffes, zebras, Grevy zebra, impalas, elands, secretary birds and bustards, the heaviest flying bird. I was also lucky enough to be reacquainted with the two cheetah brothers who Lavinia and I had seen. Later, I was able to type up my diary while sitting on the raised deck, looking out at the wandering animals. It was another stunning day in this African paradise and I felt fortunate to be invited again to absorb the experience.

I enjoyed more breakfast and lunchtime discussions with Willie and Sue and then said goodbye to Willie with his best wishes for the rest of my journey, as he was flying his aeroplane to Nairobi for a meeting. Well rested, my 4:30pm game drive was with Ngila. He could sense that there was a predator about; the eland was looking shifty, walking away and looking back nervously, and birds of prey were perched patiently in the trees around. These signs were like pointing fingers to a seasoned Maasai and Ngila easily found the two cheetah brothers (while I photographed), devouring a fresh warthog kill: absolutely amazing! We saw both white and black rhino and I took good pictures to make a Facebook post on the successful rhino protection scheme run by *Lewa Wildlife Conservancy*. There were, at the time, 68 individuals of both black and white rhino in the conservancy, guarded against poaching, which represented about 13% of Kenya's entire rhino population.

The next day, Sue supplied me with fruit, biltong, nuts and vegetables, before I took off for a 10-minute flight to Il Ngwesi Eco-lodge. After descending from about 5,500 feet above sea level to 3,700 feet, it was much hotter. I landed in another cloud of Kenyan dust to a truly amazing Maasai welcome, including the jump dance and guttural chants, which I was encouraged to join.

I was met by Kip Ole Polos, the chairman of *Il Ngwesi Group Range*, James Kinyaga, a guide of 20 years who I had met last year, and James Kasso, the lodge manager. I was hosted in the same lodge and toilet with the incredible view over the water hole that I'd enjoyed before! I was there for two nights with these most hospitable people in the only Maasai community-owned and operated lodge. Lunch was by the pool with Kip and a few others. We discussed the *TJR* journey and *Il Ngwesi's* future revenue and infrastructure development plans. *Il Ngwesi*, meaning 'people of wildlife', is home to the Laikipia Maasai, and they were celebrating 20 years of wildlife conservation, eco-tourism and community development in northern Kenya.

Later we all squeezed into a truck for an evening game drive, spotting zebras, giraffes, giraffe gazelles (the ones with the really long necks), impalas, jackals, guinea fowl, vultures and eagles. Arriving at the high edge of a dry riverbank, we talked as the sun went down. Kip sprung a champagne toast to long life, *Il Ngwesi* and tailwinds all the way home for me. It was a great surprise and I learned that the Maasai actually don't drink alcohol that much. Traditionally, you get permission from your father, which is a ceremonial thing, and usually it's only the elders who really have a drink. I was reminded jokingly, that because I was over 50, I was considered a senior elder! As the sun set, we counted four hyenas skulking around the riverbed below.

Dinner was a braai on the ground below the main viewing veranda at the Il Ngwesi Lodge; goat for all, ugali (sudza) and delicious vegetables, with soup to start and chocolate mousse to finish. It was an excellent meal and a discussion about Maasai traditions (for example, they don't eat fish) led to the discovery that there was a local wedding the next day. It was apparently good luck for strangers to drop in at a Maasai wedding!

Up early, I used the wonderful outdoor shower with my head torch hanging from a branch. It was brilliantly dark just before the African dawn. After a quick coffee, James (the guide) and I jumped into a truck and drove off to the wedding. It was being held at the manyatta, a Maasai settlement that was being maintained as a full-time, working model of traditional life. I took pictures of another gorgeous sunrise on the way.

Proceedings for what was a two-day wedding were well under way. Dixon and the elders welcomed us and I was introduced to the groom and best man, who was the principal at a local school, and who lucidly described the difference between traditional and modern ways. I was given a tour around the traditional hunting, fire-lighting, beekeeping and animal-trapping, although hunting and trapping are banned in Kenya nowadays. Real life is a mix of traditional and modern such as tin roofs, solar panels and TVs. The groom told me that he had paid a dowry of nine cows for his bride! We watched the ritual slaughtering of a ram in all its gory detail, before politely taking our leave.

We took a slow game drive back to Il Ngwesi and a look at the Rhino Sanctuary to see two white rhinos, which were being protected by 16 armed *Northern Rangeland Trust* rangers 24/7: that is certainly taking conservation seriously. In 1960, there were about 20,000 rhinos in Kenya. This was my second magical experience at Il Ngwesi Eco-lodge with the 'People of Wildlife', and I was very sad to be saying goodbye.

I lifted in a cloud of dust, flew a circuit of the lodges to get aerial footage and then set course back to Nanyuki where I was able to personally thank Jamie Roberts, the

MD of *Tropic Air Kenya*, for all their help. Jamie suggested a geologically scenic route to *TBI – Turkwel* on Lake Turkana in northern Kenya. Lake Turkana is the world's largest, permanent desert lake and the world's largest alkaline lake. I departed Nanyuki early and flew low-level northwest for an hour to Mount Silali (1,528 metres), the largest, dormant caldera volcano in the Gregory Rift Valley. Silali was south of the Suguta Valley, which reached northward to Lake Turkana.

It was flat scrubland, mixed with cattle and wild animals from time to time. I saw elephants, giraffes, buffalos and buck. It then became forested and featured as I got closer to the Rift Valley. When I turned north at Silali, the lava flows, cracks in them and craters were fully visible. It was uncomfortably thermally turbulent for taking pictures. I flew up the Suguta Valley, which is an arid part of the Great Rift Valley in Kenya. It was much hotter now at 30°C and the barren, light sandy or dark, lava flow rocky landscape unfolded in front of me for miles. There were dust devils, volcanic craters and 'moonscapes': it was impressive. Flying high over Lake Logipi, I was privileged to witness literally millions of flamingos, waves of them, below me. It was a wonderful spectacle that I had only ever seen on documentary programmes.

I made one last climb and crossed low over a broad, volcanic complex with lava flows that separates the Suguta Valley from the bottom of Lake Turkana. I flew to and around the two beautiful craters at the bottom of the lake and then up the western side following it shore-wise and low-level northwards. I saw some fishing boats but no real habitation at first. Then small signs of life close to and around the more arable land increased. Lake Turkana was stunningly beautiful: it was so hot and dry here that there were even camels. The houses were round, domed-shaped dwellings, from which people waved at me. I followed the lakeshore right to the mouth of the Turkwel River and then followed the river very low-level to *TBI – Turkwel*. Both sides were cultivated, with camels and goats roaming around.

TBI – Turkwel was right on the GPS coordinates and it was another dusty landing, with me flattening my rotor blades quickly. I was welcomed by Timothy, the camp's manager, who settled me into the research station accommodation.

Here, I was lucky enough to meet with Dr. Marta Lahr, director for *Duckworth Laboratory, Leverhulme Centre for Human Evolutionary Studies and Cambridge University*, along with two assistants from *TBI – Turkwel*, Fran and Alex. They had spent three months in the field collecting data and were back at *Turkwel* analysing their findings. I met Marta in her lab area with many boxes of hominid specimens laid out and all sorts of other relevant finds, including ancient animal remains and tools. The time with Marta was fleetingly brief but I was also able to join the crew for dinner and breakfast.

While researching for *TJR*, one of the facts I discovered was that Africa has the most cultures and languages (over 2,000, 25% endemic) of any continent: I now know why. Life as we know it began in Africa. The migration out of Africa (which started 200,000 to 70,000 years ago) had led to the successful and diverse population mix we have today on Earth. But from 400,000 to 70,000 years ago, there were 'hunter-gatherer' migrations going on inside Africa. The many different groups that would have splintered off in different directions had led to the plethora of different tribes we know about. Amazing! This encounter with scientists, uncovering and interpreting Africa's secrets, was everything I could have wished for when I planned and asked to visit *TBI – Turkwel*. There were so many similarities with my late father's modus operandi and, his rubbing shoulders with numerous palaeontologists all the time, had had a huge impact on me, growing up.

I slept well out on the veranda of my accommodation, as did everybody else, and the mosquito net kept the bugs at bay. I was soaking my hat and shirt in water and then putting them back on to keep cool because it was uncomfortably hot. The next morning, I flew a circuit around the camp and waved goodbye to Marta and her team as they stood on the balcony of the research lab.

My first visit was to Central Island in the middle of Lake Turkana with its beautiful, coned volcanos and a myriad of flamingos. Then I turned northwest, crossing a big conurbation of domed houses at the tip of Ferguson's Gulf, which I could see on Google Earth too. I continued across the barren scrub, before arriving at Lokichoggio (known as Loki), nestled between two big hill ranges.

Loki is a town in northwest Kenya and the local people are mainly nomads of the Turkana tribe, deriving their livelihood from looking after indigenous cattle. Loki's heyday was as the base for the aid relief support to Sudan during the civil war years of 1983 to 2005. The base was wound right down soon after the civil war ended, with just a few *Aim Air* and *MSF* (Médecins sans Frontières) flights left nowadays, plus a few passing travellers.

I protected DIGA with all her covers against the hot, direct sun, before I was driven down the potholed, dirt roads to the guarded 'Camp 748' by David who worked there. Camp 748 consisted of a series of little, thatched-roofed bedrooms with a central dining area; the owner and staff were all friendly and helpful. Only the rooms had air-conditioning, and the electricity was switched off from 12 midnight to 5am, to conserve energy, but it also failed from time to time. Wi-Fi bandwidth was narrow and intermittent. My plan for the following day had been to fly into Addis Ababa but I learned from Ahmed that I didn't yet have a permit.

Getting up at 7am, Ahmed still had no confirmation from the Ethiopia *CAA* and so I elected to stay at Camp 748. A group of local teachers was using the camp for a two-day seminar, so I chatted with them during their free time. The food was a good buffet style that allowed me to sample many of the local dishes.

Ahmed didn't know why the Ethiopia *CAA* was making it difficult to night stop at Addis Ababa and exit to Damazin in the southeast of Sudan, but he wasn't surprised. In addition, Addis was high, as were the routes in and out and, together with the limited Wi-Fi, it was tricky to gauge how bad the rainy, cloudy weather might actually be from my forecasting apps.

I researched a Plan B with what turned out to be the two-day delay unfolding. I considered a long flight, direct from Loki to Damazin up the western border of Ethiopia. I would need an Ethiopian permit to cover this too but if I had to, I could fly low-level and avoid detection. I had already ruled out visiting a *JAM* project in Juba during the planning phase of *TJR* because fighting had broken out and all aid agency staff had pulled out at that time. I took security advice from David Brown *(JAM)* and Cissy Walker's husband, who both had local contacts, and I asked the tower at the airport what areas the aid flights were avoiding. This gave me a good picture of what was sensible. Plan B developed into a double hop when Sudan announced that I was not permitted to overnight at Damazin and should fly straight on to Khartoum.

The hours ticked by as Ahmed toiled to get my permits and I scrutinised the weather. I also used the time to visit the airport. Boniface and Joash of *Air Total*, who were also based at Camp 748 (apparently for security reasons), gave me a lift there and back. The tower controller confirmed that Ethiopia had good radar and gave me useful frequencies; an *Aim Air* pilot who flew for *MSF* confirmed the same but said that below about 10,000 feet, I would be too low for radar detection and would not have radio communications.

Late on Tuesday evening, I made my decision to route from Loki to Damazin for refuelling and on to Khartoum. My Ethiopia permit also finally arrived. I would be legal for this long double hop and the weather looked good enough for the next day. Boniface and Joash took me to the airport again to file my flight plan and to clear Immigration and Customs so that I could depart at first light without any fuss. This was all very convenient for me. I ate dinner with the *Air Total* guys: an assortment of ugali, beans, cabbage, meat and soup. All very tasty but I could see a pattern developing!

As the sun first broke on the horizon, I took a picture with DIGA and then lifted from Lokichoggio in the beautiful early morning. I was pleased with the good tailwind component of 10 to 15 knots. The Kenyan terrain was flat and deserted, then I crossed the 50 nautical miles of South Sudan, a similar landscape, and finally flew into Ethiopia heading north. Here the terrain rose to hills, much greener and with a few signs of people appearing. There were bigger mountains to the east and I flew between 3,000 and 7,000 feet, skimming the cols between them. It turned out to be smooth air all the way and so I could fly close to the hilly ground with impunity.

Western Ethiopia was very scenic, reminiscent of southern Nigeria and at about the same latitude. There was some forest mist around, with the temperature dropping to 19°C but with high humidity. Crossing into Sudan, the hills subsided ahead and it became very flat, still green and essentially farmed. Sudanese towns started to appear; basic rural settlements at first with all the houses in an organised town and the flat, surrounding landscape farmed and irrigated. This was very different from the rest of Africa where the houses were dotted chaotically all over the arable land.

At Damazin, I was refuelled from a 200-litre drum and it was as hot as hell on the apron for the hour I was there. The fuel drum had come from Khartoum to Damazin in a round trip of 12 hours on muddy roads and I thanked the driver. The formalities here were easy and all of the assembled officials each wanted a selfie with me. Approaching Khartoum, the organised towns were getting bigger and the land more parched. About 13 miles west of Khartoum, I was held for 20 minutes to give way to the big jets that needed to land, then in I came. Khartoum itself was impressively big from the air and I could see that the Sahara Desert started almost immediately to the north – an amazing transition.

Conducting my post-landing inspection, I was concerned to see oil sprayed over DIGA's engine bay and then relieved to discover that it was only due to a crack in the rubber engine breather tube – a messy but minor problem, thank goodness! After a short delay, I was soon in my hotel with my usual regime of work to do and planning for another double hop the next day into the Sahara again; Khartoum to Dongola to Aswan (Egypt). I also needed help from Lavinia to unfreeze my *InReach* device. It had stopped working in the heat just before Damazin, cutting my tracker and messaging with Eddie. Both he and Lavinia had been worried and fortunately, Lavinia found a way to hard reset the device, so I was back in action.

At the airport, my handler sorted out all the paperwork while all I had to do was prepare DIGA, surrounded by white *UN* aviation and *World Food Aid* aviation assets once again. I had flown over seven hours the previous day and today would be about six hours of desert flying in the haze, with the sun coming directly into the cockpit. I was ready, but a little apprehensive as I climbed to 4,500 feet and followed the Nile north out of Khartoum, before turning northwest to Dongola. The desert started abruptly and this time, there were many black ground features and hills to fix on, looking down. The haze developed and it was 30°C but not at all humid. The sun was beating down on my right arm, *iPad* and *InReach*. All my 'cover tactics' were in place, but my *iPad* and *iPhone* were complaining, and I knew that I would have to move my electronics across to the shaded left seat for the Dongola to Aswan leg.

The desert view was stunning and I was able to follow the Nile again into Dongola. It was very interesting to see the cultivation, life and dwellings, and to see how the desert encroaches on the land, pushed by the wind. The inhabitants had planted trees to defend against the relentless sand.

Dongola International Airport was a small place. It was 40°C on the ground and I positioned DIGA to avoid the sun on the cockpit, ignoring the marshaller. Nobody wanted to hang about in the heat and I was soon ready to move on again, after a quick toilet stop (which was interesting!). I lifted from my current position to enjoy the view of the Nile to my left as I flew northwest now to Aswan. Khartoum control insisted I climb to FL085 for the crossing to Egypt, talking to Cairo control: 7,000 feet above ground level felt a long way up! However, the haze wasn't too bad, there were very interesting desert features to keep my attention and help with my horizon control and it was only 20°C. I flew the length of Lake Nassar, capturing pictures of the beautiful desert features such as various veins on either side.

As I had done for Damazin, Khartoum and Dongola, I packed my video cameras away before I landed. I wasn't taking any chances with having my equipment confiscated (a common phrase I heard was, "You may not take pictures!"). Landing at Aswan, I noticed my foot pedals were a little sticky in movement, but on inspection, nothing seemed to be causing any restriction. Samy, working for *G.A.S.E.*, took me to my hotel after a short city tour in the taxi. My hotel, on an island in the Nile, gave me a memorable view of the city of Aswan on the eastern bank as the sun set.

From my room and the restaurant, I was able to absorb the river activities of Aswan. Talking to the staff, it appeared that the fickle tourists had abandoned Egypt due to safety concerns, which was a shame. It's a culturally awesome country, geographically wonderful and very friendly.

I suffered cramps in my lower leg muscles again, which reminded me to recommence hydrating with the *Cotswold*-supplied tablets in these intense conditions. I rose to catch the sunrise and was soon rushing to catch the water taxi and meet up with Samy again to ride to the airport. I couldn't believe that my journey around Africa was nearly over.

Aswan Approach routed me north to Cairo control at FL085, all under squawk (a squawk code is assigned by *Air Traffic Control* to an aircraft and is used for radar identification purposes); Egypt has a good radar system and control knew where I was. It was actually quite cool at 17°C and, with much less haze, the desert views were again beautiful. I could see all sorts of squiggles and watercourse effects without water, mountains, then the Nile and its green borders and conurbations. Now and then, the odd motorway cut a straight, black path across the sandy-coloured ground. At about 80 nautical miles from Cairo, I could see the thick city smog on the horizon and wisps of cloud above. As I approached, this became a bank of cloud with a base about FL065 and decreasing. So, I asked for a descent and confirmed that I was a special VFR flight! I did this a couple of times as the cloud base continued to descend.

About 40 nautical miles south, the ground was like a small version of the Grand Canyon. At about 30 nautical miles, Cairo control vectored me to the west, bringing me round in a series of headings for an oblique entry to Runway 05 Right. I was controlled progressively to 1,200 feet, which seemed low over the city buildings. The view showed the huge, sprawling capital city of Egypt, a metropolis of about 20 million people. There was industry, restricted areas and hundreds of apartment buildings, with the Nile on my left boasting greenery and desert dunes. The sky was smoggy and horrible to breathe, with poor visibility due to the pollution. Eventually the massive parallel runways came into view: where the concrete stopped, the sand began. I was taxied progressively to a *Follow Me* car, which led me to the general aviation apron of Cairo International Airport.

Basel met me on the apron and I soon had DIGA refuelled and covered up for her stay. Once again on landing, the pedals felt a bit sticky to operate. Something wasn't right but I couldn't see what it was. With formalities completed, I went through Terminal 4 to meet Eddie from *G.A.S.E.* for the very first time. Eddie settled me into the Fairmont Heliopolis Hotel and we chatted downstairs over a thirst-quenching beer, while agreeing the immediate route from Cairo to Crete for Tuesday 27th September, allowing Ahmed time to sort the permits. I was getting ready for the big Mediterranean water hop and then 2,000 miles across Europe. Anthea, Eddie's wife, joined us for dinner, and we had a relaxed evening, discussing life in general and their love for Egypt in particular.

I planned to spend three days in Cairo, with my homecoming scheduled for Monday 3rd October. Eddie wanted to show me a bit of his beloved Cairo and leave the Monday free for planning my round the world journey. Eddie's loyal taxi driver, Abdullah, drove us to Giza, the site of the iconic pyramids and Great Sphinx, dating back to the 26th century BC. Saturday was the weekend, so the traffic was apparently 'modest' by normal busy, frenetic weekday standards but distance was still measured in time, not miles! There was a lot of horn-honking, lane-changing, stop-starting and then fast driving: it was crazy. We met an old man in an *On the Run* store when we stopped for supplies and a good discussion about life ensued over the nicest coffee of the Africa journey so far. Eddie had delivered this tour over a hundred times to visiting friends and pilots and, with the help of Ragab and his team, I too had great pictures of my ride on Charlie Brown, a white camel, and the pyramids. Natalie and Donya, managing their stalls at the Sphinx, were also adept at the tourist photos, still beautifully cheeky and bouncy at the end of a hot day. It was a pity that tourism has been so badly affected by the recent unrest. The Egyptians I met couldn't have been more polite and helpful, speaking good English when I couldn't speak their language. Bizarrely, I fell asleep at least twice on the car journey home; maybe the traffic wasn't so scary after all!

On Sunday, Abdullah drove us to the Citadel with its incredible panoramic view of Cairo. We took our shoes off to enter the Mohamed Ali mosque, with its ornate, high dome as the centrepiece both inside and out. He drove us over to Khan Khalili for a walk about, which is the famous suq on the crossroad of the Spice Road (east to west across the Sahara) and the camel trade route. On each side of the street there were people trading everything from knick-knacks, to clothing and spices. It was brightly-coloured and bustling. I spotted mother of pearl inlay boxes that I had always associated with my mother, Margaret. Eddie and I stood at the crossroads a moment to absorb the atmosphere; it was wonderful to take it all in. We then walked to the Naguib Mahfouz restaurant and ordered koshari, the Egyptian national dish and a glass of kharkady, the drink made from hibiscus. It was a lovely, calming place, in contrast to the bustling streets outside. Finally, we visited El Fishawy, which is a café that had been in the same family for 250 years. There was all manner of memorabilia hanging on the walls depicting the history of the place.

The Fairmont Hotel was a massive, air-conditioned space with 17 restaurants and Wi-Fi everywhere, so it was a great environment to catch up with my administration and prepare for getting home. On Monday, Eddie and I discussed the timing of the next two journeys for weather windows, and the airport routing and antipode positions of the Round the World journey. It was good to get his experience in real time about fuel, Customs and such like. My weather analysis was also showing serious rain in France on the coming Saturday, so that would have to be a no flying day.

After a good night's sleep, I said goodbye to Eddie, thanking him for all his and *G.A.S.E.'s* hard work. Basel saw me through to DIGA and soon I was following Cairo control instructions and maintaining FL085. I climbed quickly through the smoggy layer, taking pictures as I went. The weather above was fine; the views of the delta, with all the populous sections and cultivation in between, were spectacular. About 40 million people live in the Nile Delta region and outside of major cities, the population density in the delta averages a staggering $1,000/\text{km}^2$. I was heading northwest up the western edge of the Delta to Borg El Arab, the airport serving Alexandria. As I kept flying, the views kept coming, with the Nile snaking beneath me. Gradually, the cloud built up to a broken cumulous coverage and the controller was sympathetic on the second time of asking, letting me thread a path between and around down to 4,000 feet, safely below the clouds.

Egypt Air staff were there to meet me as I landed at Borg. My turnaround was rapid with the usual wait on the radio to get permission to start. Then I was off. I was conscious of 'coasting out of Africa', which was a satisfyingly big deal for me. As I climbed, the cloud shadows showed a scattered pattern so I knew I would be OK on top; I established myself at FL085, enjoying the unbelievable views across the Eastern Mediterranean. The horizon was clear and I was finally getting used to flying high in DIGA.

G.A.S.E. and I already knew that Heraklion Airport was not going to allow me to park DIGA overnight. So as to avoid any hassle in Egypt, I had just set Sitia as my alternate destination on my flight plan, diverting there once I'd talked to Athena inside Greek airspace. Refuelling and administration was easily sorted in Sitia, but those sticky pedals were still a concern on landing. My handlers, *Skyserv*, informed me that Greek airports often open for two-hour slots only to service a commercial arrival and departure, especially at the end of the holiday season, which it was. I would potentially not be airborne until 1pm the following day. This was out of my control, so I decided to just enjoy my simple hotel with both a great sunset and sunrise, a tasty seafood meal and the now pleasant temperature.

Ahmed let me know in the morning that Kefallinia's opening hours were not going to work either. We chose Araxos a little further north and I adjusted my knee pad PLOG (the plan and the log of the flight on my knee board) and submitted my *Rocket Route* flight plan, thinking I was good to go. *Skyserv* came to see me off but when I called the tower, I was told that Araxos required 48 hours' notice of a slot to land, which I hadn't given them. Dammit! I had under an hour and I needed a solution. *Skyserv* took me back to their office and the frantic digging began. The answer was Corfu, further north still, making a big flight with strong headwinds initially, abating en route. *Skyserv* secured a slot at Corfu and I readjusted my PLOG and submitted a new flight plan, hoping dissemination would be quick. I needed to get going and I would be landing close to official darkness. Rushing back through Security, I called the tower for start again. They hadn't received the plan yet! I explained that it was coming and why I needed to get going fast. Kindly, the controller let me start. I called *Rocket Route* on my phone to make absolutely sure that they had delivered the flight plan and at the same time, I was reading back take-off clearances and lifting into the windy day. Before I was transferred to Heraklion, my flight plan did arrive and Sitia tower was happy.

Now that I was under way and en route, controllers helped with a more direct route at altitude to economise on fuel. I landed at Corfu about 30 minutes before sundown, getting some lovely pictures but having to leave refuelling until the next day. My leisurely start to the day had turned into a long evening. I set the alarm for 6:30am to walk to the airport early to see the *Skyserv* representative. I left the flight plans as drafts in *Rocket Route*, allowing me to accommodate any problems and phone in changes if necessary.

My plan for that day was a fuel stop in Bari, Italy and then on to Elba. Bari was a lovely airport and turned me around swiftly ahead of schedule. I flew north northwest right across the spine of Italy. The views of the conurbations and farmland unfolded beneath me, as did the wind farms. At 7,000 feet above sea level, the mountains were spectacular. Roma radar routed me around the eastern and northern part of their zone and then once again, I was low out over the sea flying towards Elba. There, the airport folks all came out to take pictures of the first R66 helicopter that had landed in Elba.

That evening, I worked to find a route to Caumont Airport near Avignon through the complicated French airspace, using my *iPad* and the maps from *Airbox*. I filed my flight plan and programmed the lot with frequencies for my knee pad, *RunwayHD* and *Garmin 795*. I felt ready to face the morning and reach Avignon before sitting out Saturday's stormy weather. I was flagging and slept like a log that night.

The next morning, I flew across the water, north of Corsica, heading in the direction of Monaco. I was planning to pick up the Riviera Heli route from Monaco down to Cannes, but Nice control were having none of it! They kept me a lot further offshore than I had wanted to be for sightseeing. I made landfall and continued northwest flying over the Verdon du Valley area and took some nice pictures of gorges, rivers and lakes.

I negotiated my way into Caumont Airport and landed into wind. While my pedals felt fine in flight, they were now concerningly sticky and jerky when taxi-ing. On the ground, when I pushed them by hand right forward, it was hard to get them to return and I just couldn't work out what was causing it. All the sliding mechanisms looked fine, but this issue was playing heavily on my mind with only two flights to go. I cleaned the windscreen, refuelled and put on both covers. Eddie had arranged for me to stay at Hôtel du Palais des Papes next to Avignon Cathedral, within the ancient walls of the old city. There were plenty of restaurants and sights to see, including the River Rhone and all the famous bridges.

It was pleasantly cool now. I went to bed early, knackered after the last three days crossing Europe, which were tiring in a different way to Africa. Here, I needed to respect the weather, the routes were full of restricted areas at different levels and the radio work was very busy. In comparison, Africa was tiring once you'd landed, with all the bureaucratic challenges which took hours to sort out, and always having to be on your guard.

I was woken early by the thunder and lightning and a hard downpour. I got chatting to an American couple from Minnesota at breakfast who were about to join a Rhone cruise up to Lyon. While it wasn't raining, I managed to walk around the busy sights but at about 4pm, the heavens opened again with thunder, lightning and pouring rain. This sent everyone running for cover and lasted well into the evening, so I sorted my administration and went to bed early. The next day promised the possibility of low cloud but flying looked feasible.

It was only just getting light as I arrived at the airport. The fog was on the ground and the weather for Lyon, further up the route and in the same long valley, was no different. The tower expected it to improve by midday. I was stuck north of Dijon last year for two days with François Mias, delivering his helicopter. Being a Sunday, the airport was deserted, and the security guard kindly bought me a coffee as I settled in to wait. My drop-dead time for leaving was 2pm.

At 10am, I prepared DIGA and tested the pedals. To my astonishment, they were completely free in movement. I stared accusingly at the horizontal slider on the tail rotor. I learned later that, in dusty environments, sticky pedals are a known problem. Clearly Saturday's storms had provided a thorough cleaning!

At 11am, the weather was good enough for me to get away and I was soon past all the relatively high ground with power lines and mobile phone masts and cruising at 2,000 feet above sea level into improving weather, working all the radios stations. There was still rain about but visibility was perfect and the little traffic there was seemed to be other G-registration aircraft heading home to the UK. I left DIGA in Le Touquet and headed to my last night's stay in an hotel.

I was excited to be up early for the sunrise, which was glorious. It bode well for the visibility and my final flight home from Le Touquet to Wycombe Air Park. Talking to

Eddie, the weather was perfect for my planned arrival at 10am.

The day was a beautifully sunny 12°C. I flew up the coast to Cap Griz Nes and coasted out with Lille information. Mid-channel, I changed to London information and coasted in at Folkstone, changing to Southend-on-Sea before Rochester and then to Farnborough North at Lamborne. There was a constant chatter with Eddie by *InReach* messaging. London looked splendid in the morning sun from the east and I took some great photographs.

I changed to Wycombe and it was much harder than I expected, getting the words out past the lump that had suddenly appeared in my throat: "Wycombe tower, this is Golf-Delta-India-Golf-Alpha." It was lovely and sunny, with no wind, and my touchdown was smooth.

I dismounted from the *TJR* configuration for the last time on the Africa 2016 journey and climbed out to be greeted by Lavinia, staff and students from *Helicopter Services*. My head was spinning. I was tired but happy, knowing that I had accomplished the physical mission safely. Lavinia came over and hugged me and I shook hands and hugged folks. I handed Thingy back to Leon for safe keeping: Thingy had done his job. Eddie and Ahmed were the first to congratulate me by Facebook Messenger and Lavinia and I went into *Helicopter Services* for a coffee and catch up, before Hannah phoned for a chat. Then Lavinia and I took the car round to DIGA for a methodical unload. Lavinia had to go home to catch up with Fraser and his driving lessons, while I stayed on a bit longer to make sure that I got my *Fédération Aéronautique Internationale* (FAI) paperwork certified by *Air Traffic Control*.

8

Focus

Wow! I had just returned from a solo VFR helicopter flight from London to Cape Town return, landing in 22 countries and flying 16,600 nautical miles in 73 days. However, I was absolutely knackered and still living inside the bubble of the journey. I was happy to be home safely, but it was boring compared to the adrenalin, excitement and regime of the journey and I felt a bit lost. Africa had been utterly spectacular. I had seen first-hand the stunning contrasts: the generous peoples, cultures, levels of development, weather, deserts, forests, coastlines, rivers, volcanoes, animals, history and much more.

I spent Tuesday 4th October writing down actions as I was jogged to remember them and taking calls from well-wishers. There was a lot to do in order to 'unpack' this journey and plan for the next one. On Wednesday, I flew DIGA over to Denham for maintenance and caught up with David Cross, Quentin and his team at *HQ Aviation*. DIGA was dusty and in fact, to this day, we still find parts of her fuselage where the dust of the Sahara and East Africa managed to penetrate. She needed a bit of TCL and within a couple of days, David had her back at *Helicopter Services* ready for her day job. Her 100-hour service wasn't due for another 25 hours. Lavinia took me home. I had hardly driven for over 70 days. For the rest of the day I unpacked my bags, cleaned my cameras, sorted the pictures and updated my diary.

It took me about two weeks to feel rested but what I found really hard was trying to decompress and refocus again. However, since I had only six months to be ready for my *Round the World* (RTW) journey, in order to fit the weather window for a four-month circumnavigation, I needed to buck my ideas up! I started my gym training again and the long road to getting fit.

I wanted to learn from the experience of nearly dying in the desert between Tamanrasset and Agadez and do something about it. I talked to Leon about my experience. Analysis of my GPS and *Iridium* track data showed that my height and direction control had been erratic, as I tended to follow my magenta line to Agadez. I had been very lucky to remain within DIGA's flying parameters and maintain sufficient altitude so as not to hit anything. We discussed how, even with the best weather forecasting, I was still going to inadvertently end up in marginal VFR conditions, or worse, from time to time while flying long range.

I would continue to practice in the flight simulator and ensure that I was completely familiar with all my equipment in order to be able to remain calm. Leon and I discussed the merits of having two pilots, which would certainly reduce the workload. Two experienced pilots sharing alternate legs would help to reduce the planning and flying workload. When you inevitably have to divert or obey different instructions arriving at a busy airport, it's easier and faster to make good decisions simply by sharing and being there to help the flying pilot. However, the real safety solution would be a 'stability system': an autopilot. I had only chosen solo flying for Africa at the last minute and apart from the workload issues, I had thoroughly enjoyed it. However, Lavinia was much happier when I said I would choose to fly *RTW* with another pilot and investigate the autopilot possibilities.

I also felt that the weather delays in Nigeria and then Cameroon had moved all my downstream visits to the right uncontrollably and had immersed me in time-consuming communications, often with poor connectivity, to let everyone know I was changing my dates. My planned Africa journey had extended from 62 to 73 days! I needed a better strategy for *RTW*, which would be a longer journey at about 120 days. I needed to position buffer days where I would either just stop and rest or be involved in a longer planned visit. I would always advise safety first and only fly in the right weather conditions but positioning buffer days every 30 days would mean that I could make the majority of my appointments on time and hold the end date more accurately.

When Charles Stewart had dropped out, I had made a shortlist of people I knew who might step in; I had also talked to Charles McCann. All of the people on my list had said that it was, understandably, too short notice. However, a few had said that, given more time, they would definitely consider the next journey, so this is where I started my co-pilot search. I added about four people to the list who had messaged me while I was in Africa and had expressed an interest. I needed a co-pilot to join a team who had the resources, time, commitment and someone who provided no surprises! With each candidate, I discussed the challenges and explained what it would take to be involved. I was as open as I could be.

Charles McCann was himself interested in joining from

the UK around to California, thereby completing his own circumnavigation distance. Matthew Gallagher, with whom I had gone to 'Hell and back,' was also interested. Matthew had previously harboured a desire to fly long range and my *RTW* opportunity would fit well with his objectives. Both Charles and Matthew needed the blessing of their respective partners. Charles' other half was understandably cautious, after his crash in Nairobi. It was of course my choice in the end and a solid team for the whole journey was what I needed.

I hardly knew Matthew, but by way of introduction, we discussed and explored flying configuration, weight and balance, man-machine-interface, equipment on DIGA, clothing, documents including licences, medical, passports and visas. We also covered the regime for preparation, logistics en route, getting the story, fitness, wrapping up and thanking people. Matthew really appreciated the principle of 'no surprises' and that worked both ways to eliminate any skeletons or impediments. So it was decided that Matthew would be my co-pilot.

I was building on a successful formula but planning a completely new and longer route this time with three service stops, including all the cold-water equipment, as well as weight and balance calculations to include two crew. Matthew threw himself into a fitness regime to make his 85-kilo berth and we attended open water survival courses together at *Andark Diving*; Matthew went on the dunker course too. I shared equipment lists with him and we both went back to Maraid at *Cotswold Outdoor* for her advice and our resupply. All the same people could help us. Updates to the medical kit, vaccinations, visas, additional beacons and so on were all added to the to do list and shared. The mission doctor was still Robin, another brother-in-law. The helicopter systems would be the same and we just had to work out how we would work together in the cockpit and who would have which piece of equipment to hand. In Russia, Charles Stewart and I had taken up the right-hand seat when in command of the helicopter, flying alternate legs. Matthew and I agreed to dedicate ourselves to always having the same seat in our flying office, independent of who was the pilot in command, to minimise disruption.

Matthew was an experienced pilot and he held licences for both helicopters and fixed wings in both Europe and America. He had significant flying experience in America where he had been an instructor in a previous life. Crucially, Matthew was an instrument-rated pilot and was well-versed in procedural flying, filing the corresponding flight plans and using the fiddly *Garmin 420* GPS that was installed in DIGA.

From my experience of two-person operations, I decided to implement a whole list of minor improvements. I replaced suction cups with light brackets that wouldn't ping off, split the grab bag contents into two bags to make them more easily available, bought some black hand towels to use against the sun and eliminate reflections for camerawork, moved to the *iPhone* 8 because of its enhanced camera features and waterproof capabilities, blackened anything white to reduce reflections for camera work and used black cables throughout the cockpit. We exclusively packed quick-drying, insect repellent clothing and attached epaulettes on all of our shirts to make us easily distinguishable as pilots. I also switched to a single rock crystal underarm deodorant which didn't stain my shirts and a small, solid shampoo bar to cut down on weight. None of this was rocket science but it all helped!

It was a steep learning curve but I tried my hand at preparing presentations, short videos and selecting the best pictures for my *TJR* website, in celebration of my Africa journey. I also produced a coffee table book, learning to use the software on my Mac. The last thing I produced was an A1 poster, to hang in the offices at *Helicopter Services*. It was all good fun and allowed me to revisit the experience through the images and to follow the satellite track of my journey on Google Earth. First though, I had to review every picture, establish its location and give it a sensible name. I could access all the meta data automatically on my *iPhone* with the right technology. This was something I resolved to do religiously and daily en route next time because it was a mind-numbing job to complete retrospectively. Matthew and I would have the additional challenge of each having *iPhones*, which would mean more organisation and categorising of pictures.

Back in the UK, I re-established contact with Brad of *Pacific Avionics* in Australia to see if there was a practical, affordable HF radio solution. Brad knew of a couple of solutions that had been installed on a Robinson R44. However, the first problem was that the items required were not currently in manufacture and were therefore rare! The second problem would be a costly process of getting approval from UK *CAA*. I had to ask their permission because an HF radio permits communication over long distances in remote areas, while normal VHF radios only work over 20 to 40 nautical miles with a good line of sight. So for me, communications in remote areas were impossible except by relay to an overflying commercial jet or by satellite telephone, which was acceptable and required for 'Operations Normal' calls in Greenland and for calling control in Russia's remote east.

For *RTW*, I also sold the handheld *Satphone* I was using and bought an *iGO* device still linked to the *Iridium* network. It created a Wi-Fi in the helicopter that both Matthew and I could use with a *Satphone* app to make satellite telephone calls through our headsets anywhere in the world. This turned out to be a perfect solution everywhere except in Gabon, but I wouldn't be going back there!

When I started researching an autopilot, I found that *Genesys Aero Systems* had just had their *HeliSAS* Autopilot system certified for use on the R66 and it was retrofittable. I worked with James of *Sharman Electronics* and Paul of *Helimech*, who maintained many of *Helicopter Services'* helicopters, to understand the configuration for DIGA. We arrived at a specification that would provide me with stabilisation and control of my heading and height. I discussed it with Leon and he seemed happy to augment DIGA's capability. I then reached an agreement directly with *Genesys* for their sponsorship to install the autopilot on DIGA, in return for marketing materials contrasting my experience of nearly dying in the desert brownout with its performance while flying around the world. I was grateful for their support. The next challenge was to assemble the various components and get them installed on DIGA. The supply lead times were long and, even with encouragement from *Genesys*, I began to bite my nails as my *RTW* start date approached!

I was now back to working seven days a week and very busy planning the logistics, visits and farming the pictures and video assets. Experience told me that I needed to lay down my routing as soon as possible. I had already worked with Eddie in Cairo to get his input to my now-familiar spreadsheet and we had a complete route option. There were still many variables such as fuel availability, permissions, flying viability, the position of my visits, maintenance stops and so on, which would need to be assimilated and accounted for through numerous iterations. What might look like a doable route on a map, sitting in Buckinghamshire, could end up being impossible to fly if a permission was denied, an airport had a problem, the local military restricted airspace, the fuel supply became unavailable or the weather was poor. If I could, I wanted to give myself options to make progress and keep single point of failure routing to a minimum at the planning stage. All of this depended on the actual range of DIGA. Matthew and I were going to have to stop and refuel over a hundred times. *G.A.S.E.* and I were also trying to choose the lower cost and more efficient airports. So once again, our team had its work cut out.

To reduce the impact of delays that I had experienced in Africa, I deliberately added extra buffer days where I would either just stop and rest or be doing something different, which could soak up any delay and minimise the impact on the downstream schedule. I investigated my possible visits and researched the weather to confirm that I was choosing the best time to fly through the tropical conditions of Malaysia and Indonesia, and the higher latitudes of Eastern Russia, Alaska and Baffin Island, Greenland and Iceland. I didn't want to meet any cyclones or hurricanes, so I planned to thread my way in between those seasons too. I also researched and chose my antipodes, two places on opposite sides of the world with airports.

G.A.S.E. chased down the practicality of my proposed route using their vast experience. Eddie and Ahmed knew that crossing India from Ahmedabad to Kolkata would mean stops at internal airports requiring fuel and overnight stays. This would require a 'diplomatic flight clearance' because helicopters were regarded as 'air drop' capable and thus subject to tighter security regulations. Matthew and I would also need visas in our passports. It would have been easier if we were only landing at the point entry/exit airports of Ahmedabad and Kolkata because permits and visas could all have been done online!

At this point in time, not many people had been able to fly from the north of Japan through Russian to Alaska in the previous 10 years. However, it appeared that the situation for general aviation was relaxing due to the great efforts of the helicopter pilots I had met in Moscow, including Mikhail Farikh. Eddie introduced me to Evgeny Kabanov of what became *MAK General Aviation Services* (MAK GAS). Evgeny also flew R66s and he and I worked out a routing, communicating back and forward between October 2016 and February 2017. The international airports in Russia were straightforward but the smaller, national ones needed investigating. The further east we went, the more remote it would become. At this time, Russia still required all pilots to file IFR flight plans and fly IFR routes. We would be expected to fly DIGA at about 10,000 feet. Pure VFR flying in Russia was extremely limited at the time and almost non-existent for foreign-registered aircraft. Evgeny suggested that we fly through Russia quickly because airports close at the weekend. With his help, we decided on a route, airport opening times, all the coordinates, places that would have English-speaking controllers, *Satphone* capability and all the necessary invitation papers to secure a six-month business visa. Evgeny was so professional, helpful and patient and we couldn't have been in better hands.

With Matthew now involved, we also accommodated

his suggestions and introduced the Cayman Islands, which added the opportunity of Havana and Kissimmee, routing north in the USA. *Hayward Aviation* were able to confirm that, with certain conditions, we would be insured to take DIGA into Cuba. Michelle Hilsdon and the *World Fuel Services* team analysed the route and made suggestions of where they could provide contract fuel, again minimising the cash we had to carry.

The theory of positioning the maintenance was easy: service DIGA before we left and pick a spot every 100 hours. But DIGA was due for a maintenance service about December time and might not fly a full 100 hours before Matthew and I would leave in April 2017. I had to juggle three maintenance stops this time, which was very different to one at the bottom of Africa, which had been easy for David Cross to reach. Originally, I was thinking of Ahmedabad in India for the first maintenance stop. I researched the R66 dealer's base from *RHC* along the draft route and made contact to explain what I needed, as well as to establish capability and willingness to help. It wasn't straightforward and took time to get traction. I just had to live with the ambiguity for a while longer!

Matthew and I both had British passports which certainly helped to reduce the number of visas needed for travelling through all the planned countries. However, flying a General Aviation non-scheduled aircraft did require visas in Russia and the USA, and because we intended to stay in Bangladesh for a few days, we needed one there too. For India, we also needed a visa in our passport and 'diplomatic flight clearance'.

At the beginning of November 2016, I couldn't find anyone to help me obtain diplomatic flight clearance for a non-scheduled flight across India. The UK *CAA* didn't have a department for it and the *MOD* only arranged it for military flights. I turned to Peter Drissell, who was the father of my daughter's school friend and Director of Aviation Security at the *UK Civil Aviation Authority*. He had enjoyed following the *TJR* story on Facebook through Africa and said he would see what he could do.

Via *G.A.S.E.*, our handler, Bobby, of *Aerotech* in India, said he could apply for the permit in the normal way to the *DGCA* (India's *CAA*) but because of the 'special security' requirement, the *DGCA* would have to seek a 'Note Verbal' from the *British High Commission* (BHC) in Delhi vouching for the flight. Peter Drissell's meeting with the Air Advisor of the *India High Commission* confirmed that process and the fact that it would take up to 20 days to clear it, with all the correct paperwork. It helped that Peter was a retired Air Commodore! Peter contacted military personnel in the *BHC* in Delhi who confirmed that they would see what they could do for me but stressed that they only dealt with Her Majesty's Government flights and they didn't know anyone there who did the same for general aviation flights. I succeeded in getting a letter confirming my flight intentions from the UK *CAA* General Aviation Unit. But frustratingly, time passed, emails went back and forth and out of office replies filled the electronic highway.

In early February 2017, Peter contacted the *Indian Ministry of Aviation* and they also confirmed the procedure to follow and supplied key contacts at the *DGCA*. Bobby used those contacts and on 9th February, he confirmed that the *DGCA* had indeed contacted the *BHC* in Delhi and received a Note Verbal. We now had all the necessary papers and could apply for our diplomatic flight clearance. To this day, we don't know who in the *BHC* in Delhi vouched for us but we know it wasn't our military contacts. However, this was indeed the breakthrough we needed and *G.A.S.E.* and Bobby took over the submission and chasing. Simply "add 20 days" and we expected to have the necessary permit!

DIGA had gone to *HQ Aviation* for her service on 7th December. I had planned with David Cross that this would be a service to pull all the maintenance requirements forward so that the next three services in the field would amount to scheduled inspections. However, while everything else with the service went smoothly, the 400-hour engine vibration analysis showed up an anomaly that required investigation. Just before Christmas wasn't a great time to be needing to take the engine out and get it checked as part of a thorough root cause analysis. David and *HQ Aviation* coordinated the effort of both *RHC* and *Rolls-Royce* to solve the problem. But in the end, the elapsed time that unfolded, including the normal Christmas shutdown of two weeks, equated to about three months, so *Helicopter Services* only got DIGA back at the beginning of March 2017. This meant she wasn't available for *Helicopter Services* to use for type ratings, Matthew and I had no time to fly her together and my assumptions about where DIGA would need her next services were now incorrect.

In addition, the people installing the autopilot had all the parts ready but the installation booking date was slipping as they waited for DIGA. When she did finally go on 9th March, the completion date stretched until 29th March. I nudged and cajoled but it required nerves of steel as our early April departure date loomed ever closer. Actually, the knock-on slippage of delays in the UK meant that DIGA had sufficient hours remaining to fly all the way to Malaysia before her first en route maintenance check would be required. This turned out to be advantageous and I finally settled on maintenance in Kuala Lumpur (where James Greaves of *Cempaka* offered to help), on Vancouver Island at *E&B Helicopters* (where Ralph Richier and Ed Wilcock offered to help) and in Québec at *Capitale Hélicoptère* (where Christopher Stapor offered help). Hopefully, I had calculated all my planning hours correctly. I made the necessary travel arrangements for David and, by comparison with South Africa, he was going to have to cover some serious distance and time zones.

In my continued discussions with Nigel Winser, he suggested that I should research thoroughly the three signed Rio Conventions on *Climate Change*, *Biodiversity* and *Land Degradation/Desertification*, which underpinned sustainable development. These three Rio Conventions were derived directly from the 1992 Earth Summit, which was a conference on 'Environment and Development' in Rio de Janeiro, organised by the *United Nations*. Despite its name, desertification is not "equated to desert expansion", but "represents all forms and levels of land degradation occurring in drylands." Each convention represented a way of contributing to the sustainable development goals, and the three conventions were linked, operating in the same ecosystems and addressing interdependent issues. I also learned that scientific work on biological diversity and conservation, climate and the greenhouse gas effect, and land degradation/desertification, originated way back in the late 19th and early 20th centuries and that there were many actors involved.

The *World Meteorological Organization* (WMO) was established in 1950. WMO was dedicated to international cooperation and coordination on the state and behaviour of the Earth's atmosphere, its interaction with the land and oceans, the weather and climate it produces, and the resulting distribution of water resources. The *UN Environmental Programme* was established in 1972. *UNEP* coordinated the *UN's* environmental activities and assisted developing countries in implementing environmentally sound policies and practices. The *WMO* and the *UNEP* established the *Intergovernmental Panel on Climate Change* (IPCC) in 1988, which to this day provides the world with an objective, scientific view of climate change, its natural, political and economic impacts and risks, and possible response options with periodic reports.

A guy called Tomasz Wojtowicz contacted Eddie in November and December 2016. He explained that he was flying an old Cessna 152 around the world in stages and asked if we would like to hook up. It looked like he'd be making the final leg from Thailand to the USA where he lived at about the same time we would be passing through Japan and the Philippines. We promised to keep him posted. I also re-contacted Rene Chamorro, who the Wilson family had met in Belize on holiday. I had kept in touch and Rene was my inspiration on the final route planning through Central America. I also contacted Dean Grieder, who I knew reasonably well through his brother, Martin. He lived in the Dominican Republic and arranged a local visit to the *DREAM Project*, which educated children there.

Nigel Winser introduced me to Hein Gerstner, Park Manager at Gunung Mulu National Park, which was a *UNESCO* World Heritage site in Sarawak, on the island of Borneo. Hein then introduced me to the Mulu Marriot Hotel and I made plans to land right in the park. Nigel also put me in touch with Mark Evans who was the General Manager of *Outward Bound Oman*; he had lived in the Arabian Gulf for 21 years, 12 of those based in Muscat. Mark was a serial explorer in his own right and we also made plans to meet up at a *Royal Geographical Society* (RGS) lecture on his recent crossing of the Empty Quarter, following in the footsteps of Bertram Thomas. Nigel also sounded out some contacts in India, however it turned out that they didn't fit our timescales, along with the uncertainties of our diplomatic flight clearance.

David Constantine of *Motivation International* introduced me to Valerie Taylor, the founder of the *Centre for the Rehabilitation of the Paralysed* (CRP) in Bangladesh. CRP promoted an environment where everyone with disabilities should have equal access to health, rehabilitation, education, employment, the physical environment and information. Valerie helped me to make plans for visiting her operation in Dhaka.

Keith Ketchum of *MAF* kindly provided more introductions to various *MAF* locations, including Bangladesh, Myanmar and Haiti. A *MAF* floatplane was being used to bring patients to floating 'Friendship' hospitals in Bangladesh, but in the end, we couldn't finesse a way of getting DIGA close enough. However, Mark Bloomberg, the *MAF* Country Director for Bangladesh, offered assistance and made an introduction to Mark Pierce of *Save the Children* (STC) in Dhaka, who helped organise visits. This was a much more effective introduction than any response I was getting from *STC* in the UK. I had gone to meet *STC* in London and explained that I really needed a few good visit introductions since they hadn't helped in Africa but I remained frustrated by their half-hearted approach and constant changing of staff. Adding Dhaka to our route rippled through my route planning.

Back to 4th February, and Nigel and his wife, Shane, had kindly organised tea at their house for a lovely group of planetary caretakers. This was a wonderful opportunity for me to show off my Africa journey and have discussions with people who had dedicated their lives to exploration and conservation issues. I was like a sponge, soaking up their stories, comments and ideas, which inspired and encouraged me enormously.

In particular, I met Andrew Mitchell, who was founder of *Global Canopy* and an international thought leader on natural capital, climate change and tropical forests; he would later help me on the subject of forests and provide critical introductions for visits in Latin America. I also met Steve Jones who was an expedition manager for *Antarctic Logistics & Expeditions*, which offered air transportation and logistic support, and guided experiences for those venturing to the interior of Antarctica. He would also help me enormously later with crucial advice, introductions and ideas for flying around Latin America. Finally, I met John Ingram, Food Systems Programme Leader for the *Environmental Change Institute*, University of Oxford, who helped me understand the subject of food security. He would later direct my research and reading to the work of David Tilman and Michael Clark, which I had time for on return from *RTW*.

The day before Nigel's tea party, my wife, Lavinia, broke her femur quite dramatically and badly while skiing with her girlfriends. I became her designated driver, ferrying her back and forth to doctor and physio appointments. She was only cleared to drive again the day before Matthew and I set off on *RTW*. Matthew's wife, Maria, had also just had a hip operation and so there was some vague amusement in having our partners both hobbling to see us off!

There was now a lot happening for the final preparations, including travelling in and out of London to get visas, putting logos on clothing, organising our equipment and supplies and reweighing everything. I was obviously updating the website with changes as I went, which was still all home-designed and built.

Steve Brooks and Joanna Vestey unfortunately couldn't make it to Nigel's tea party, but they invited me to meet up in early March. In fact, it was my first flight with DIGA and her autopilot. I picked her up from *Helimech* and flew over to Steve and Joanna's house! Steve was a real character: he was an engineer too, as well as an avid explorer and had made the first helicopter flight from pole to pole. Quentin Smith from *HQ Aviation* had joined him for the two polar legs and Joanna had joined him for their honeymoon to fly the length of the Americas! We shared stories and I graciously received a beautiful, signed copy of their book called "*Due South – Through Tropics and Polar Extremes*." I could learn a lot from their South American leg for my third journey and Steve was interested in what would be my *RTW* experience for his next project. He was restoring a Spitfire and preparing to fly it around the world: *The Silver Spitfire* project. I left their house buzzing with excitement.

Eddie was organising visits for us too, including the *Experimental Aircraft Association* in Kuala Lumpur, *The Evergreen Museum* at McMinnville, Robert DeLaurentis in San Diego, *AOPA* in Frederick, Maryland, and the *Nantucket Flying Association* on the island of Nantucket, off Rhode Island.

I sent Tomasz Wojtowicz my most up-to-date schedule. *G.A.S.E.* would be handling us both and if we could meet up, we would. With the journey planned to last 120 days, many of the visits were still tentative. However, Matthew and I were as ready as we could be and had a 'plan to re-plan' en route. It was the beginning of April and we still didn't have the diplomatic flight clearance for India yet, but Bobby seemed confident and the *DGCA* weren't asking for any more information.

9

Arabia, 300 people per km²
and Asia

On Saturday 8th April, family and friends assembled at the *Helicopter Services* offices at Wycombe Air Park. The weather looked good and I felt ready and less nervous than I had been before my Africa journey.

We posed for photographs and then said goodbye with hugs, handshakes and waves. I accepted Thingy from Leon once more before Matthew and I climbed into DIGA. We knew that our rusty starting routine would get slicker over time. I got the *InReach* tracking working and established messaging communications with *G.A.S.E.* Eddie and Ahmed would once again follow all of our flights, providing support, permits, logistics and first response for *SAR*. As with Africa, the mission would simply not function without them as team members.

With a smile on my face, I called the tower for a flight "Outbound around the world, back in August!" and with their best wishes, we lifted fully loaded for the first time. Matthew was initially 'pilot in command' (PIC) and it was a straightforward flight to Le Touquet, albeit hazy all the way. Le Touquet wasn't busy and I was soon flying our second leg to Avignon, working all the different radio stations. We were flying the reverse of my Africa return route to Cairo. The haze finally lifted, affording us great views of the Alps about

50 nautical miles north of Avignon. Eddie had organised the airport hotel and we settled in there to plan our route through the dense airspace in the south of France and I filed our fight plan using *Rocket Route*.

The following day, we had a leisurely start for our short flight to Elba, after washing off all the squashed biodiversity from DIGA that we'd collided with the day before! We climbed away southeast towards Saint Tropez. We tried our luck with control to get permission to fly the Heli Lanes down to Monaco but, just like my return from Africa, the answer was a firm No. Shame! We struck out across the sea to Elba routing north of Corsica. Matthew tested the navigation function of the *HeliSAS* autopilot on the way. In Elba, we reused my routes to Bari and Corfu and, by adding the landing slot information from Ahmed, we could file our flight plans in advance. I then had plenty of time to process the day's photographs, do my hand washing and sort my administration.

I hadn't been sure whether I would like two-pilot operation because I was so used to solo flying. However, it felt good to have another skilled pilot with whom to share the workload and experiences. We recognised that we might get on each other's nerves, but we were both tolerant and happy to talk through any issues that might arise.

The next morning, we skirted around Rome and across the gorgeous plain to the west of it, climbing high to cross the spine of Italy southwards to Bari for our refuelling stop. We again crossed Casoli and Luco dei Marsi, the lovely cultivated area that I'd photographed before. Lifting from Bari, we had to taxi downwind to join the runway, which was a great experience for Matthew to see how DIGA performed when it was hot, and she was heavy. Most controllers don't understand the effect of flying downwind on the performance of a heavy helicopter and it performs very differently while taxi-ing compared to an aeroplane pulling itself along the ground. It was beautiful down the coast to Corfu. Installed in our next hotel, I sorted my photographs and Matthew worked out how to get his *Rocket Route* account to file flight plans with me as crew, which my account already did; this process further streamlined our teamwork.

Bizarrely, Corfu Airport had changed owners overnight, which resulted in a small delay to our departure for Iraklion, but it was gorgeous flying down the islands of Greece to Crete, crossing the Ionian and Aegean seas. Working together, Matthew and I made light work of the radio, navigation and reporting with the autopilot, providing good hands-free time for photography. It made me realise just how hard I had worked to 'stick fly' Africa solo!

While flying, I made an urgent telephone call to Peter Drissell to once again enlist his help. We needed him to push for our diplomatic flight clearance for India which we still didn't have, according to messages from *G.A.S.E.* Peter called the Director of the *DGCA* (India's *CAA*) in his official capacity as Director of Aviation Security at the UK *CAA* and followed that up with a letter, attaching all the relevant supporting documents. He travelled to his London office off his family holiday to do this for me, which was embarrassing but greatly appreciated. We all crossed our fingers because India was a mission-critical routing bottleneck!

That evening, we met a lovely couple at dinner: the husband was originally from Pakistan and his wife from Sarawak, Borneo, where we were headed. With Ahmed's help, we filed our flight plans to Borg El Arab (Alexandria) and then on to Cairo the next day.

Iraklion tower let us lift directly south through the misty hills and off across the Eastern Mediterranean Sea. Matthew was PIC and he had an horizon-wide smile for his first 'continental coast out' in a helicopter. We anticipated a slow climb to FL085 (about 8,500 feet above sea level) above the broken cloud layer. Approaching Africa, the clouds dissipated but the dusty haze increased markedly as we coasted in at Alexandria.

A very friendly group from *Egypt Air* greeted us on the ground at Borg El Arab. They also wanted photographs and assisted us through formalities, chatting and laughing. They remembered DIGA from 2016. After refuelling, we waved goodbye and climbed slowly to FL085 again to cross the Nile delta. The dust haze, mixing with the fog of Cairo, was making visibility atrocious and I requested successive descents to keep the ground in sight; the controller obliged, vectoring us to the runway. The conditions were marginal VFR and certainly not for the faint-hearted, but our two-man crew configuration and the autopilot made all the difference.

The *HeliSAS* autopilot could control heading and height while the pilot is left control power and trim. This meant that we could let go of the cyclic stick (while maintaining trim with our feet and setting a friction on the collective lever for power) and DIGA would fly herself. This reduced flying workload and allowed us to use two hands for messaging, photography, grazing and hydrating. Using the *HeliSAS* navigation function, the 'heading' could be a flight planned route in our *Garmin GPS*, which was even more helpful.

Landing directly at Terminal 4, another cheery entourage from *Egypt Air* wanted photographs sitting in DIGA. She was dusty and Cairo was experiencing poor weather conditions. With rain threatening, we applied both covers and the tail rotor cover (my new addition to DIGA's protection).

Once through Customs, we settled into our regime at the Fairmont Heliopolis Hotel and then joined both Eddie and Ahmed (who I was meeting for the first time) for a pizza. It was nice to thank Ahmed face to face for his support. Ahmed also helped Matthew and I with our flight planning to Hurghada and then on to Hail and Al Ahsa in Saudi Arabia.

The next day, the sky was beautifully clear for our visit to Tahrir Square, the Egyptian Museum and the Pyramids of Giza. At the museum, we headed straight for the artefacts of the most famous Egyptian pharaoh known today, King Tutankhamen. He is chiefly known for his intact tomb, discovered in Egypt's Valley of the Kings in 1922 by Howard Carter. Being mummified and buried with all sorts of goodies and gold seems amazing to us but it was quite popular at the time! We walked around Tahrir Square, which had become infamous during the revolution of 2011. Eddie and Anthea lived in Cairo throughout that difficult period but now the only noise was from the frenetic, horn-honking traffic.

On the way to the pyramids, we once again met some interesting people at our coffee stop, namely a university professor who was working on getting the food value out of the crops before then using the remainder for biofuels. He was familiar with the *UN Sustainable Development Goals* and his wife had worked on *Save the Children* projects – it was indeed a small world!

Ragab and three camels, Charlie Brown, Scooby Doobie and Mickey Mouse, entertained Matthew, Eddie and me at the pyramids. On revisiting the Sphinx, we caught up with the crazy Natalie and Donya who worked on the stalls and who brightened up the day for tourists. We had a good day in the hot sunshine before Abdullah drove us safely back to the Fairmont.

We said goodbye to Eddie and Ahmed at Terminal 4 while *Egypt Air* sorted out all the formalities. We prepared DIGA and negotiated our permissions to lift directly to the south and climb to FL100. The views of Cairo were spectacular in the lovely weather conditions and we used the cameras and videos we had mounted just after take-off. At 10,000 feet above sea level, Matthew could finally see how stunning the desert was. We had direct views of the many changing colours, from white through to black. The diverse shapes often looked like ferns laid flat; these were the water courses which had been created by the infrequent rain. It was mesmerisingly beautiful.

We could see the Red Sea to the east most of the way and landing at Hurghada, it was a windy 25 knots, which gave Matthew something to think about. Smiling *Egypt Air* officials welcomed us through all the formalities after their photo session and randomly bombarded us with the usual questions. We soon had our daily regime underway at our tourist hotel, with the Red Sea lapping at the shore about three metres away from our feet.

Looking ahead to our next stop in Saudi Arabia, Hail, the weather there was poor: '4000m DU BLDU', which means 4,000 metres visibility in dust and blown dust. We had experienced this on arrival in Cairo and it seemed we might be catching this weather up as we chased it eastwards across Arabia!

We left for the airport after a good night's sleep, in spite of the belly dancing and music that went on until 5am. *Egypt Air* had arranged everything for our departure and we were cleared to FL085 flight for Hail, taking pictures of the beautiful, blue Red Sea as we departed the coast. We had good radio communications coasting in Saudi Arabia and while we still had the spectacular, remote desert views, there were many more small settlements and roads here in Saudi Arabia. As we descended the last 50 miles into Hail, a little airport at 3,300 feet above sea level, the haze had begun to build up again. Hail is largely agricultural with significant grain, date and fruit production and a population of about 310,000.

We were parked on a helipad and waited for our handlers, *Saudi Ground Services* (SGS). Four soldiers walked over to look at DIGA and take selfies. Customs officials came over and wanted our passports. At last, a friendly, English-speaking *SGS* representative attended us and understood that we needed to refuel, then clear Immigrations. After another delay, a young Saudi lad arrived in a brand-new, German-made fuel truck, which he couldn't operate! Later, the same truck returned with an English-speaking Philippine driver who could finally deliver our *WFS* contract fuel.

Once inside the air-conditioned terminal, we were served tea while waiting for our passport checks and stamped papers allowing us to leave. It was explained to us that these papers were our "most important documents" so we must not lose them! Finally, after three hours, a staff member kindly gave us a lift to our hotel, and we could start our daily wrap-up regime.

It actually rained hard during the night, which woke me up and my grumbling stomach that required three successive Imodium tablets also kept me awake! In the morning, the weather ahead at Al Ahsa was low visibility, blowing dust and sand, which stood for serious Instrument Meteorological Conditions and necessitated that we delay one day in Hail.

I wanted to arrive in Muscat on 19th April to honour a speaking slot for Mark Evans at the annual dinner of sponsors of *Outward Bound Oman* (OBO). At the previous stop in Al Ain in the UAE, I also planned to meet a school friend, John Ramsell. Matthew was hooking up with Andy Woodford, a friend now working at *Horizon* who had offered to host DIGA at their facility 'off the international airfield'. Matthew and I looked at rescheduling options and I alerted everybody of our unplanned one-day delay.

We decided to taxi to the airport and meet *SGS* to dry run our departure formalities for the following day. Few people spoke English and we looked decidedly out of place, to put it mildly. We asked to be dropped at a large shopping mall near our hotel to mosey around. It was pretty much deserted, but we couldn't really figure out the working hours, the praying hours and when men and women went out. It was quite a bizarre experience. Anyway, we bought a small towel each to cover ourselves against the direct sun in the cockpit and walked back to our hotel.

Ever the inquisitive pair, that evening we asked our hotel for a return taxi to a restaurant in town. There, sitting on the floor of one of the many booths on a pink, plastic cloth, with chicken and rice on a plate, drinking Sprite, was possibly our most surreal dinner of *RTW*! In 2016, the only visa travel permitted to Saudi Arabia was by businessmen and pilgrims to the Hajj.

The next day, our passports and papers 'allowing us

to leave' were returned to us in a sealed envelope to be handed to officials in Al Ahsa. We were cleared from the helipad to FL090, direct to Al Ahsa; light, dirty rain made the windscreen muddy as we climbed slowly. It was really murky but the sun came and went and the features on the ground moved from dark rocks to yellow sand and back. We crossed many irrigation crop circles in the early part of the journey. Compared with the Sahara, the Arabian desert seemed to be more heavily populated, even in these remote areas between oases with little conurbations and their own dusty tracks.

The radio was just a frequency to monitor and we could hear the commercial jets above us. The visibility deteriorated as we approached Al Ahsa and the ground was hard to see from FL 090 except for the dark features and towns, which gave some relief. The Al Ahsa Oasis lies about 60 miles inland from the Persian Gulf and is one of the world's largest oases, with millions of date palms plus gardens, canals, springs, wells and lakes.

Abruptly, Riyad control blurted out, "G-DIGA" on the monitoring frequency. Riyad wanted us to divert northeast around some military activity. We took up the new heading immediately but already knew that this diversion could give us a problem with range. I requested an easement when possible and received the response, "Fly direct to Al Ahsa and contact Dhahran Military control". So, we did – panic over. Then unusually, Al Ahsa tower asked us to talk directly to another commercial aircraft to sort our own order to land!

Al Ahsa had two aprons and we were directed to the edge of the most convenient one in front of the terminal building. It was very windy, 34°C and humid, causing Matthew and me to sweat profusely. English was well-spoken and we were inundated with polite officials posing questions as we wrestled with refuelling and securing DIGA. Once inside the air-conditioned airport, we were discussing the next day's flight plan when the airport director announced that we must move DIGA to Apron #2 because they were expecting royalty on Apron #1. With a sigh, we went through the whole sweaty process of moving DIGA. Everyone was very apologetic but anticipation didn't seem to be a strong point in decision-making.

Our taxi eventually found our accommodation, although none of the airport staff had heard of it and were very interested to hear about our experience! Luckily, it was a fine two-bedroom apartment organised by Eddie. However, we did have to buy dinner and breakfast, which involved us walking down a small, dusty high street looking for shops, with men staring at us and women wearing abayas with the niqabs covering all but their eyes, shying away from us. A solitary tree on the dusty road provided a roost for hundreds of noisy small birds. We were definitely strangers in a foreign land!

Day 11 started well with Peter Drissell giving us the very welcome news that India had granted our diplomatic flight clearance. This drama had gone to the absolute wire and had taken so much effort from so many. My relief was palpable: Peter had saved our mission!

The Al Ahsa airport manager, dressed in his splendid white thobe, greeted us at 8am and we took a pleasant tea with officials as our agreed flight plan, directly southwest across Qatar to Al Ain in the UAE, was faxed to various locations for confirmation. Finally, with an accepting nod, we were through Security and driven to Apron #2 to prepare DIGA. After goodbye pleasantries, we were cleared to fly the flight plan with our squawk code. We lifted late at 9:30am and established contact with Dhahran Military for our crossing of military areas and into Qatar.

After about 20 minutes, we were questioned about our route and clearances by an apologetic Dhahran Military controller. We had all the necessary permits but Dhahran wanted us to route further south if we had the fuel, which we did. The visibility was deteriorating and we lost comms, but by relay, Dhahran instructed us to return to Al Ahsa under vectored headings to "avoid military activity". Oh! We obeyed sensibly. Dhahran offered us an alternative route, to the northeast of Al Ahsa, north of Bahrain and Qatar, and then southwest across the Persian Gulf. We didn't have sufficient fuel to mess around and opted to return to Al Asha first.

Eddie had already spotted our unusual *InReach* routing and, having landed back at Apron #2, Ahmed suggested a routing that was acceptable to Dhahran Military. The airport manager met us again, apologising profusely. Matthew and I had worked out that if we could lift within two hours, we could still just about make Al Ain before dark. All we had to do was go through all the necessary processing and refuelling to get airborne again! Minutes ticked by and with only five minutes to spare, we lifted to execute the new flight plan.

We climbed to 5,000 feet, heading northwest this time. Once Dhahran passed us over to Bahrain, we were free. It was a great flight, albeit a long way around and over the sea to avoid the traffic using all the famously big, busy airports of the region. In the Persian Gulf, we flew over many oil rigs with helipads. On making land fall with the UAE, we could see Abu Dhabi to the south (on our right), but not Dubai (further away to our left) as it was a little too hazy. Al Ain was busy with circuit training traffic but they were perfectly happy with us slotting in. We secured DIGA and scooted through Immigration and Customs because it was too late to organise going to *Horizon* tonight but just as the sun was setting, we were greeted by Andy Woodford of *Horizon* and John Ramsell, my school buddy from Rhodesia, who I hadn't seen for 40 years.

Andy looked after Matthew while John drove me to his house where we pieced together the jigsaw of the last 40 years! John and his wife, Lyn, entertained me with a braai, a few beers and some good stories. John and Lyn went to bed at 10pm while I uploaded photographs, sorted the flight plan for Muscat and coordinated the schedule to give us time at *Horizon* before heading to Muscat. I then went to bed myself: I was completely knackered after an epic day!

John worked as Quality Manager at *Horizon* and started at 7am. I agreed with their helipad operations where they wanted DIGA to land later. Then, back at the international terminal, I negotiated clearing Customs and a departure from *Horizon* directly for Muscat. Perfect!

Landing at *Horizon*, we were entertained with tea and Arab delicacies, talking to the staff and students about our journey, while DIGA was refuelled and pampered outside. Then we all assembled for marketing photographs and goodbyes. As we climbed away, we could see the sand dunes around Al Ain again and the spread of the city. We climbed up over the beautifully rugged Al-Hajar Mountains and Muscat control routed us down the coast. The sea had less haze to the east (our left), there was a green ribbon of conurbations underneath us all the way, and to our right lay the desert with its dusty haze. Our welcome at *Outward Bound Oman* (OBO) was warm and friendly from the staff who were comfortable with international visitors. We chatted with Mark Evans and then we had time to settle into the *OBO* accommodation before the annual sponsors' dinner.

With two rest days planned, Adil took us on a guided tour of Muscat. It was really hot, about 40°C and not even summer yet! He drove us to the Muscat I recognised from tourist pictures: a spotlessly clean city squeezed between jagged hills and the coast. We stopped at the mosque, explored the suq, admired the King's Palace and visited the Museum of Omani Culture. After lunch, we met with a local newspaper. There had been quite a bit of local press organised by *OBO*. Back at our *OBO* accommodation, we tried desperately to keep cool while planning the next series of flights through Pakistan and India, taking us to Dhaka in Bangladesh. We would be heading towards humid, tropical weather again. In the cooler evening, Matthew and I walked round a bit and found a Holiday Inn for our dinner.

On Friday morning, we enjoyed breakfast in Muscat with Mark. The mountains looked beautifully chiselled on this clear, blue-sky day. We discussed *TJR* and Mark's various projects. He had been a geography teacher before his current job with *OBO* and his life had been punctuated by some amazing expeditions across deserts, round coasts by kayak and across ice caps. He had a determination to recreate the great journeys of history and retell the story. Crucially, Mark introduced me to his friend, Mikael Strandberg, an explorer planning to spend time in Greenland when we might be passing through. Little did I know that this would be the beginning of my love affair with Greenland!

Friday and Saturday are the weekend in the Arab world, and we had the accommodation to ourselves to finish domestic and administrative chores. We would be up early on Saturday to cross the Gulf of Oman to Pakistan.

Lifting from Muscat, we were immediately into our long water hop, which at one point had us five nautical miles from the corner of Iran's airspace. Our slightly risqué plan was to clear Customs at Gwadar, which didn't have fuel, file a flight plan to Karachi and then divert to Pasni en route, which did have fuel (according to research by *G.A.S.E.*). The tiny Gwadar Airport existed in an expanse of bleak desert but we were overwhelmed by the friendly welcome from all the airport employees who came out to see DIGA. Officials quickly prepared the paperwork for our 72-hour, General Declarations-based stay in Pakistan, in the only, small, air-conditioned building. Within an hour, we were flying east, coastwise to Karachi, soaking up the absolutely stunning mountain scenery and geology of the arid desert Balochistan region. Sandy beaches and massive hard features rose up like sections of the Grand Canyon.

For *TJR*, I'd planned our range and fuel consumption based on 100 nautical miles an hour ground speed but wind was by far the biggest influence on this. While Matthew tried in vain to raise Pasni Airport, I messaged Eddie to get the wind speed aloft ahead of us because we needed help if we couldn't find fuel! At Ormara, we turned direct over the sea and managed to find a stonking 130 nautical miles an hour ground speed to Karachi! Scattered clouds greeted our approach to the amazing views of Karachi, a metropolis of about 18 million people and spectacular buildings. We were soon safely in our hotel dealing with our daily regime, feeling that we had definitely ridden our luck on this flight!

Handlers had already prepared our flight plan for the following day but there was still a delay wrestling with Pakistan for clearance and then Indian military. Our handler made frantic telephone calls and listened in on one of our headsets as we all sweated away in the unbearable humidity. With smiles of relief, we were good to go, only 30 minutes late. The visibility was frankly horrible and we could actually smell the fumes and haze. We flew over a mangrove-filled, marshy delta which became an arid landscape as we continued and crossed the Indus River. We actually crossed the Indus three times as we negotiated with Ahmedabad via Karachi and messages to Eddie, allowing us to land directly on the apron not the runway, which was now apparently closed for maintenance during our planned arrival.

The fumes and haze made for poor photographs. Crossing into India, the terrain below was really weird: our maps said there was water, but it was dry below, so possibly tidal. With Eddie's help, we realised that we were flying over Great Rann of Kutch, one of the biggest salt marshes in the world! Where there was a bit of land, we could see brick-built housing with tiled roofs. Eventually the land became inhabited and despite being very dry, it all looked farmed, divided into parcels like the UK with conurbations. Nearing Ahmedabad, conurbations grew larger and more numerous, and the ground became less parched and more cultivated with railway lines and major roads.

With *Aerotech's* support, the formalities were very relaxed. Eddie had organised a respectable hotel with great Wi-Fi. We had time left to walk around in a stiflingly humid 34°C, assimilating the raw humanity: four to a motorbike, horn-tooting, kamikaze driving and sacred cows wandering about the roadside. It was intoxicatingly chaotic. Dinner in the hotel was mainly vegetarian and we discovered that Ahmedabad was in the alcohol-dry state of Gujarat!

Aerotech guided us through the throng at domestic security and we could still smell the fumes and haze of the poor visibility (reported at 3,000 metres), caused by the uncomfortably hot weather and the burning of fields. A patchwork of dry, farmed land unfolded with brick and tile-roofed houses, which looked to be a step up from the poverty of Africa. We spotted wells dotted about where communities obviously took much-needed water and progressed over bigger conurbations, viaducts, irrigation schemes and railway lines. We saw kilns producing bricks and, as we approached our refuelling stop at Indore, the conurbations were bigger with factories and burnt-out wheat fields after the harvest.

After a pleasant three-hour delay in the new Indore airport building, we could proceed to Raipur. Past midday, it was stinking hot with a lot of bumpy thermal turbulence, which our autopilot didn't handle well. The *HeliSAS* autopilot maintains height by moving the cyclic stick, which also controls speed. So, with big drafts up or down, we normally reverted to manual flying. I had seen thermal turbulence like this while flying solo in Africa.

The city of Indore, with a population of 4½ million, was soon replaced by the cultivation of every bit of the flat landscape. The haze subsided and our photographs were clearer, capturing the changing greenery to arid-looking agriculture with more cropped and burnt fields. There were small communities far and wide and every square inch of the land appeared to be used, with wells dotted around the more arid areas. I supposed this was how you feed 1.3 billion people. We passed over sizable wooded areas, reservoirs and rivers from time to time, before being routed around military activity and cleared into Raipur.

The taxi journey was a 10km experience at night through the traffic chaos, avoiding sacred cows and families on weaving motorcycles. By contrast, our hotel was gentle and our hosts calm and friendly. Although the place was dry again, the buffet was delicious.

On our daytime return to the airport, we could really see how loosely road users were observing the highway code to the accompaniment of their horn-tooting. It was crazy! *Aerotech* quaintly issued us with boarding passes for DIGA and we progressed through domestic security to prepare her.

Climbing to 5,000 feet as requested, we encountered similar smoggy conditions and scenery to the day before. The land was populated and heavily cultivated as far as we could see in all directions. We passed over huge industrial regions, counting 10 coal-fired power stations close together at one point. We flew over the industrial town of Jamshedpur with an amazingly dirty factory and through the thickest, smelliest smog I have ever encountered. We were routed around to land from the north at Kolkata and met by an entourage of 15 smiling officials. Anticipating our international departure to Bangladesh the next day, Customs sealed DIGA's doors with masking tape – the first and only time I have seen that!

Aerotech had lots of paperwork to complete for us but we were at our hotel by 2pm and had done all of our chores by 3pm. We elected to taxi to a mall and see some of Kolkata! We assessed that it was probably a middle-class area with shops full of everything imaginable, but outside the mall, it was the usual fatalistic pandemonium, with thousands of people going about their daily business. The mall and our hotel were spotless but from the windows, we could see rubbish everywhere and a whole underclass living under the concrete highways with their own cafés and services. The sun was supposed to set at 6pm but by 3:48pm, it had already disappeared down into the fumes and haze of the horizon, creating an eerie twilight. A great advert for climate change.

Before going to bed, I received an email from Captain Phil Wilkinson, a British Army helicopter flight instructor serving in the Sultanate of Brunei with No. 7 Flight of the Army Air Corps. He had been following our journey. When in Mulu, he said we would only be 30 minutes away from their base. He invited us to visit during the Army Air Corps 60th anniversary year and Matthew and I weren't going to pass up this unique offer, so I investigated the feasibility of making it happen.

We chatted to the crew of a camouflaged border patrol helicopter as we waited for our clearance papers to Dhaka. It was humid and the visibility at Kolkata was low, at only 2,800 metres. The airport was under instrument flying rules; however, we were granted special visual flying rules to get away in the fumes and haze.

Our next short flight was over the amazing Ganges Delta, the world's largest delta which empties into the Bay of Bengal. The scenery grew ever lusher, with bigger rivers meandering and oxbow lakes everywhere. Little strips of land were either cultivated or built upon, with the remainder either forested or simply water, totally different to the dry landscape of central India. The weather had changed too with multiple cloud layers to negotiate and embedded CBs building up. An appalling smog hung over Dhaka, but while being held orbiting before landing, Matthew and I still had a murky overview of this absolutely massive city of 22 million people that we would be visiting for two days.

On the ground, the 95% humidity kicked in and we sweated profusely when refuelling and securing DIGA with covers, before clearing Immigration and Customs. I had arranged to meet Masud from the *Centre for the Rehabilitation of the Paralysed* (CRP) and we were driven 24 miles across Dhaka and out to the *CRP* compound at Savar. Masud pointed out landmarks and we saw busy side streets, shop fronts, rickshaws and throngs of people. The congestion was hideous. We continued past the debris of life: unfinished buildings, businesses from popup shops to steel girder sales yards, and everything in between. Speed wasn't excessive, but it was mayhem, yet a wonderful experience at the same time. Our senses were assaulted with the incessant horn-tooting. Suddenly, we were in a tight side street, squeezing past more colourfully dressed women and decorated rickshaws, to enter the 13-acre *CRP* compound.

We were welcomed by Dr Valerie Taylor who founded *CRP* in 1979, in response to the desperate need for services for spinal injury patients. She had developed it into an internationally respected organisation. That afternoon, Masud gave us a tour of the main medical departments, service units, hospital, operating theatre facilities, and supporting therapies and rehabilitation services, including social welfare, counselling and vocational training. We spoke with the Assistive Devices and Technologies department who helped children with prosthetics and wheelchairs. The compound was full of smiling faces as people were encouraged to strive and endeavour.

Settling into our accommodation in the compound, Matthew and I both reflected on the day's assault on our senses and sensibilities and the juxtaposition of our so very different lives.

At *CRP*, we were looked after by Shamoly. She had arrived 25 years ago with her seven-year-old niece who, after falling from a building, was paralysed from the neck down. Her niece had lived until she was 17 and was helped by *CRP* in many ways; she is celebrated to this day through her extraordinary mouth paintings. Shamoly had stayed on working at *CRP*, bringing up her own child as a single mum: she was a real inspiration. After breakfast, Shamoly guided us down some back streets toward three schools where the children seemed excited to talk and possibly look at our white legs! We returned along the main road capturing images of the side-by-side continuum of rubbish and commerce and scramble for life. The horn-tooting was incessant and the battery-assisted rickshaws had especially loud horns. The big buses with battered front, back and sides just beeped and drove when and where they wanted to!

At midday, we gathered for lunch, kindly organised by Valerie, to meet the *CRP* leadership and all the other volunteers, mainly occupational therapists and physiotherapists on placement from the UK. After interesting discussions, farewells and group photographs, Valerie saw us to our waiting car. The traffic was chocka block and we were going to be very late for our afternoon meeting with *Save the Children* (STC).

The car took us to our hotel to check-in and drop off our bags, before Sultan from *STC* whisked us off to see the *STC Education and Youth Employment* (EYE) programme.

We were rushing to leave when the hotel's X-ray machine showed that Matthew had a gun in his bag. A second pass revealed nothing at all and we wondered what the devil was going on! Security seemed horizontal. Then it dawned on us: it was just a random introduction in the software to keep the security personnel on full alert! We laughed – relieved – and joined Sultan.

Arriving at the *STC* programme site, we were ushered through the school gates and down a narrow walkway. There were drummers and lines of children each side, singing with gusto and throwing flowers at us. It was a little bizarre and quite overwhelming. Embarrassingly, we had kept everybody waiting two hours to meet and greet us, brief us with slides and documents and then show us round the classroom facilities and meet the school children. We saw how children from the slums or domestic workers with no education were helped into an accelerated education programme and then into employment. We met the children, saw the training and felt the passion of the successful graduates to whom we spoke. In a local scooter repair shop, we met 'the child labourer turned owner,' now employing *EYE* programme graduates himself. The fact that about 190,000 children were now entering the *EYE* programme annually and the government was scaling up the approach with *STC* technical help showed that Bangladesh was making progress to become a developed country. Fighting for the rights of children to participate and succeed represented the very essence of *Save the Children*. I could tell that this humbling experience had profoundly affected Matthew too.

We got back late and slept well, in spite of the 24/7 noise of humanity outside. The humidity was still oppressive and our handwashing remained damp in the morning. We were off to visit the *Inclusive Protection and Empowerment Project for Children with Disabilities* (IPEP) with Rafika from *STC* and some of her contemporaries from supporting organisations. It was Friday, the first day of the weekend, and we were grateful for their time with us. *IPEP* was a pilot programme designed to help communities overcome poverty, malnutrition, birth complications and prejudice to include disabled children in everyday activities.

We drove 30 miles outside Dhaka to visit a school that was being assisted by *IPEP* to integrate disabled children into community activities. Rafika had previously worked for a disabilities charity and had a psychology degree. We discussed the *TJR* project and Rafika's dedication to the disabled who always seemed to be the lowest priority in any society, particularly those living in extreme poverty. Even the rickshaw drivers might earn only 3 USD for a full day's work. I recounted Nelson Mandela's poignant words: "There can be no keener revelation of a society's soul than the way in which it treats its children."

We met the community council comprising parents, disabled children and a cleric. Rafika translated and vigorous discussions and questioning ensued. We then met the children in the kids' club which was now integrated with the able and disabled kids, all of whom were using the school facilities on the weekend to have fun. Again, Rafika translated and the children were uninhibited in their questioning. I asked Rafika what the main causes of the disabilities were and received the shocking but frank response: extreme poverty; malnutrition; and home birth complications, including cerebral palsy and interbreeding.

Travelling back to Dhaka, we discussed with Rafika

the logic and feasibility of solving UN *Global Goal #1*, namely, eliminating extreme poverty. She said it was a delicate balance between 'pump priming', creating a 'safety net' and expecting people to self-determine. Rafika was very clear on one point though: if women could choose to have smaller families, they would do so.

Our final visit was into a poor area of Dhaka to meet a 15-year-old boy called Rabbi, who suffered from muscular dystrophy. His mum admitted to being abusive, cruel and to neglecting him, until she and Rabbi enrolled in *IPEP*. They were found by the house-to-house survey for the pilot programme. The family has not looked back since; Rabbi was a lovely, cared for child now. With his wheelchair, he was helped to join the normal school system and enjoyed his friends, schoolwork and art.

We thanked Rafika sincerely for the amazing experience but getting back late in the evening left us little time to process it, before preparing for the following day's flight across the Ganges Delta again.

We were cleared at 500 feet, which was a perfect height to see the city and transformation to urban fields, waterways and conurbations lining the elevated sections above the delta. Rice cultivation broke out below us and was punctuated by water, housing and factories. It was a short flight, with the lush green delta below and a fumy, haze-filled horizon. The visibility fluctuated but there were hardly any clouds. We crossed bigger rivers and a short, muddy portion of the Bay of Bengal, before spotting the coast to our left, then Chittagong and the many container ships on the Karnaphuli River.

It was a nice, new airport with the first free Wi-Fi of

the journey, so Matthew and I cleared our messages while waiting for a taxi to the hotel section of the Chittagong Boat Club, founded in 1880. There, I used my time to catch up on administration and to anticipate the arrangements for servicing DIGA in Kuala Lumpur. I also had to follow up on plans for meeting the British Army Air Corps in Brunei during their 60th anniversary year, which also happened to be my 60th year too!

10

Beauty, diversity and destruction

The next day, we were leaving the Indian sub-continent and moving on to the torrid, tropical countries of South East Asia. We planned to make our way to Myanmar first and then on through Thailand and Malaysia to South Sumatra. We headed over more interesting and forested terrain and, although the fumes and haze were still there, the visibility was improving in parts. The ground developed some satisfying shapes as we rose to about 2,000 feet; when the scattered clouds thickened around us, we chose to climb to 5,000 feet on top.

We passed just 23 nautical miles east of Cox's Bazar where all the trouble for the Rohingya people unfolded in the world news in October (more than 600,000 Rohingya refugees had arrived in Bangladesh since 25th August after fleeing violence in Myanmar). We crossed into Myanmar which was not as densely populated as Bangladesh. We were talking to Chittagong until we lost them, then picked up local military airfields along the way who were all helpful. As we journeyed down the coast, we crossed islands and beaches, passing villages and fishing boats, and the sun reflected off the numerous, shiny-blue, tin-roofed houses. Turning towards Yangon, we crossed a huge low plain, the Irrawaddy River, and cultivated fields with harvesting activity underway. The unusual shape of the fields was influenced by the previous beautiful curves of the now dry, reclaimed oxbow lakes of the meandering river.

We had elected not to use a handler at Yangon but that resulted in a time-consuming delay at the airport and finally an indication that we should pay 900 USD cash the following day! No-one spoke English and it was all a bit frustrating. By contrast, our hotel provided a very pleasant experience and everyone chatted to us in English. We managed to calm down in the comfort of the air-conditioning, finally attending to our end-of-day regime.

The next morning, an English-speaking airport official did kindly expedite us through all the formalities, explaining that our bill had been miscalculated based on DIGA weighing 12 and not 1.2 tonnes! With faith in humankind restored, we prepared to depart and feasted on views of Yangon city and the container vessel-filled tributaries. As we headed for a crossing of the Andaman Sea, the haze, clouds and muddy waters combined to reduce visibility, so we climbed above the scattered clouds again. Rain and cloud could become our new challenge, especially when mixed with the higher ground of Taninthanryi National Park ahead, before crossing the Gulf of Thailand, south of Bangkok.

Using our *Garmin* terrain software and working together, we found an optional route through the hills if the weather did close in. Luckily, both weather and visibility continued to improve, and it seemed we might finally be clear of the blown sand, fumes and haze that had started in Egypt. At last, our horizon was blue again. The high ground was forested and carved by rivers, reminding me of beautiful west Ethiopia as I headed between Lokichoggio and

Damazin, skimming the hilltops at about 300 feet above ground level.

Thailand seemed more populated and developed and big Buddhas replaced the temples of Myanmar. Approaching U-Taphao Airport, serving Rayong (formerly Rangoon), we could now see clearly for 50 miles; the view was of a beautifully built-up shore, blue sea, beaches and rolling, green hills. All we wanted was fuel and formalities sorted quickly, but every man and his dog turned up and we were given another big draft handling bill! However, waiting on the apron, we had front row seats, watching 12 Thai Air Force jet fighters taking off in groups of four and then landing back, which made Eddie jealous.

At the Lord Nelson Hotel on the seashore, we could hear the waves crashing above the road traffic, which was virtually silent because horn-tooting isn't rampant like in Dhaka. We found the Thai experience welcoming and friendly and we enjoyed the more relaxed, freer social surroundings, listening to familiar Western music for the first time in 25 days. Myanmar, Thailand, Lois and Cambodia are largely made up of the Buddhist religion.

With Cambodia and Vietnam to the east, our direction the next day would be flying south down the Malaysian peninsula. We reached DIGA after satisfying ourselves that our extortionate handling bill was merely highway robbery and not mistaken for corruption. We counted 19 jet fighters and Eddie's research showed that their type (Northrop F5s) played the part of the Russian aircraft in the movie *Top Gun*. Unbeknown to us, there was a major exercise underway.

The tower cleared us but we were held for a long time at different positions as the military jets received priority, followed by two landing commercial jets and finally, the spectacular arrival of a formation of eight military helicopters (including Blackhawks, Hueys and Jet Rangers) – it was quite a show. We had wanted to fly coastwise, but we were routed directly across the Gulf of Thailand, flying over six warships; we half expected to be intercepted!

We passed the island of Ko Samui and the sea changed to a lighter green as its depth shallowed. As we crossed the Malaysian peninsula, the clouds were building up on land, which was flat but with significant chunks of rock sticking up into the air. Eddie told us that these geological features were from the Devonian period about 300 million years ago. The ground was lush and planted with big trees and palms, and the crops looked like rubber and sugar cane. Reaching the Straits of Malacca, we had another 50 nautical miles south across the sea to the island of Langkawi; the clouds ahead looked ominous and heavy with rain. We passed beautiful, little islands and more geological features jutting up out of the sea. The airport we were approaching was hidden behind hills and we were so low over the water under the rain clouds, we couldn't get comms with them on the radio. We checked our radios and frequencies again. Finally, rounding the headland, with only four nautical miles to go, we established contact and slotted in behind a landing passenger jet. It was raining properly for the first time since a little rain had muddied our windscreen in Saudi Arabia. Here, the airport formalities were very relaxed and we paid a total of 20 USD. We now looked forward to easy VFR flying into Kuala Lumpur (KL) the following day. Langkawi is the 52nd *UNESCO* global geopark: a site of special geological interest and beauty, and the scenery and rocks were indeed spectacular.

We saw even more of the beauty of Langkawi on our next

flight, lifting early to fly east across the island. Back on the Malaysian peninsula, the scene was of wet, cultivated, low-lying fields stretching inland and down the coast, with the early morning sun glinting invitingly. We were due to be met by Captain Siva and his wife Rani of the *Experiment Aircraft Association, Malaysian chapter* (EAAM) on landing. We were heading for our first service at Subang, the smaller, international airport serving KL, and Rani had already kindly sorted our hotel and settled in David Cross prior to DIGA's service. With a mixture of fading radio signals and indecipherable accents, we zigzagged south down the coast, avoiding restricted areas while attempting to follow our incomplete, photocopied map of the VFR waypoints for the Heli route. We passed Kedah Peak and flew low between Panang with all its beachfront high rises, and the mainland over the causeways and fisheries. Then we continued zigzagging inland and back to the coast until finally, through the haze of KL, we were nearly there.

On landing at the hangar, we were greeted by the *Chempaka Helicopter Corporation* team, Siva, Rani and David, a photographer and a journalist. It was mayhem for a bit, then Matthew, David and I set about cleaning DIGA, watching a huge thunderstorm with lightning unfold, before preparing for her inspection with help from supporting *Afjets* staff.

We agreed to meet James Greaves, who owned both *Ascend* (helicopter tours around KL) and *Chempaka*, for an evening meal along with Trine, one of his helicopter pilots. David opted sensibly to go to bed because he was on a completely different time zone. We were warned about KL's commuter traffic and the gridlock meant we arrived late, but it was an evening of great company and delicious seafood.

The next day, David tackled DIGA's inspection and it was my job to help him as and when required. It was very humid and noisy with commercial jet engines running on the apron. I was perhaps acclimatised but David was suffering, with the only respite being in an air-conditioned storeroom! James was keen to meet David at lunch and they soon discovered that they had many mutual contacts in the helicopter industry. That afternoon, there was an awesome thunderstorm and lightning. I thought to myself that there could be interesting flying conditions ahead in the Inter Tropical Convergence Zone (ITCZ), perhaps as far as Japan! Siva and Rani had organised an *EAAM* dinner and Matthew and I were invited guests. We were entertained like family and proud to be the thirteenth guests that *G.A.S.E.* had introduced. The hospitality was wonderful, meeting fellow general aviation and professional pilots, sharing stories and learning.

By way of a test flight, David and I were excited about a combination flight with another helicopter for ship-to-ship pictures. Another of James' pilots, Barry, who had local knowledge, came with me, David and a photographer in DIGA, while Matthew went with James and a second photographer in James' air-conditioned R66. The route was first to the south (via Klang and Tanjong Sepat), then southwest along the coast (via Bagan) to Port Dickson, then east to Kampung to Palau Subang, then north via Seremban to KL city itself. We landed at the Lexis Hibiscus Hotel, which holds the Guinness World Record for each of its 643 rooms having swimming pools and 522 of them being water villas on stilts. We flew low-level over the palm oil plantations, which pretty much cover Myanmar, Thailand and Malaysia. The iconic building that we wanted to see was the Petronas Twin Towers. We 'hover posed' each helicopter in turn and captured some great photographs, before landing in the city at the Titiwangsa helipad for a quick sandwich. Recovering back to Subang, we left DIGA primed for our Monday morning departure. That evening, David left to return to London, we said goodbye to James, then enjoyed a meal with Barry and his wife, sitting under an outside awning as the heavens opened again.

For the Saturday and Sunday, Matthew and I planned rest days. I chose to visit a huge mall to resupply, get a haircut and people watch. There was a broad mix of Malay Malay, Indian Malay and Chinese Malay, plus all the Asian tourists and the outlets serving their different preferences. Women wore anything from Muslim headscarves to the shortest, flimsy shorts and blouses suitable for the hot weather. It was a wonderful rich tapestry of humanity, not European obviously, but also not Indian sub-continent or Arabian. Back at the hotel, I wrote up my diary, messaged Ahmed, returned emails, attended to Facebook, prepared my PLOGs and watched the weather for the route ahead. By 3pm, it was raining cats and dogs again. That evening, *G.A.S.E.* messaged to say that we would need an alternative point of entry for Japan and suggested routing through Taiwan, which started a ripple effect through our logistics planning and spreadsheets.

Our next two destinations had been forecast regularly as Instrument Meteorological Conditions because of mist and low cloud which could just hang around because of the high humidity combined with lights winds. I started to monitor the stations ahead with each hourly update and overlaid the forecast from my *Windy* app to get the best understanding. Luckily, the weather looked pretty good for our departure, and onwards. After a final 'thank you' conversation with Rani, I fell asleep to be woken by the hotel phone ringing. A person also calling herself Rani wanted to know if I'd like a drink. Confusion ensued until I realised that I wasn't talking to the 'real' Rani and the caller also realised that I really didn't want to go for a massage and cut the call off!

On Monday morning, we said hearty goodbyes to everybody at *Chempaka*. We already knew our way out and we turned south southwest across the Strait of Malacca direct to Palembang. Indonesia is the fourth most populous nation in the world, behind China, India and the US, and it's scattered over either side of the equator comprising more than 17,500 islands. Reportedly, half of its population lives on less than 2 USD a day, representing about 100 million extremely poor people.

Initially, we encountered misty cloud which cleared as we travelled when the temperature rose above the dew point. Sumatra was full of flat plantations and rarely did we see any remaining pristine forest. The tropical forests had been cleared to make room for a vast monoculture of oil palm trees and we flew over big bulldozers clearing the land for new plantations, causing horrific devastation. Indonesia is in fact the world's largest producer of palm oil.

The practice of draining and converting tropical peatland forests in Indonesia is particularly damaging as these 'carbon sinks' store more carbon per unit area than any other ecosystem in the world. In addition, forest fires set to clear vegetation for oil palm plantations is another source of CO_2 released from land clearing. With this practice, Indonesia is the third worst emitter of greenhouse gases in the world, behind China and the USA.

We crossed the Equator with about 150 nautical miles to

run to Palembang, our first antipode. The South Sumatran province is very flat with a mean elevation above sea level of only eight metres. We began to see more conurbations and roads as we drew closer. It's a city, port and district in the south of the island of Sumatra, twinned with its antipode, Neiva, where we would also be going. 'Palembang' literally means 'the place which was constantly inundated by water' and it's the oldest city in Indonesia, dating back to the 7th century.

The airport was really efficient and we were in our hotel within an hour. We had time for a walk around the mall which was quite a different experience to KL. Fewer people spoke English and we were the only Caucasians. Interest in us was keen and everybody stared, especially the children. We had a coffee and soaked up the atmosphere.

During our morning taxi ride back to the airport, we glimpsed the waking city traffic. Three and four to a motorbike was common again and, like Thailand, speeds were modest. As the traffic merged and weaved, there was still an absence of the incessant horn-tooting seen in Bangladesh and India!

I had my *FAI* paperwork certified by *Air Traffic Control* (ATC) and we were soon ready for our short domestic flight to Pontianak on Borneo, the third largest island in the world. The weather reports at both airports were Instrument Meteorological Conditions but improving and we could already see the sunshine at Palembang. We flew northeast across the flat palm oil plantations towards Bangka Island with a bit of low cloud and mist to cope with. Eddie messaged that Bangka Island was the setting for Joseph Conrad's book 'Lord Jim' – also a cheeky nickname for my father. We could now see for 50 nautical miles and avoid the thunderstorms ahead.

Approaching Borneo and Pontianak, the monolithic-type peaks of Gunung Batuwangking rose majestically out of the otherwise flat ground. In Pontianak, it was quite hard to get a conversation going because English wasn't a commonly spoken language, even in the hotels, but people were happy to try and communicate and help us as we took a short walk around our hotel district.

The next morning, the good forecast seemed accurate, with excellent visibility in between the inevitable diurnal CB build-up and rain pattern. Our first flight was northwest into Sarawak (East Malaysia) past Kuching, Sibu and then coastwise from Bintulu to Miri. Although the ground was hillier initially, the oil palm plantations were almost continuous on this part of Borneo.

Bintulu was a small, coastal fishing village, now developed following the discovery of oil and gas. We flew low over the beaches and the palm oil trees for about 50 miles approaching Miri, an even bigger oil city. We passed the Lambir Hills National Park, which had lost 40 species of mammals down to 22 in only the last 20 years, according to Eddie's research. Our handler helpfully made arrangements for us to clear Immigration and Customs at Mulu, direct to Brunei, which was very convenient. After a quick turnaround in the pouring rain, we lifted to pick our way through the rain showers and hop just 40 nautical miles eastwards to Mulu.

We saw plantations right up to the Gunung Mulu National Park border. Beyond, the park turned to rugged and protected pristine forest. We landed on a grass patch, slushy under foot, and it was really humid and sweaty hot. We were expected by our hosts, the Mulu Marriott Hotel and once settled in, we dashed off to the Mulu Park offices to organise outings for our four-day stay.

Mulu is a *UNESCO* World Heritage site in the heart of the amazing Borneo rainforest. The humid heat of the rainforest supports a stunning range of flora and fauna, and the geology of alluvial clays, sandstone and limestone formations produces dozens of specialist environments for plants and animals. We were here to experience unique cave environments and see the jagged peaks rising to above 5,000 feet.

Our first morning's excursion was to ride a boat up the river. I was carrying a handwritten letter from Nigel Winser to Nyapun, one of the original Penang who supported the *RGS* expedition in 1977/78, 40 years ago, when the *RGS* was surveying the biodiversity in Mulu. It was an honour talking to Nyapun, who was by now an old man. Since then, the Sarawak Government has committed to developing world-leading conservation practices to protect Mulu's biodiversity and high-quality, nature-based tourism activities to support Mulu's integrated community. We continued to the Cave of Winds and Clear Water Cave with their cool, dark interiors providing relief from the sweaty, humid heat outside.

At a local restaurant for lunch, we met a young couple from Singapore; it sounded like Singapore was a unique experiment in how to run a country efficiently, yet the couple remained cautious in their commentary. It rained hard before the baking sun reappeared.

In the afternoon, we used raised walkways through the rainforest to visit two more caves and I met Melissa who worked in climate change policymaking for Australia. Lang Cave was full of spectacular stalagmites and stalactites and amazing colours. Deer Cave was enormous, with possibly the biggest single cavern cave in the world and housing three million wrinkle-lipped bats. We got soaked walking to the bat-viewing gallery. Not expecting the bats to exit in the rain, we nonetheless enjoyed discussions with two young doctors touring Vietnam and Cambodia. Simon and Nina, both police officers, were also taking a five-year sabbatical from work to travel widely.

The following morning, we took a boat to Lagang Cave, talking to two young engineers from Penang as we walked through the extensive cave system to its separate exit. These two weren't even born when I had graduated as a mechanical engineer! It hadn't rained all day and many people were now gathering to observe the mass bat exodus from Deer Cave in the evening. We spotted Simon and Nina again and got chatting to others also on lengthy journeys. The wrinkle-lipped bats came out in short streams that lasted a minute or so: three million bats on the move was a stunning show, drawing gasps from the crowd. You would think that there would be loads of biting insects and mosquitoes, but these lovely bats apparently kept the bug population under control. Everyone left at the same time as if a local football match was finishing. We caught up with Simon and Nina and legged it back to our 'local restaurant'. Joined by our new friends, we were eight for dinner, swapping stories until late when it started to pour again.

Early on our third morning, we went for a rainforest canopy walk, 30 metres up, which gave us a good vantage point. The proboscis and macaque monkeys only visited in the fruit season, which it wasn't. What we heard instead was the cacophony of Nature: birds, bugs, amphibians and more, all tweeting, cracking, chirping and singing. It was actually quite noisy. Mulu was the first place where we had really heard Nature alone making more noise than humans. That night it poured down again for a good two hours.

On Sunday, we went to the airport. DIGA seemed fine after all the rain and we agreed the process with Customs and our flight plan with *ATC*, which all seemed straightforward. Using the hotel's Lobby-Fi, I had been nudging administrative messages morning and evening. Nigel had suggested that the easiest way to see the hidden valley and the limestone pinnacles would be from DIGA and, if the weather was good, we would try. We also had our Russian permit now and I had prepared my PLOGs for the journey ahead. Upon leaving Brunei, we would be flying through the Philippines, Taiwan, Japan, Russia and into Alaska, witnessing some wonderful geology and geography along the way.

By staying in Mulu for a while, I had been able to get a sense of local personalities shining through and to understand local issues better. I was in no doubt of the friendliness of the Malays but having a longer stop in one place was a learning point for me when designing my next journey.

After days of rain (Mulu receives nine metres per year), the next morning was dry and we could see the mountains clearly. We were excited to be preparing DIGA and Peterus (who worked at the airport) pushed his camera through the door with his thumbs up, smiling. We climbed to fly through the majestic hidden valley, twice, and after a bit of searching, past the pinnacles. Circling the Marriot and airport facilities, we settled on the apron to return one camera and, with *ATC's* blessing, set off north for our 30-minute flight to Brunei International Airport. The squiggly Sungai Limang River looked like a varicose vein and outside the park, the palm oil plantations scarred the land again. Approaching the airport, we had views of the beautiful city of Bandar Seri Begawan with its glistening palaces and mosques.

Within 30 minutes, we were flying west in the direction of Miri, becoming the first civilian aircraft to land at the base of the *No. 7 Flight of the Army Air Corps* (7 Flt AAC) in Brunei. We were looking forward to celebrating their 60th anniversary in my 60th year. The base is home to three Bell 212 helicopters used to support the British Army's jungle training. Captain Phil Wilkinson and Major Tom Harbottle welcomed us warmly. DIGA was hangared with her new friends and we were shown around the operations. The pilots were interested in our safety survival equipment which, apart from flak jackets, was small, modern, light versions of all their military issue – this gave me comfort too! We were put up in the Officers' mess of the Gurkhas based nearby and after settling in, we joined a social evening including *BP* Offshore Operation pilots revelling in helicopter and flying stories.

Our Officers' mess experience was like a club, hotel and employer all rolled into one, with Gurkha history, traditions, memorabilia and people moving through. Breakfast was accompanied by more interesting people and stories.

Back on the *7 Flt AAC* base, we hooked up with *British Forces Radio Services* (BFRS) who wanted a story on *TJR* and our *RTW* journey. We worked with reporter Lisa David and a photographer to get what they needed. Then we talked to the engineers, fire crews, doctors and medical crews before taking some team photographs. We watched the medics practicing winching dummies up and down from the Bell 212 (11,200 lbs maximum all up weight), hovering at 100 feet.

Tom dropped us back to the Officers' mess and there were more new faces to talk to over dinner. I could see that Matthew had topped up the sunburn he started in Mulu and had also managed to sprain his ankle. I sat next to Izzy who described her journey to becoming a military doctor and what ailments troops get on jungle training, including Dengue fever. Izzy said that Dengue is widespread throughout the tropics and is a mosquito-borne viral disease transmitted by female mosquitoes of a species that also transmits yellow fever and the Zika infection. This was all very interesting and the symptoms sounded rough. We were on *Malarone* for protection against malaria but apparently, the only real safeguard against contracting Dengue was not to get bitten in the first place!

On Saturday morning, we were on our way to the Philippines and made sure we had selfies beside the *7 Flt AAC* regimental signage. Lisa captured more material for *BFRS*. We said goodbye and followed a Bell 212 taking off to shadow us partway back to Bandar. With some great photographs in the bag, we continued to the international airport just as it was opening, in order to clear Immigration and Customs. We almost achieved a fast turnaround, except that a VIP flight with the Crown Prince onboard unexpectedly closed the airport for one hour!

We flew northwest across Brunei Bay, which was a parking lot of oil and gas ships, and into Malaysia, passing Kota Kinabalu. To the right of our track (south) we could see Mount Kinabalu (13,500 feet) from miles away, the highest peak in Borneo and, in terms of topography, the twentieth most prominent mountain in the world no less. Kinabalu Park was another World Heritage Site, protecting 6,000 species of plants, 326 species of birds and more than

100 mammal species. Then we struck out across the Sulu Sea to Palawan Island. The sea was a wonderful blue, with idyllic, small islands, floating pontoons and lots of fishing boat activity. The weather started off fine with a typical tropical cloud build-up and interspersed CBs which we managed to avoid.

Airport formalities at Puerto Princesa were easy. We found the heat sticky and clammy and opted for a tricycle motorbike taxi to our hotel, which turned out to be very basic, with an open-air restaurant and reception area and motel-style rooms with trees and jungle around them. It reminded me of Camp 748 in Lokichoggio (Kenya) but without the guns. The people were very friendly though and I agreed to meet Matthew at the restaurant, the only place where the (poor) Wi-Fi worked. It started to pour down loudly before Matthew could cross the tiny courtyard; within minutes, it was under a foot of water, which he had to paddle across. It was some sight and pedestrians were just getting soaked. Sitting in the restaurant, dry as a bone, I was bitten to death by mosquitoes under the table as I tackled my administration, to a chorus of bullfrogs, croaking in appreciation of the soaking.

During the night, the air-conditioning had thankfully masked the sauna that greeted us the next morning and we breakfasted amidst the fickle cats who meowed until we'd finished. The same smiling tricycle taxi driver chatted away to us, avoiding puddles and pointing out Jeepney buses made from leftover US military jeeps. The Philippines was an interesting and friendly place, with English widely spoken and a lot of American influences, including music.

We continued flying northeast up the archipelagic Province of Palawan, crossing beautiful little islands, isolated beaches and fishermen criss-crossing the sea. In 2016, Palawan was rated the 'most beautiful island in the world' by readers of *Travel & Leisure* and at the top of Palawan, we flew over El Nido, rated the 'most beautiful beach in the world'. It was indeed stunning and in perfect visibility too.

After more of the China Sea, we crossed to the main island of Luzon. About 40 nautical miles out of Manila, we could see a dome of smog hanging over the city. Manila is the most densely populated city in the world, boasting 66,000 people per km². The airport sounded very busy, operating both runways; getting closer, rain added to the smog to reduce visibility considerably. We were vectored round at 300 feet to approach over Manila Bay from the west side of the airport. Crossing the shoreline, we weaved our way through multi-storey buildings under construction with many tall cranes. We landed on a taxiway and hovered over to John of *Airmach*, who kindly handled us. Formalities were relaxed, being a domestic flight. I was exhausted and ready for an early night after I'd completed my evening administrative regime.

We departed Manila Airport at 300 feet to the west, dodging all the buildings and cranes. Reaching Manila Bay, we dropped to 100 feet over the water and turned northwest. We crossed on to wetlands which looked like reclaimed land using rubbish to infill, with remarkable lines of stilted villages just above the water. Soon the visibility cleared up and we transitioned to dry, agricultural land. We passed Mount Arayat, an extinct conical volcano, then Lingayen Gulf, which was the site of two major amphibious landings in WWII. After a lovely clear spell, it became hazy again north of San Fernando and we saw pontoon-fishing boats, villages and beaches as it became more remote.

We were heading for our point of exit from the Philippines, a small city called Laoag, at the north of Luzon Island. The airport was very quiet and we were granted permission to fly over the beach before landing and sorting formalities. Our only hotel choice was in a bizarre setting, aimed at Chinese tourists who love their gambling. It was grand yet tacky at the same time, with gardens, function rooms, restaurants, money exchange stations and casinos. I managed a short walk around, but I felt absolutely drained of energy. After sorting the minimum of my domestic and administrative chores and checking in with *G.A.S.E.*, I went to bed at 6pm without eating and slept for 12 hours straight!

In the morning, I felt suitably revived and was looking forward to the reducing temperatures and less humidity of the higher latitudes ahead. During breakfast, *Airmach* and Ahmed organised a handler for us in Kaohsiung, which now seemed a condition of our permission to enter Taiwan. Anyway, we didn't speak a word of Chinese and the assistance would be welcome at a complex airport.

We took off to fly 250 nautical miles across the South China Sea. When we left, it was clear but various layers of clouds developed, so we descended and climbed, eventually flying VFR on top. As the cloud thinned and we talked to Kaohsiung, we descended for our approach. We were held north of Lambai Island close to the mainland where the visibility was atrociously smoggy and hazy. Kaohsiung was a heavily industrialised city and, with a population of nearly three million, the second largest in Taiwan. The airport was IFR, reporting 3,000 metres visibility. We were cleared across the industrial, ship-building portion of the docks and landed on the busy apron. Freda, who had probably never dealt with a small general aviation flight, was our handler.

After having my temperature taken in the quarantine area, I was suspected of carrying Dengue fever! I was interviewed and a nurse took blood immediately for analysis. The quarantine authorities explained the barrier precautions I should take to avoid infecting any of their local mosquitoes, and they arrived smartly to fumigate my hotel room! They seemed happy that I would be leaving the following day and I was asked to stay indoors. Ironically, while I didn't feel 100%, I did feel much better than the previous day in Laoag and my appetite was back. My recent mid-afternoon energy slumps made sense to me now and based on incubation time, I had probably been infected four to 10 days ago in Mulu or Puerto Princesa. My discussions with Izzy at the *7 Flt AAC* base had been timely; Dengue fever might slow me down a bit but fortunately, it wouldn't kill or maim me! Rest was the best remedy, so Matthew got to walk around Kaohsiung, while I ate my dinner next to a mosquito coil and went to bed early again.

Once again, I felt revived in the morning and hungry. However, we were flabbergasted at breakfast; the Taiwanese are not quiet queuers, nor eaters! It was like the scrum of a school dinner and Matthew and I had to quietly smile to each other.

There was a fuss at the airport and, while Freda was personable, it was the flight information office that understood what we needed. Apparently, military use of airspace dictated that we must first fly to the south of Taiwan, before going direct to Okinawa. Freda could have told us this yesterday! It left us with an even longer flight into forecast headwinds and some weather and, for the most part, a very long water crossing. Only Miyako-jima, about 160 nautical miles from Okinawa, presented a refuelling alternative although it wasn't a point of entry. Using *Rocket Route* and *Windy* to get the latest forecast wind and weather, we checked our calculations for PONR and refuelling. We would also be making regular assessments based on the actual weather en route.

Kaohsiung City was sunny, and the smog of the various industrial townships cleared as we approached the south of the island and set course direct to Naha (Okinawa's airport). We adjusted altitude to give the least headwind, Eddy updated us with *Windy* forecasts and Mother Nature delivered as advertised. We only experienced two marginal VFR patches where the *HeliSAS* autopilot helped. We used our *Satphone* for 'operations normal' calls to Taiwan control and then picked up Naha control at an incredible range. We saw some of the beautiful Okinawa islands and Haterume-Shima, the geographical southernmost point of Japan. We flew on past our PONR and the island of Miyako-jima, ducking below the overcast cloud cover for the last 50 nautical miles.

We were met at Okinawa by our amiable handler, Gem, and a pleasant temperature. After DIGA's status was converted to 'domestic flying', we refuelled and secured her. Soon we had some local currency and a taxi to our hotel, where registration was very, very polite, but surprisingly slow – too many people involved, too few of whom knew what they were doing – it wasn't what I had expected of this mighty industrial power.

I was hungry again and ate well at dinner, then attended to my chores and flight planning with Matthew. With only one short flight the next day, I felt I was getting better, but still went to bed early as a precaution. I was looking forward to exploring some of Japan's thinking, although I wasn't underestimating the language barrier.

There was a lot of military activity at Naha Airport in the

morning, including transport planes, F15 jets, Chinook and Apache helicopters. We were vectored around it and then to the east of the island, low over the city and through the rain. However, the weather brightened as we followed the impressive 'ring of fire' chain of volcanoes northwards to Kagoshima in the south of Japan. Some were active with a strong smell of sulphur. It was a little hazy, about 22°C, but feeling humid and certainly gusty and turbulent around the volcanoes.

Eddie messaged a running commentary all the way while following our beacon tracker. The island of Iwo Jima, one of the Japanese volcano islands south of Japan, is small by comparison, but it sure has a massive history. More than 18,000 Japanese and 6,800 American soldiers died on Iwo Jima in the last land battle of WWII and it was the reason that America decided to use the atomic bomb. Approaching the island of Kyushu, we could see and smell the dominant active volcano in the bay, Mount Sakurajima, rising to 3,365 feet. As we passed Kagoshima, it was built up with golf courses, lovely surrounding hills and lots of greenery, and boats and ferries crisscrossed the beautiful bay itself.

We had a friendly greeting at Kagoshima's small airport further north before taking a taxi to our hotel, situated midway between the airport and the city. Nagasaki was about 80 miles northwest on the same island. Our hotel was quintessentially Japanese and we were the only non-Japanese people there. We had a great deal of fun communicating and, in my room, the 'wash-everything-heated-toilet-seat' instructions in Japanese meant that I had no chance of mastering its full functionality!

I still felt underpowered by the lasting effects of Dengue fever and looked forward to our rest day here. The breakfast was a proper Japanese-style experience for me. There were the usual juices, but unusual coffees and teas which suited my taste. There was a wide choice of chopstick-sized meats, salads and potato. Sticky, steamed rice of course and eggs, which I thought were hard-boiled, but some apparently broke a raw egg onto their rice. I of course broke mine on the plate, to the muted amusement of the other guests and the smiling waitress, who came over with a hard-boiled one and cleaned up my mess! There was also a variety of soups, goulash and noodles, as well as bread, toast and jam. We ate well and had fun.

We decided to visit the Sengan-en Gardens and Museum and, as our taxi skirted Kagoshima Bay, we could see the Sakurajima volcano. The weather was warm and sunny, and the gardens were spectacularly ordered and very beautifully laid out. We learned that in the 1850's, the 28th Lord Shimadzu Nariakira felt threatened by the expansion of Western countries and their colonisation of Asia. This feudal lord of the Satsuma clan embarked on a path of military and industrial modernisation by aggressively introducing Western technologies through the Shuseikan project, which marked the beginning of the process of Western technology transfer to Japan. We climbed to the viewpoint of Kagoshima Bay and visited the preserved, traditional Japanese residence of the 32nd generation lord. Many visitors seemed interested in two pale Westerners and we talked to people from Hong Kong and to a Japanese couple who had travelled from the north to see Kagoshima.

Returning to our hotel, we prepared for our next flight to Yao Airport, east of Osaka on Honshu island, often referred to as the Japanese mainland. So far, we had been shocked by the destruction of Asia's ecosystems, but delighted by its diversity, and now impressed by the scale of its beauty.

11

Provideniya

After another delightful breakfast, our airport taxi driver was a wonderful, old-school Japanese gentleman in a meticulously clean, old car with white seat bibs and plastic foot trays.

We flew northwest across the green, forested hills of Kyushu island and over the sea to Shikoku island. It too was beautifully forested, reminding us of Devon in the UK. We continued on to Honshu island, making landfall at Wakayama. The extraordinary build-up of civilisation began with ships in the bay, immense conurbations and industrial operations. We crossed modest, forested hills east of Kansai International Airport and unfolding before us was Japan's second largest metropolitan area, Keihanshin, with a population of 19 million. It stretched way out ahead of us and all the way around Osaka Bay to our left. Where the beautiful forested hills stopped, the incredible building started on all the flat land available. We were flying at 1,500 feet over a simply awesome megalopolis heading for the general aviation airport at Yao.

We were greeted by our now familiar *Noevir Aviation* handlers, where we completed domestic formalities, hangared DIGA and celebrated with everybody wanting selfies. It was a 45-minute taxi to our hotel in Osaka and, on completion of our usual regime, we dashed out to meet

Tomasz Wojtowicz, who was also in Osaka. Polish-born, Tomasz lived and worked in the USA flying helicopters. In his holiday time, he was flying around the world in his 30-year-old Cessna 152 and now hoped to reach New York to complete his staged circumnavigation. Tomasz was a likeable character, with smiling eyes and a passion and energy to make his adventures happen. His Cessna was being serviced at Yao Airport and Tomasz wanted to get pictures of DIGA leaving the following day. We arranged to hook up again in Russia on our common leg to America.

Early in the morning, we delayed our flight to Akita by a day because of the poor weather forecast. However, by 10:30am, it was much brighter and the forecasts showed that conditions the next day would actually be worse for flying into Akita. So, we changed our minds and judged that, if we took a train to the airport with Tomasz, we could be airborne by 12:30pm at the latest.

However, we had sorely underestimated how long it would take us to decipher the underground map in Japanese, and we had unwittingly wrong-footed our handlers, who struggled to bring forward our delay permission! So, we had plenty of time to show Tomasz around DIGA and to look over his Cessna. Finally, at 2:45pm, we departed for the north of Honshu island.

We flew northwest at 1,200 feet and were hit with an immediate sensory overload with the enormous views of Osaka and the Keihanshin megalopolis. The amazing scene continued all the way up to Kyoto. The high-density order and scale of Japanese conurbations was a wonderful sight from DIGA. We flew north up the western edge of Lake Biwa, then over the hills and towards Komatsu, another immense metropolis. We followed the coastal, urban sprawl to Toyama and then flew across the sea to Niigata and on to Akita. The vistas were impressive. Every flat valley was used for cultivation, with rice paddies everywhere, and all the surrounding hills were wearing lush forest coats and the high mountains were snow-capped.

We landed at the small airport southeast of Akita city and found ourselves in Omagari, a modest, little town about 35 miles southwest of the airport. We enjoyed a lovely ride through rice paddy fields to the hotel that Eddie had found us. Later, at a Japanese restaurant, we ate simply what we pointed at! Then it was back to sort photographs, diary and get to bed.

After breakfast, Matthew helped me cross-check the accuracy of our PLOGs and flight planning paperwork for Russia, which Evgeny of *MAK GAS* insisted was essential. We had fun at dinner, again eating anything that we pointed to.

We judged it flyable and with our clearance, we lifted at 12:15pm. The weather was unfolding as per the forecasts and it was now partially sunny at Akita Airport and poor in Tomakomai (our destination on Hokkaido island), but due to improve in Tomakomai before our arrival, two hours later. Immediately, the tower radioed saying that our handler wanted us to return, with no reason given. Thinking we may have forgotten something, we just swooped back onto the apron, confusing the handler who was still standing there. Calling our handler's office at *Noevir Aviation*, it transpired that they only wanted to tell us that the weather was poor in Tomakomai! Our flight plan lapsed while we were explaining our strategy and frustratingly, we lost our weather window. We recovered back at our Omagari hotel and bought a selection of food from the local supermarket to eat in the hotel. I was now feeling back to 100% fitness and we were looking forward to enjoying our leg across Russia.

However, the next day, the weather just wasn't good enough for making it to Tomakomai, never mind considering a double hop on to Sakhalin. But it looked perfect for the day after, Sunday. This delay meant that we would still enter Russia within the 48-hour window granted by our permit, but one day later than planned. I nailed down the arrangements with the *Noevir Aviation* office to avoid any more misunderstandings in Japan. At lunchtime, after the rains in Omagari, Matthew and I went for a walk to the end of town where we found small electric and hybrid cars for sale. They were definitely environmentally-friendly and made by companies the West has never heard of – possible future competition, I thought. It was 16°C and 10°C in Sakhalin, our next destination. I bought sushi for my dinner again and also made time to exercise, by running up and down the stairs.

The following day, we finally flew north with a strong tailwind, skirting the edge of Honshu island, and on to Hokkaido. We overflew Tomakomai and landed at its older airport of Chitose, straight after two military jets. We were processed seamlessly for our international departure to Russia in a pleasant 18°C. As we approached Waianai, the northernmost point of Hokkaido at FL080 (about 8,000 feet above sea level) as instructed, we were VFR on top, with Rishiri volcano poking way above the clouds to our left. Also talking to Sapporo control, we heard a Boeing 737 from Waianai on a reciprocal heading being restricted to 6,000 feet until it was south of us. Matthew and I looked at each other and trained our cameras down and ahead. The 737 broke through the cloud base 2,000 feet below and whizzed south underneath us: an amazing sight!

We were already talking to Russia as we coasted out of Japan and when the cloud below us dissipated, the sea looked cold, and our outside temperature had dropped down to 5°C. We crossed La Perouse Strait and coasted into Sakhalin Island at Cape Crillon, getting used to the Russian radio's accented English and their way of doing things. We were back to height in metres from feet, and wind speed in metres per second from nautical miles per hour.

Khumotovo (serving Sakhalin city) was a typical Russian airport with a massive runway and apron, an eight-storey tower building and MI8 helicopters parked around. We were met by an amiable entourage of Immigration, Customs and security officials, fuellers and handlers – about 12 people in all – and we were soon getting Russian roubles from the local ATM. Eddie had booked us into a wooden-built, ski resort hotel with stuffed bears all over the place. While there wasn't any snow, the roads looked like they were exposed to harsh winter conditions. At dinner, we met two American oil rig workers and shared stories and experiences.

Later, we saw Evgeny's Facebook post of the airport's security camera footage of DIGA landing and with his help, we wrestled to get our flight plan accepted. *MAK GAS* had worked extremely hard to secure our permissions and everything was agreed with the Russia *CAA* for us to fly a long way, during the weekday opening hours, through remote Eastern Russia, including refuelling at airports without spoken English. We were looking forward to covering 2,500 nautical miles in four flying days, subject to the weather.

We felt the time shift as our bodies were forced up two hours early. Although the sun streamed in through our hotel windows, there was fog at the airport, delaying our departure. Sasha made sure that our documents were correct and we people watched normal commercial passengers in the airport lounge, assembling for their flights to Vladivostok, Tokyo and Moscow. The Russians here looked very European. Since the Arabian, Indian sub-continent and Asian countries, we really hadn't seen any Caucasian features except for a few tourists here and there.

Six people and two vehicles watched us prepare DIGA and call for clearance. Soon we were climbing slowly to FL100 (about 10,000 feet above sea level), flying northwards up Sakhalin island and bound for Nikolayevsk on the Amur River in the Khabarovsk region of the mainland of Eastern Russia. At this time, foreign aircraft were required to file IFR flight plans following IFR airways. It was understood that we were only VFR capable, but the altitudes were expected for communications. Sakhalin island is Russia's biggest and it was part of Japan in the 19th century. It is sparsely populated compared to Japan, with snow-capped mountains and few roads. We could see both coasts and flew above scattered clouds and patches of sea fog with the temperature outside dropping to -2°C. As we made our long cruise descent, we had fantastic views of the surrounding geography, the estuary, the Amur River and the town of Nikolayevsk.

Here, the English-speaking controller guided us right into the airport and we landed near small, commercial planes and a few Mi-8 helicopters on the large apron. English wasn't spoken but, after a couple of calls to *MAK GAS* and using Google Translate, *ATC* arranged everything we needed. We then found an apartment-hotel in town that amazingly took credit cards. However, with no Wi-Fi, our administrative chores were limited and completed quickly. In the afternoon, we walked around the rundown town and suburbs. Fishing was the main industry with canning facilities everywhere, the second biggest industry being reindeer herding, apparently! Nikolayevsk-on-Amur has no land transport connections, so traffic to and from the town enters via the port on the Amur River or the airport. At the side of the river, there were various monuments honouring the war dead. Vehicles were classic, old Russian-style vans and trucks. We had a couple of cheap microwave meals and a bottle of water in our hotel restaurant for dinner. Subject to weather conditions, we had double hops planned for the next three days.

At Nikolayevsk Airport the next morning, it was overcast with a base of 1,800 feet topping out at about 4,000 feet. It was perfectly clear at Okhotsk and Magadan, according to the station reports provided by ATC (we had no other source of weather information). ATC seemed happy with our flight plan and watched us prepare DIGA on the freezing cold apron. We donned our *Typhoon* dry suits for the first time because we had freezing cold water crossings ahead of us. After the ritual selfies, we waved goodbye.

We flew over the estuary and climbed up through the cloud layer continuing to FL110 (about 11,000 feet above sea level), where it was sunny and hot inside DIGA, even though it was -7°C outside. We flew northwest VFR on top of the clouds across the Sea of Okhotsk. With 120 nautical mile visibility, we saw the amazing snow-capped mountains of the Dzhugdzhur range, which ran southwest to northeast on the mainland ahead. Making landfall at the settlement of Ayan, the clouds had all gone and we turned northeast to follow the coast, with the beautiful mountain range on our left and the Sea of Okhotsk on our right. It was awesome, remote scenery with very few settlements at all.

Once again, the English-speaking controller guided us all the way into Okhotsk, a small, national airport where no English was spoken. He told us to land, refuel and call him when we had altitude again. He explained that he had contacted Okhotsk *ATC* by telephone. As we approached, we could see that the runway and apron were made from interlocking, heavy metal sheets sitting on top of the permafrost, which was unstable ground in summer. This was a first for Matthew and me! We were looked after fabulously by the friendly airport manager and took selfies in his office, with a portrait of Putin as the backdrop. We couldn't speak to each other but we were generously treated with respect and curiosity. Our second leg was gorgeous, sunny flying, with more beautiful, tundra-like scenery. Again, we could see for miles from FL090. It was a short flight to Sokol Airport, which was an English-speaking airport serving Magadan.

Tomasz had arrived two days earlier and was there waiting to greet us with Anastasia, our handler, who joined in our fun while sorting our paperwork. Tomasz actually spoke some Russian and had met Inga, an English student, who wanted to help us all and practice her English. We bussed it for the hour-long drive to the town of Magadan, which was 60km away. With Inga's help, we checked in to an unbelievably good value, Russian-style hotel then went out to sample the cuisine at a local restaurant. Magadan was founded in 1930 as a port town servicing mining activity in the area. After an epic day's flying, we all agreed that we would combine our flying with Tomasz the following day.

We arrived early for the airport security and managed to

get onto the apron to prepare. With separate flight plans, we still wanted to fly 'together' and get some air to air pictures. Tomasz was ready before us and our flight plan clearance was delayed too, so he set off. About 15 minutes later, we gave chase with our better speed (by 10-15 nautical miles an hour) and climb rate. We had a two-stop strategy while Tomasz could reach Anadyr with his range.

At FL110, we were on top of broken cloud, heading in generally the same direction but out of sight of one another, talking to each other and the same controller. Matthew and I routed more over the Shelikhov Gulf than Tomasz. Visibility was perfect as the cloud came and went below. Once again, our English-speaking controller guided us into the 'national airport' of Manily. Using our *Satphone*, the controller informed us that Manily was "not exactly" an airport and we were to just land, refuel and go! From 11,000 feet and -11°C, we dodged the rain, using only GPS coordinates from Sergey. Manily turned out to be the community helipad of a tiny, remote fishing community, with Jet fuel! We were greeted by hardy locals wearing only shorts and t-shirts, who just smiled and refuelled DIGA while we got out of our cold-water gear, which was not needed for the next overland leg to Anadyr. We were ready to start within 20 minutes when Matthew received a *Rocket Route* message via Manily's GSM mobile coverage (believe it or not), saying that our flight plan had been rejected. I called Sergey to verify the situation.

In the meantime, Matthew had been honoured with the gift of a huge frozen fish wrapped loosely in thick plastic. We felt bad declining it but we both knew what would happen when it thawed inside DIGA!

After a 25-minute wait, Evgeny messaged, telling us to take

Round the World
The Journey

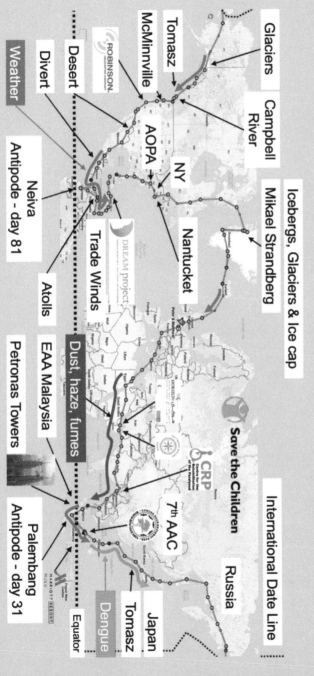

Near Limkheda en route to Indore – India

Desert rain at FL075
Hail – Saudi Arabia

Shamoly and school kids at Centre for the Rehabilitation
of the Paralysed, Dhaka – Bangladesh

DIGA at Mulu on Borneo

Matthew and me on the metal apron, Okhotsk – Russia

Hovering at Petronas Towers, Kuala Lumpar – Malaysia
Photograph by Tien Chew

Evergreen Aviation and Space
Museum, McMinnville – USA

Matthew and I reached
Neiva, Antipod – Colombia

Beautiful landscape,
Fukui Honshu Island – Japan

Clothing market,
Port-au-Prince – Haiti

Tomasz, Matthew and me at the Explorers Club, New York

Iceberg landing, Ilulissat – Greenland

Ahmed, Evgeny, me and
James at Friedrichshafen –
Germany

Robin, Jørgen and me in
Illulissat – Greenland

off immediately! Our double hop had been ambitious within the published airport opening hours and we didn't want to be stuck here or arrive too late at Anadyr Airport. We lifted, talking to the controller through a relay by Tomasz, who was 50 nautical miles ahead. We climbed dutifully to FL110 again on top of the clouds. It was still -11°C at altitude but sunny. The clouds dissipated and we finally had gorgeous views of the frozen and deserted tundra below with snow and ice: it looked paradoxically beautiful and brutal. It was just the beginning of June, and so early summer. The 'white nights' never really get dark here and it would warm up a bit more. About 50 miles from Anadyr, we managed to undertake Tomasz and commenced a long cruise descent over the most beautiful, harsh frozen scenery.

Anadyr is the most easterly town in Russia and very remote. The airport apron was characteristically big with many planes and MI-8 helicopters. We had landed one hour after the airport had closed and a small group of officials split between both our aircraft to make checks and to see us out of the back door! Tomasz's Russian helped arrange accommodation at the pilot hotel opposite the airport and we left everything else until the following morning. The stilted buildings looked like they were built to survive the long, brutal winters and the main town, which we overflew, was on the other side of the estuary and couldn't be reached except by hovercraft across the sea ice.

After a second epic day of flying, we hoped that Evgeny could organise Immigration and Customs here with just a fuel stop at Provideniya for DIGA, before flying on to Nome in Alaska. Once again, Tomasz had the range for a direct flight.

We all slept well, even with the twilight and our skylights

open to balance our room heating. We could tell that *MAK GAS* and *G.A.S.E.* had worked hard to get our flight plans and necessary documentation sorted for entry into America. We suited up for our flights across the Gulf of Anadyr and Bering Sea and then we waited patiently to be processed through Immigration and Customs. After some delays, we were both calling for clearance. This time, Tomasz was delayed, and we took off first over the sea ice, flying east and climbing back to FL110. It was mostly beautifully clear and we had stunning views across the frozen landscape.

Provideniya is the eastern-most settlement in Russia and the continent of Asia and I wanted to say that we had been there. Matthew took video footage of us crossing the 180° line of longitude on DIGA's GPS. Our long, cruise descent into Provideniya was absolutely gorgeous with the remote, snowy, mountainous scenery. English was well spoken and after a confirmatory call to *MAK GAS*, we were on our way within 45 minutes. Tomasz radioed that he was now 45 minutes ahead of us as we climbed to FL110 to give chase and we crossed the International Date Line, which later proved confusing in our logbooks! Transferring from Russia to Anchorage control marked our triumphant progress to the American continent. Yet it also marked the end of an absorbing experience of the largest country in the world, which certainly has much more to offer up.

Landing at Nome, the formalities were relaxed and friendly. Nome is a tiny settlement without road connections to the rest of Alaska and, because of our move from GMT +12 hours to GMT –8 hours, we were forcing our body clocks to bed four hours earlier than the previous day. The local entertainment seemed to involve alcohol, gambling and fighting. We'd had three consecutive days of flying but the weather ahead, down the coast to Vancouver Island after Anchorage, looked more challenging.

We started with a hearty breakfast in a local café, then we chatted to other pilots at the airport as we prepared DIGA in a sunny 12°C. From now on, it would be VFR flying, low-level without administration and we could easily fly in combination with Tomasz. Both Tomasz and Matthew had significant experience of flying in North America. After crossing the bay, the flat tundra-like scenery below was so inviting. We crossed the winding Yukon River and other smaller, squiggly ones too. Tomasz suggested getting out of our dry suits at a tiny gravel strip called Takotna, after which we skimmed the treetops, slaloming the meandering Takotna River to drop into McGrath for refuelling. Continuing southwest and at about 7,000 feet in the mountains, we again worked to get our aircraft close together for some more photographs against the sky, mountains and snow. Low-level again across the Susitna River Delta, thousands of aphids splattered our windscreens as we headed for Anchorage.

Merrill Field Airport was a busy general aviation haven for all types of 'outback' and amphibious aircraft. We were enthusiastically helped through all the self-service facilities, secured DIGA and Tomasz's Cessna and soon the brilliant hotel Wi-Fi was gorging on our backlog of Russia photographs. Walking into town, we enjoyed a familiar meal in a rowdy bar and saluted our fourth fantastic day in a row. The evening was a complete contrast to everything we had experienced since leaving the UK.

Lifting at 9:30am, we flew over cloudy mountains and descended into Princess William Sound. It was huge with crystal-clear water and green-treed, little islands. The weather was misty with layers of cloud and raining in parts, so we had to pick our way carefully. We were flying low over the water and Tomasz was at about 3,000 feet. Suddenly, we glimpsed Columbia Glacier and that changed everything – we turned back to explore! The sea changed to ice chunks and the water was a glorious glacial melt, azure blue in colour. We flew up and down its glacial wall and circled up over the huge cracks. It was absolutely amazing to see Nature at work from DIGA. Tomasz had pressed on ahead, more concerned about the poor weather conditions; when we caught up with him, we were both very low, crawling our way carefully down the coast to Yakutat. The conditions were horrible and it was slow-going at the Cessna 152's slower cruise speed.

After refuelling for both us and our aircraft at Yakutat, the weather looked to be brightening all the way to our next destination, Sitka. We flew low in combination, following the coast and taking air-to-air photos and videos of each other against the gorgeous shoreline scenery. Eddie messaged us to say that we would be passing Glacier Bay National Park and suddenly we could see Grand Plateau Glacier. This time, Tomasz could join us to take pictures and video and it was a wonderful experience to be flying together. We explored another three glaciers and then weaved our way through the various forested valleys and beautiful waterways to Sitka, still flying low. The weather continued to brighten into a beautiful, long evening sunset. We struggled to find accommodation but finally, after a great day, food, exchanging photographs and sorting the administration to cross to Canada, we were ready for bed at midnight. The next day's weather was our only concern.

Our plan was a short, direct flight over the hills and islands to Wrangell in the USA to clear Immigration and Customs, then on to Port Hardy on Vancouver Island. However, while flying in the deteriorating weather, we reverted to a much longer sea-level route in the rain and misty conditions. At Wrangell, we reassessed the situation and decided that our only option was to crawl down channels between the islands to Prince Rupert in Canada instead. Matthew and Tomasz sorted new international flight plans while I arranged the necessary border authority's information changes.

Togged up in our *Typhoon* dry suits, off we went again. It was slow-going under the low cloud in the rain, hugging the coastlines with all sorts of craggy-shaped inlets and islands. The geography reminded me of a supersized north of Scotland. At Prince Rupert, we discovered that the most convenient way to get to our accommodation on the main island was to ferry ourselves to the heliport, using DIGA, which was a fun ending to our flying day. We toasted meeting Tomasz and a lot of spectacular flying together through Japan, Russia and Alaska. He would continue his journey to New York the following day, while we stopped at Campbell River for DIGA's next service.

The next morning, we reversed our ferrying operation in poor weather and waited in the Prince Rupert Airport terminal for it to improve; we looked out of place in our dry suits as it filled with commercial passengers. When the weather looked like it wasn't going to change, we decided to fly towards the better forecast where we were headed. We said an emotional goodbye to Tomasz and wished him good luck. His energy and enthusiasm for adventure reminded me of Martin Grieder, a good friend of mine who had climbed Mount Everest. Tomasz and I would always keep in touch and hopefully meet again.

We adopted our working strategy of following the coastline and flying over the water where there was nothing to run into. As promised, it brightened up and the visibility improved to a good 30 nautical miles. Our journey was between and beside all sorts of inlets and islands that make up the western coast of Canada: it was remote and beautiful. As we flew south down the channel between Vancouver Island and the mainland, we started to see isolated pockets of people living remotely, before evidence of the logging industry, people fishing and isolated houses became more frequent. The tides looked powerful and a place called Tremble Point apparently has the fastest flowing tides in the world. Tomasz left us for Port Hardy and, continuing to Campbell River, we had to climb suddenly over wires – a sage reminder of the dangers of low-level flying!

Ralph Richier welcomed us as we landed at *E&B Helicopters*, which comprised two big hangars and about 12 helipads. Matthew and I cleaned DIGA in the now-glorious afternoon sun as helicopters came and went regularly, carrying people to and from the lumber industry. We joined the *E&B Helicopters* crew with Ed Wilcock, the boss, for a beer in the hangar and chatted until David Cross texted to let us know that he'd arrived at our hotel.

In the morning, David and I got to work on DIGA's 100-hour airframe inspection and a 200-hour engine inspection. I fetched and carried and liaised with Ralph. It was a lot of work made easier by David's expert knowledge, preparedness and the very helpful services of *E&B Helicopters*. It was another beautiful, sunny day and Daniel arrived to help. He had worked for David at *HQ Aviation* in the UK and was in the process of emigrating to Canada and actually lived in Campbell River, of all places. By 5pm,

DIGA was ready for flight testing and we all joined the *E&B Helicopters* team in the other hangar for their social unwind. Later Matthew, David and I, along with Daniel and his girlfriend, Sam, sat on the hotel deck overlooking Discovery Passage. We watched the bigger ferries and little water taxis move back and forth between the islands across the fast-flowing tidal waters.

First thing, I managed a service laundry and a haircut, then bought a few supplies. For the test flight, David and I flew Daniel and Sam over Strathcone Provincial Park to see their new home from the air. With the service completed early, we bought a couple of fishing rods and tried our luck at fishing with Daniel in one of the nearby lakes. David's stress was dissipating and as we relaxed, we had more success drinking the beers in the tackle box than catching fish! The following day, Matthew and I would be heading a short distance south and I would be staying with family friends on Vancouver Island.

Mid-morning, I drove David to the airport for his flight home. I would next see him in Québec, and I thanked him sincerely for all his support and dedication. It was still raining uninvitingly as we got DIGA ready outside for photographs. We thanked everybody at *E&B Helicopters* for their support and flew 45 minutes down the east coast of Vancouver Island to Qualicum, which serves Parksville. Rick, Sheri and their daughter had arrived by ferry from Vancouver to meet us just as the rain stopped. We all had lunch together before Matthew set off to his chosen hotel to concentrate on filing a VAT return, while I joined Rick and the family at their Parksville hideaway in the Madrona Beach Resort. We toasted marshmallows on a driftwood fire and ate well, catching up on family news. Sheri and I talked about sustainable development; she was familiar with the issues of population growth, climate change and the UN *Sustainable Development Goals* in her line of work. It was a great evening that ended late.

I rose early to get pictures of the sunrise. While Rick and the family had to be back in Vancouver, I had a rest day to catch up on everything and plan our way down the west coast as far as Guatemala, flushing out issues and posing questions of *G.A.S.E.* I also responded to Kurt Robinson, CEO of *RHC*, to let him know the timing of our visit to the factory at Torrance and some of the items that David Cross had suggested *RHC* might want to check out on DIGA. We would re-enter the USA the next day and be back to the country of the 'USD', the currency which we had been using in most other countries anyway!

I picked Matthew up on the way to Qualicum Airport and the weather was good. We flew an hour to Bellingham on the mainland where we refuelled and cleared Customs. Then we were off towards McMinnville, which took us over similar island and water scenery as we routed south. I called Terry Naig on my phone to let him know we were inbound and he marshalled us right onto the *Evergreen Aviation & Space Museum* car park. Eddie had kindly arranged this fantastic visit with his friend, Terry, who was the maintenance supervisor for the museum, and landing there was part of the treat. Terry gave us a quick, private tour of the two main museum hangars and tickets to return the following day for a slower walk around, enabling us to read the plaque information. We saw the famous Lockheed SR-71 'Blackbird spy plane' and the Hughes Flying Boat, Spruce Goose, close up.

Then Terry and his friend, Angel Mendoza, treated us to supper at the Legion before taking us to our hotel.

Matthew and I used Sunday to revisit the museum just as a flight of five Blackhawk helicopters from the National Guard was doing the same. I enjoyed my time, reading about the development of space travel, from Sputnik right up to the modern day. The museum presented Russian history side by side with the US developments, which emphasised the space race!

12

Claustrophobic emotions

Before setting off the following day, we assembled for a group photograph at DIGA with the museum volunteers who waved us off, along with Terry and Angel. After refuelling at McMinnville, we headed for Medford following the I5 south, which meant avoiding hills en route. As we picked our way carefully through cloud, the layers kept coming and finally we climbed through a thin layer of cloud to be VFR on top at 8,500 feet. In the seconds of exposure to the cloud, we accumulated some ice on DIGA's windscreen and leg fins. At Medford, we descended through a hole to refuel and, feeling chastened, we accepted that what we had done hadn't been very clever!

However, with much improved weather, our second flight to San Francisco was less fraught. Upon reaching Lake Clear, it was finally a sunny day. We flew over the Santa Rosa and Napa Valley vineyards and headed across San Pablo Bay, passing Richmond and Berkeley. We could see over to the Golden Gate Bridge, Sausalito, Alcatraz and San Francisco downtown. We were routed down the Nimitz Freeway past the Oracle Arena stadium and orbiting news helicopters for the National Basketball final that evening (which the local team, the Golden State Warriors, won). Steffany Kisling, who I'd met in Virunga National Park, had organised for *Signature Flight Support* to look after us at Oakland Airport.

Soon, we were seamlessly on our way to our San Francisco hotel and enjoying the gorgeous weather set for the week, having seen some iconic sights.

Matthew visited an old friend that night and I didn't expect to see him up early! So, with all my errands and administration complete, I took a city bus tour, finishing at the lively Fisherman's Wharf. Steffany Kisling is a passionate entrepreneur who, in 2010, launched *SkyAngels*, a cabin attendant development and staffing company based at Oakland Airport. That evening, we went out for dinner and continued the discussion we'd started at Mekino Lodge in Virunga National Park in the DRC, Africa.

On our second rest day in San Francisco, another of Matthew's local friends, Marc, kindly flew us around the Bay area in his fixed wing aeroplane which was also hangared at Oakland Airport. This was a real change for me as I had only every flown in helicopters: the big difference between pictures from DIGA and a fixed wing, was the wing! Now feeling totally relaxed, we took an Uber taxi to Oakland early to avoid the million people expected to attend the Golden State Warriors parade. *Signature Flight Support* was our Fixed Base Operator (FBO). FBOs pay to manage and provide services on a section of airport aprons. *Signature Flight Support* kindly waived their fees in support of our TJR project and, after we were shown around the *SkyAngels* facilities, Steffany and her students waved us off.

We flew our own personal San Francisco Bay tour past Oakland Bay Bridge, across to San Francisco, around Alcatraz, and then out and under the Golden Gate Bridge. Turning south, we enjoyed the beautiful Californian coast to Los Angeles, avoiding the sea mist and passing memorable places including Monterey, Carmel and Santa Barbara. We passed the huge landslide closing the coast road at Big Sur. Pismo and Glover beaches looked perfect and the cultivated areas on Nipomo and Santa Maria were stunning.

We climbed high over the hills around Santa Barbara and managed to get some excellent pictures of the metropolis of Los Angeles, in spite of it getting quite busy in the cockpit! We landed at Torrance Airport right in front of the *Robinson Helicopter Company* (RHC). Keith Newmeyer, the flight test manager, was going to look after DIGA for two days and his team whisked her into a hangar while Tim Tucker welcomed us warmly. We were treated to a guided tour of the factory, met the CEO, Kurt Robinson, and gave an interview for the *RHC* magazine.

Later, Tim drove us to a very nice restaurant where we met Kurt and Pat Cox, the Engineering Manager. We discussed our *TJR* experiences and DIGA's performance in different conditions and it was a great trade for a delicious dinner with helicopter experts.

The next day I was in the factory early with Keith. DIGA was being pampered and thoroughly checked over by experts, who were understandably very interested in learning from her condition after all the flying she had done. In the meantime, my best friend from my Rhodesian school days, Roy Holden, was driving over to the factory and Matthew hooked up with his friend who worked for *RHC*. Roy and I were catching up on nearly 36 years. We'd talked on the phone when I was at the Plantation Lodge in Tanzania last year with his brother, Trevor. We had lots to cram into a short space of time and we picked up like we'd never really been apart! Roy was a helicopter technician in a previous life and the *RHC* repair bay was a perfect backdrop for our discussion, which criss-crossed back and forth with questions to and from the *RHC* engineers. Roy jumped in the back of DIGA for her test flight over the harbour and we could see the horizontal build-up of smog, which happens when 13 million people all drive fossil fuel cars in a relatively small area called Los Angeles!

Roy and I then had the afternoon to ourselves and we continued our discussion in the glorious sunshine until early evening. When it was time, our goodbyes were a little emotional and, after wishing each other well, Roy was waving and driving off. Suddenly strong emotions hit me really hard. There I was, standing outside in plenty of open space on a clear blue-sky day, yet feeling claustrophobic in a way you do when something traumatic has happened. It was a horrible feeling of loss and I went back to my room and cried.

On a glorious Saturday morning, Keith helped us prepare DIGA for our next short flight down to San Diego. We flew from Torrance over the harbour to Long Beach, past Huntingdon Beach, then Newport, Camp Pendleton, Solana Beach and Torrey Pines. At Camp Pendleton, navy vessels and smaller boats were out to play, and light, general aviation traffic was building up too – everybody was enjoying the weekend sunshine.

Robert DeLaurentis welcomed us to his home airport of Montgomery. Robert is a great storyteller and was interested in our experiences for comparison. He flies fixed-wings, IFR and high, which is very different to our VFR helicopter approach. He has circumnavigated and is author of *Zen Pilot*. He very kindly offered to host us in San Diego, helping us with accommodation, sightseeing around the splendid Balboa Park and crucial administrative advice on flying in Mexico. That evening, we joined a small gathering at his penthouse overlooking San Diego and enjoyed a fun evening. There were all sorts of debates and with one guest in particular, Robin Doten, who had travelled widely.

On Sunday morning, after thanking Robert for his wonderful hospitality, we headed east into Arizona. Leaving the cool greenery of San Diego and crossing some hills, we were suddenly over scrubland and desert with rising temperatures (31°C at 5,000 feet) accompanied by thermal activity that pushed us around. We essentially followed the I8 and the Mexican border, avoiding restricted military areas. A patchwork of irrigated cultivation bordering a few rivers was the only greenery against the stark desert conditions. Arriving at Tucson, we could see across to the 'Boneyard': a large area covered by thousands of disused aircraft. Landing was uncomplicated and as we refuelled, it was a dry 40°C hot. In the evening, we prepared for several double hop flying days through Mexico, heading to Central America. The weather looked good for the early legs.

We saw the beautiful desert dawn since we had to be up early for a long day of flying, a Customs entry at Chihuahua, then on to Monterrey, losing one hour at each stop moving from GMT –7 to GMT –5. F16 jets from the *Air National Guard* were already thundering into the blue sky ahead of us! Both flights were unpleasantly turbulent with thermal activity, similar to my experience in Africa. We flew high between 5,500 and 8,000 feet above sea level and the desert scenes were awesome: dry riverbeds, harsh mountains and sometimes the contrast of irrigated agriculture in a river valley. I never tire of seeing Nature in these environments.

Chihuahua was an efficient, small, friendly airport and, well-prepared as we were, formalities were straightforward, enabling us to catch up some time. There were no Chihuahua dogs to be seen though! On our second flight, it was even hotter than the first, as we grappled with the turbulence, chose routes between massive and stunningly beautiful mountains and topographical features, and took pictures. We arrived into Monterrey at 6:30pm and the last hour gifted us gorgeous scenery with the sun behind us, over my right shoulder. Eddie had unwittingly booked us a hotel close to the 'other' Monterrey Airport, which added a longer journey through the interesting, developing infrastructure of Mexico, before we set about our evening regime.

The following day, we had another double hop through Tampico to Veracruz. I had time to take pictures of the stunning mountain scenery around Monterrey in the morning sun, before Keyla Zuniga arrived, a journalist from a local magazine. Then we flew southwest over a green, cultivated landscape with lots of orange groves and some big cattle farms. Monterrey city looked impressive, nestled up against the mountains with its smog halo. Tampico was a small airport on the coast of the Gulf of Mexico and the airport manager bought us a Coke, waived our fees and swapped selfies with DIGA. With *WFS* fuel, we lifted again. Our second leg was essentially coastwise low-level. We flew the impressive long beach of Laguna de Tamiahua. Veracruz airfield welcomed us to their city and we hoped for a great stay. It was exceptionally friendly and Eddie had found us a hotel on the beach. The following day, our plan was to head into Guatemala via Tuxtla, our port of exit from Mexico; we were going to need local advice there for a good route through big mountains to the Pacific coast. Having attended to our evening chores, the soporific sound of the crashing waves worked perfectly.

On the 75th day of our *RTW* journey, we flew coastwise before cutting south across higher ground to Tuxtla Airport. The scenery was again spectacular: the regular housing of Veracruz, the long beaches and the wonderful green pastures, either cultivated or grazed. There were cattle on the beach as I had seen in South Africa. At Tuxtla, we covered DIGA against the heat and set off to undertake the necessary point of exit formalities and to obtain routing advice. We couldn't speak Spanish which proved a hassle for us here. Flight Operations told us that we must negotiate 7,000-feet high mountains about 20 nautical miles southwest of Tuxtla, flying in a corridor between two active Restricted Areas, and then arrive into Guatemala City at 4,500 feet. The weather forecast was for clouds on the mountains with more clouds and possibly rain around Guatemala City. While it was perfectly sunny outside in Tuxtla, we considered our return and diversion options carefully.

We departed, assisted by the controller, and climbed steadily to 11,000 feet above sea level indicated on our altimeter (equating to a density altitude of about 12,600 feet), flying the corridor VFR on top of the clouds. As we had hoped, the clouds did gift us a clear hole to descend through on the other side of the mountains where we then hugged the lower ground and headed towards Tapachula on the Pacific coast. We crossed the border into Guatemala where the lush forestation, cultivated fields and wonderful topography continued, dotted with housing along the roads, orchards, cows and goats. However, there were heavy downpours all around us. Lightning crackled on the radio and lit up the sky towards the mountains. We were talking to San Jose, a small airport on the coast, when we reached the foothills about 25 nautical miles directly south of Guatemala City, which was inland.

All of the routes we searched were shrouded in cloud with a base of 2,500 feet and the San Jose controller was persistently requesting our intentions and fuel status. *G.A.S.E.* confirmed that we had permission to go a further 90 nautical miles eastwards along the coast to our next destination, the airport in San Salvador city (in El Salvador). I informed the San Jose controller of our intentions to divert with sufficient fuel and he still insisted that we either land at Guatemala City (not possible) or divert to his airfield (which we knew was not a point of entry). I ignored him, although it crossed our minds that we might be intercepted, so I turned off DIGA's transponder (a radio-signalling device used by radar) in case San Jose did have radar! In the meantime, *G.A.S.E.* had already updated Guatemala and San Salvador air traffic, switched the *WFS* fuel supply and changed our hotel booking: a brilliant example of virtual teamwork!

Crossing into El Salvador, the scenery was similarly spectacular: more forest, interesting topographical shapes, strips of housing along the roadsides and some modest palm oil plantations. The weather on the coast had improved as forecast but there was still cloud sitting at the base of the foothills inland as we searched for a possible route. I was talking to San Salvador Approach now and had explained my intentions. The approach controller covered *both* San Salvador airports, one 14 miles into the hills in the actual city, and the other on the coast, which was more reliable for IFR traffic in poor weather. With no way of getting up to the city airport, I made the decision to divert to the coastal airport.

With only six minutes to run, *G.A.S.E.* switched all our logistics for a second time while the approach controller calmly passed us over to the tower. We were met by friendly officials who understood why we were doing what we were doing, since other aircraft in the same boat had also landed there. This was the only time I have ever diverted twice and, on this occasion, across another country in order to do so – what a flight and day it had been! That night, in our airport hotel, I informed Rene Chamorro that we would be with him in Managua the following day and thanked both Eddie and Ahmed for their incredible proactivity. Teams perform better than individuals and teamwork is absolutely key to success in life.

At 6:32am, there was an earthquake of magnitude 6.4 in Costa Rica, further south. I was awake in bed and I felt and heard the shaking and rumbling, as did Matthew. Departing San Salvador was easy for our short flight southeast down the coast. The ground was lush and cultivated with more cows and goats. To the north (our left) was a chain of hills, many of them conical volcanoes, including a few active ones. Crossing the Gulf of Fonseca to Nicaragua, we had to avoid a huge electrical storm by routing north and round Cosigüina volcano. In the rain, we couldn't find a suitable place to land in the wetlands below and we inched our way carefully through the weather cell. We continued down the side of a string of volcanoes to Lago de Managua, right over the top of a small volcano, Momotombito. We then flew over the crater lagoon, Laguna de Apoyeque, and into Managua's Augusto C. Sandino International Airport. The scenery was spectacular.

Everything went smoothly because our host, Rene Chamorro, had organised VIP lounge treatment for us both. Two foreign, uniformed pilots who knew a prominent, local businessman caused some confusion and made us feel important...for a moment! Rene's son, Rene Junior, actually met us and cleared the way; we were soon being driven to Granada, about 45 minutes to the southwest on Lake Nicaragua and home to multiple, Spanish colonial landmarks. Rene Junior chatted away in perfect English, courtesy of his US education. Rene Chamorro greeted us at the Hotel Plaza Colon, a very nice, colonial-looking building, where we chatted with his friends and contemporaries. Rene and I caught up over dinner, discussing *TJR*, Belize (where we had met), his new catamaran project and life in general.

For months, *G.A.S.E.* and I had been watching the political troubles unfold in Venezuela and they hadn't improved after a recent moratorium on general aviation flying. That evening, Matthew and I discussed the various options for avoiding the dangerous parts of Venezuela, specifically Caracas. I still wanted to go to Maracaibo if possible and I let Eddie and Ahmed in on our thinking.

In the morning, after breakfast in the hotel courtyard, I planned to get on top of my actions and then walk around the lovely-looking town. First, I looked again at the weather for Medellin, our first planned stop in Colombia, high up in the mountains and our base to get to Neiva, our second antipode. It was still reporting cloudy conditions and, given our recent experience in Guatemala, I decided to find a low-level route to Neiva and avoid flying over high, misty mountains altogether. Using my *iPad* software, I chose a longer, low-level route through the Magdalena river system: Panama City to Cartagena, to Barrancabermeja, to Neiva, to Barrancabermeja, to Barranquilla, before exiting to Venezuela. It looked like a good option to keep us on schedule. I emailed Ahmed, asking various questions because I was about to send a huge ripple of change through our logistical plans and permit applications!

Feeling better, I rushed downstairs at midday to meet up with Rene, Rene Junior and Matthew. Rene gave us a guided tour in a water taxi through the 285 islands close to Granada and round to a restaurant on Lake Nicaragua. They were kind, generous hosts and we discussed a variety of topics, including flying, boating, Nicaragua, Managua, politics and sustainable development. Before saying goodbye at the hotel, Rene suggested that we visit the nearby Masaya volcano lava hole that night. Later, we found ourselves staring wide-eyed at the red glow of the molten lava hissing with steam: what a sight to behold! I had regretted not seeing the huge lava lake of Nyiragongo in Virunga National Park so this was a real treat.

That Friday night, Ahmed messaged to tell us that our permit for Colombia would be delayed – public holidays and working practices were hard to understand from afar! So, our Sunday entry plans would become Colombia on Wednesday, preceded by a four-day stay in Panama.

Having enjoyed our people watching during the hour-long taxi ride to the airport, we managed our own way around flight planning, payments, Immigration and Customs. We prepared DIGA in the humidity for one long flight southwest, direct to Panama City. We flew past the smoking Masaya lava hole and across Granada, recognising our hotel and the conglomeration of 285 tiny islands. We continued the length of Lake Nicaragua, past conical volcano islands, and followed the Costa Rica land border to the Caribbean Sea at about 1,500 feet, just below the clouds, dodging them, and the rain. The forest wasn't as dense as Nigeria or Cameroon but there were snaking rivers and few signs of people. We dodged a few more heavier rain cells and as we coasted out of Costa Rica, the weather was hazy. With Eddie watching our tracker and messaging weather reports, we flew directly across the sea to Panama City.

The weather was murky until about 60 nautical miles to run and at 30 nautical miles out to sea, we were faced with a wall of rain, forcing us south, low-level and under the thick of it! Reaching the Panama coast, we followed it east to the brighter weather and when the cloud lifted off the forest, we cut across it low-level and continued over Gatún Lake, where ships joining the man-made sections of the Panama Canal can pass. We followed the canal all the way into the smaller international airport. With sun from the west and good visibility, Panama City looked stunning with its huge 60-storey skyscrapers and adventurous designs. Airport officials were relaxed, and we completed formalities quickly, secured DIGA for her four-day stay and headed to the city where Matthew had booked the Trump Ocean Hotel. While Matthew explored, I attended to my nightly regime using the excellent hotel Wi-Fi.

Panama City was a good place for any delay because there was a lot to see, the facilities were excellent and I could exercise. From my 23rd floor room, I could see the big yachts moored out front; all of my life I had fancied sailing across the Atlantic and maybe one day I would! I recast the routing spreadsheet to Neiva and allowed time to meet the explorer, Mikael Strandberg, near Ilulissat in Greenland, then I fine-tuned the length of other stops. I communicated with our hosts all the way to our Québec service and started a systematic weather watch for Colombia and the Caribbean; towering CBs and popup storms would be an ongoing challenge.

Two Rotors: One Planet

On Monday, Matthew wasn't feeling well for the first time on the journey. Since I'd contracted Dengue fever, we were ever vigilant and hoped it was just a cold. I went out to the local mall for domestic chores and supplies. Finally, I could no longer avoid one huge outstanding action: to annotate all my photograph files from our Russian and Alaskan legs where I had just run out of time and Wi-Fi. Now with excellent Wi-Fi access, my normal evening regime included labelling every photograph for the *iPhone* GPS metadata and cross referencing our *InReach* route map. It was a merciless job to do retrospectively, but without it, the digital assets would be almost meaningless.

Matthew and I went out to visit the Old City on the other side of the bay. It's made up of old, colonial Spanish buildings in various states of disrepair but the renovated ones were beautiful. We found a wonderful outdoor restaurant looking back over the skyscrapers of the new city. At breakfast on our third day, Matthew was still suffering from his cold bug while I was able to exercise before getting back to my chores. Caracas still looked risky and we settled on Colombia to Maracaibo (Venezuela), to Bonaire, then on to Trinidad. So, I rippled this change through my routing spreadsheet, permits, *WFS* fuel availability, *WFS* fuel requests, my PLOGs and *RunwayHD* routing again. To avoid Venezuela altogether, we could still route from Barranquilla (Columbia) to Aruba and onwards, if we had to.

Finally, I had Wednesday to take a break. We were enjoying Central America and the prevalence of Spanish gave me the impetus to learn some of the language before my third *TJR* journey around Latin America. On Thursday, we had to anticipate our permit at the airport which the

Colombia *CAA* had said we'd receive at about 10am. We weren't confident of completing a double hop, especially with any challenging afternoon weather.

I felt guilty having insisted to Matthew that we get to the airport very early but then a combination of our Uber taxi traffic indiscretion and congestion conspired to delay our arrival to 9am, whereupon we joined a massive queue for Security in the busy terminal. We noticed a Canadian couple having coffee waiting for their flight to Cartagena. The lady was Googling our *TJR* clothing patches and when I gave her a card, she joined us in the queue to chat. They'd been travelling around in a camper van for the last two years!

When our turn came, we apparently didn't have the correct general declaration form. We should have done all of this airside on our arrival but hadn't done so because we weren't sure of our exact departure date. I was taken airside to get the necessary seven stamped and signed copies, providing five copies to Immigration and Customs, while Matthew waited in the corridor. Returning to the original queue for Security, we passed the Canadian lady again and smiled broadly to her as if we had just returned from a meeting of village idiots!

Finally, we were airside to make payments and at 10.15am, Flight Planning seemed quite relaxed about us wanting to fly the Panama Canal north and then eastwards to Cartagena. Just in time, Ahmed messaged through our Columbian permit. At 11am, we lifted on the Pacific side to follow the canal north. The early section over land was low-level as we avoided radio towers and peaks under low cloud, until we were crossing the Golfe De San Blas with its 378 beautiful islands on the Caribbean side. Here, the weather was brighter as forecast, and yachts had moored up, 'each with their own protected water and island' apparently, in one of the biggest, eco-friendly tourist destinations on earth.

We struck out northeast on an uneventful sea crossing to Cartagena, a port city on Colombia's Caribbean coast with a population of one million. Descending across a built-up area to land, we had to take avoiding action for a kite flying and then immediately avoided a second one, all caught on video! Hector, our handler, appreciated our desire for an immediate second flight but discovered that the Colombia *CAA* still hadn't lodged our permit in their own country system, meaning that our flight plans couldn't be accepted yet. The Colombian system is heavily bureaucratic and everything would work out here if we did it 'by the book'. So, Eddie organised a hotel for us and we used our time wisely, recruiting help from local pilots who regularly fly these routes between the mountains and restricted areas. Then we prepared flight plans for Hector for all our Columbian routes, planning a triple hop on Thursday and a double hop on Friday. Finally, we had a basic, local meal out and prepared to be up at 4am for a dawn take off.

13

Antipode #2

The following day, we became quite ambitious with our fifth continent, South America. Our flight plan was Cartagena to Barrancabermeja, to Neiva, then back to Barrancabermeja. Our path to Neiva was essentially down a massive river system. The river channels, wetlands and lakes are all part of the beautiful Magdalena River, the biggest river in Northern Columbia. The river was enveloped by 9,000 feet-plus mountains on either side and the valleys, colours, geology and agriculture all made for a stunning canvas. We lifted into a beautiful, early morning at sunrise and the forecast was good. However, in the tropics, humid forests and mountains can often combine to produce local bad weather, so we chose to fly under broken low-level clouds to Barrancabermeja, which is known as the oil capital of Colombia. Matthew organised refuelling while I negotiated the flight plan and we were off again within 45 minutes.

Our route to Neiva was influenced by a huge military restricted area from surface to unlimited. We skirted south down the western side of it, close to the mountains at 6,500 feet as instructed, which gave us a different perspective of the Magdalena river system in the narrowing valley, with the mountains on either side. The clouds burnt off and it was beautifully clear to and from Neiva, with only isolated CBs building on the range of hills to the east. Neiva, the capital of the Department of Huila, was our second antipode and it was twinned with Palembang, Indonesia. Our handler worked efficiently and we all climbed the tower to get the *FAI* paperwork signed and to have a ceremonial picture with the controller. Having now visited both antipodes, we had a real sense of aviation achievement! The return leg to Barrancabermeja gave us both a chance to see a different side of the beautiful views.

During the flight, Eddie and I had finally decided to avoid Venezuela completely and substitute Aruba for Maracaibo, our Plan C! Perhaps Venezuela could be back on the cards for my third journey? Reaching Barrancabermeja, we had recorded our longest day of flying at eight hours and thirty-six minutes and we readied ourselves for another early start.

It was a refreshing 19°C in the air as we lifted before 7am the next day. It was an absolutely gorgeous, clear morning to be flying the Magdalena river system again; the mountains either side wore cloud blankets and the sun glinted off the winding rivers in the valley floor. Our destination was Barranquilla to the west of Cartagena. Here, the helipad was a considerable distance from the terminal buildings, and we experienced delays processing our exit to Aruba. Finally, in the oppressive heat, Customs accompanied us to search DIGA and seemed satisfied, once their sniffer dog had finished slobbering over our bags!

We elected to climb to 7,500 feet directly over another restricted area, passing north of Cuchilla de San Lorenzo mountain (14,000 feet) which looked splendid with its cloud blanket; we then flew direct to Aruba against the stiff 20 knot headwind. We crossed the easternmost peninsula of Columbia over the Serranía de Macuira range, which stands in the middle of the La Guajira Desert, before crossing 70 nautical miles of sea to Aruba. On arrival, it was hot and humid, with a strong 20 knot wind for air-conditioning. We dipped straightaway into Aruba's rich tapestry of Caribbean culture and European influences for a meal out as the sun set.

The following day, we would face the trade winds all day. We assessed the weather carefully and made our first hop under the clouds across Curaçao to Bonaire's Flamingo Airport. Then we lifted for Trinidad and our second longest water crossing after Taiwan to Japan, climbing to 7,500 feet to find the least headwind. We were excited when we saw the first of three gorgeous archipelagos and the third was the most spectacular: Los Roques, a federal dependency of Venezuela consisting of approximately 350 islands, cays and inlets. Its range of shapes, blue hues and white sand against the ocean were stunningly picturesque. The 35,000 feet CB cloud formations all around us also made for astonishing viewing and it was a pleasant 20°C as we crossed Margarita Island. Eddie messaged us to say that Christopher Columbus had apparently arrived there in 1498 – a bit before us!

With small course adjustments, we weaved our way between towering CBs in surprisingly smooth flying conditions and started to cross the Gulf of Paria, another Columbus 'discovery'. The delta of the Orinoco River lies to the south and feeds into the Gulf. We made a long cruise descent into Port of Spain, the capital city of Trinidad and Tobago. In hindsight, we should've recruited a handler to avoid the limited Sunday Immigration and Customs services. Our hotel taxi driver was a real hustler. He accepted 10 USD after negotiating our business away from others at the airport and then spent the whole ride trying to upsell mercilessly back to the 25 USD he really wanted. It was an amusing sales masterclass in his wonderful, Caribbean-English lilt. That evening, we thanked Mother Nature for the good weather that had enabled us to avoid Venezuela and for the once-in-a-lifetime archipelago scenery. It had been a memorable day.

After all the stamping, photocopying and queuing at Port of Spain's Piarco International Airport, our objective the following day was to reach St. Kitts & Nevis, via Martinique for refuelling. We intended to progress north up the island chain and the weather over the sea was bright but hazy. Suddenly, while on the way to St Lucia, the weather deteriorated, and rain cells popped up all around us and across the horizon. I decided to divert to Argyle Airport on St. Vincent and the Grenadines to let the poor weather pass. Argyle staff were friendly, but we had another paperwork palaver when leaving. We passed west abeam of St Lucia and Martinique airports who turned us around efficiently in French before we flew northward towards Dominica. We continued to Guadeloupe, flying over Pointe-à-Pitre and then passed east of Monserrat, photographing the Soufrière Hills volcano lava flows, before continuing north westwards with a tailwind component to St. Kitts.

After refuelling, Immigration and Customs were very organised and all the formalities were expedited by jovial officials. It was a short taxi ride to The Royal St. Kitts Hotel and we had time to walk to a local beach restaurant that Matthew remembered, enjoying discussions with various holiday-makers there. We returned to the hotel later that evening for administration and diary duties. The weather had been much more challenging, which put the previous day's long flight into perspective. It was about 26°C but 80% to 95% humidity, so a bit sweaty! The trade winds had thankfully become a tailwind component.

We were going to rest for one day in St. Kitts, which meant time for my actions and exercise in the great, air-conditioned gym. I breakfasted with the owners of the hotel who were originally from the USA and had lived there for 30 years.

Moving across the Caribbean had been very interesting: from the Cosmopolitan Dutch of Aruba to the English of Trinidad, French of Martinique, and then back to the English of St. Kitts. It's a melting pot of indigenous and colonial influences, all swamped by tourists in a humid, warm environment, doused with rain every two hours. Each island is different topographically but all are verdant green with a wonderful 'Caribbean-ness' to them. Flying around the islands was a privilege, with great support from *ATC* in the popup weather conditions. However, it was a paper-heavy process with individual departments all stamping, filing and archiving copies in a serial, unproductive manner. To me this was bizarre, unthinking behaviour, since I'd spent my life trying to improve productivity!

With evening approaching, the frogs started chirping, reminding me of Maun in Botswana. We were mostly prepared for the next day's flight to the Dominican Republic where I would be hosted by Martin Grieder's brother, Dean, and visit the work of the *DREAM Project*. Matthew would be meeting up with his wife, Maria, who had flown out to see him.

We mounted up and lifted for our first short sea flight to Beef Island Airport, on the British Virgin Islands (BVI), passing Sint Eustatius and Saba Islands (pointed, volcanic islands maintaining human life, clinging to their steep sides). We were obliged to circuit in and out through Immigration and Customs to pay fees, in the heat and humidity. BVI was a pretty grouping of islands; there were many yachts around, and the Caribbean looked to be a mecca for sailors, with reliable winds and beautiful places to explore. Only two months later, Hurricane Irma (category five plus) struck the BVI causing the most extensive damage since 1988.

Our second flight was tailwind assisted, north of Puerto Rico and along the north of Hispaniola to Puerto Plata in the Dominican Republic (DR), which shares the island with Haiti to the west. The DR is known for its beaches, resorts, rainforest, savannah and highlands, including Pico Duarte, the Caribbean's tallest mountain. We needed to get a wiggle on because the forecast wasn't great, and we wanted to avoid any diurnal build-up. As we progressed, we could hear other pilots being warned about regions of rain. It was really murky at 1,200 feet and we tried ascending to 7,000 feet where we were mostly above the foggy type of cloud. It did rain from the very high cloud above us but while the horizon remained murky, we were fortunate that no heavy rain materialised. Dean picked me up at Puerto Plata and Matthew caught his transport to Santo Domingo on the south of the island to meet up with Maria, who was travelling from Punta Cana on the east. The logistics couldn't have been worse!

I hadn't met up with Dean for a good few years and we had a lot to catch up on. We went out for a meal along the beachfront at Cabarete in time for a beautiful sunset. My administration could wait as we were there for two days. I stayed at Dean's house by the sea, sleeping soundly to the backdrop of the crashing waves. Breakfast was made perfectly by Eri who kindly looked after me. I exercised by the pool and knocked off my emails and Facebook business in time to accompany Dean to visit the *DREAM Project* centre at Callejon de la Loma, Puerto Plata.

Stacy McKinnon talked about the project, while showing us around the facilities. Kids were enjoying the stimulating activities of a four-week summer camp. Stacy explained that the school system in the DR produced the lowest educational outcomes in Latin America, and more than 50% of children in the country lived in families that survived on less than 2 USD per family member per day. Families living in extreme poverty tended to have four to six children. By providing access to feminine healthcare, addressing prejudices, education and an understanding of choices, girls especially would have better life chances. The *DREAM Project* was currently providing education for over 7,000 youths and had affected the lives of over 10,000 community members. Their belief is that quality, early and continuing education is the most effective way to break the cycle of poverty and to change destinies. I had witnessed this same endeavour all over Africa and in Bangladesh.

I reflected on my epiphany, recognising three clear game changers to permit 'development within Earth's means'. Firstly, Hans Rosling had shown that raising the living standards of the extremely poor would stabilise population growth because when women have choices, they choose fewer children. Secondly, Johan Rockström had shown that mankind needed to respect absolute planetary boundaries to live within Earth's means. Finally, Pavan Sukhdev, study leader for *The Economics of Ecosystems & Biodiversity* (TEEB), had suggested that we must account for *both* Nature and people to make profit sustainably. Basically, there is no business case (never mind a moral one) for maintaining extreme poverty, and Nature's services are *not* free! We all need to think about that and live our lives accordingly. Dean then drove me around some of the back streets to see the situation for myself. We ate locally that night, swapping more stories and ideas.

I enjoyed training by the pool on my second rest day and tackled more routing details for Greenland. In the evening, I returned to Cabarete where the restaurants lined the beach and photographed the beautiful sunset again. I chatted with other tourists in the stifling humidity. Puerto Plata had been a wonderfully peaceful and productive retreat for me. I said farewell to Dean and Santo drove me to the airport. It was one of those 'where did you get your licence' kind of drives! The guy was too close to the car in front to avoid potholes successfully, using a mobile phone and just about avoiding oncoming traffic on our side of the road! It took us 40 minutes while Matthew had a three-hour transfer from Santo Domingo and shockingly, saw several dead bodies en route.

Lifting from Puerto Plata, the sea was a clear, see-through blue and our journey over the valleys and hills to the Haitian border was beautiful. It was a short flight with views of the dense housing surrounding Port-au-Prince as we approached the airport. We made arrangements for departure on the Monday and then relocated DIGA to *MAF's* parking on the general aviation apron. Bosquet (working for *MAF*) helped us secure DIGA but there wasn't anybody else from *MAF* available on the weekend, so we took a taxi through impoverished streets and crumbling roads to our little, gated hotel. We decided that being chaperoned around Port-au-Prince would be the safest way to see it! This was also a country rife with both malaria and Dengue fever.

At breakfast, I recognised voices from the previous day and started a discussion with Michael Robison who had been involved with Haiti for more than 10 years. He had also been involved in delivering aid for established charities in a few places (including Syria) and now supported projects helping the Haitian poor with food and orphanages. He spoke French and Creole. There was room in the truck for us to join Michael's drive around several Port-au-Prince meeting spots, so we could take in the sights safely. It was fascinating bumping along the roads, swerving to avoid obstacles and pushing into gaps, while at the same time discussing charitable giving (guilt), versus enabling local self-determination, versus delivering aid. Michael clearly knew his way around Haiti and Port-au-Prince like the back of his hand.

We drove with our windows up mostly. We saw some stunning street scenes of the roadside businesses and markets but also the extent of the rubbish in the drainage ditches and rivers. People lived in poor conditions with open sewers and no safe running water; it reminded me of Goma, in the DRC, Africa. 80% of Haiti's 11 million population live in poverty and therefore most people are just surviving with 'self-made' jobs. Haiti is the poorest country in the western world and there are over 600,000 orphans. We did manage a walk through an amazing multi-levelled, tin shack market, visiting an orphanage and meeting the Director of *Haiti Team Challenge*, which provides leadership development for the 'future leaders' of Haiti. We also met Josue who had ambitions to establish a school for orphans so that they could be educated and prepared for adult working life, but his resources were meagre compared with the scale of the *STC EYE* project we had visited in Dhaka. It was an incredibly instructive day and I thanked Michael for sharing the experience with us.

On Monday morning, we found the *MAF* pilots and engineers, including Tim Schandorff with whom I had been in contact, for a short conversation and a couple of selfies. *MAF* does amazing work all around the world. We said goodbye to Bosquet and as we lifted from Port-au-Prince, we managed another view of the dense housing stretching westbound and the rubbish emanating into the bay from the river. We crossed Haiti to its beautiful south shore and Pic De Macaya was the largest peak we could see at 7,700 feet. We headed out across the Caribbean Sea and flew the north coast of Jamaica, passing Falmouth, the birthplace of Usain Bolt, then landing at Montego Bay for refuelling.

Within an hour, and in sunny weather with a few CBs building, we continued west across the sea to Grand Cayman Island. We flew along the north coast and over Stingray City, then round Seven Mile Island to land. Maria and her friend, Lori, were waiting for us at the airport. Matthew and Maria had worked together in Grand Cayman for nine years. Matthew drove us to a local spot on the island called 'Hell' to close the loop on where we had first met in a place called Hell near Trondheim in Norway! We shared an apartment with the luxury of a washing machine and enjoyed an evening meal with Matthew and Maria's friends, Ferghal and Laura. We stayed out late and walked home, barefoot along the beach and carrying our shoes.

Matthew caught up with more of his friends in Cayman on our rest day. We were also interviewed by the *Cayman Compass* and timed our evening meal for a beautiful sunset, followed by a tremendous display of lightning inside one of the towering CBs about 60 miles out to sea. A humbling spectacle!

The next morning, Matthew and I looked like a couple of boy scouts as we posed for the *Cayman Compass* photographer in front of DIGA. We were looking forward to heading to Cuba, and Maria and Lori had come to see us off. After a false start to change our VFR flight plan to an IFR flight plan, we were cleared low across Stingray City again and then north, climbing to FL080 to Havana. We flew over the striking archipelagos of cays to the east of Isla de la Juventud. Between them and southern Cuba, the shallow water of the Gulf of Batabano was a beautiful, clear blue. Coasting in under the clouds over the island, Cuba was low-lying, flat, green, farmed and fertile. We were offered a direct approach to the small apron of Terminal 5 (T5) at the other end of the runway to the large new Terminal 3 (T3), which handled commercial jets.

José, a Christiano Ronaldo look-a-like, welcomed us to Cuba and suggested we wait in the air-conditioning of empty T5 while he persuaded a fuel truck to come over from T3. That gave us plenty of time to observe the four officials who were just watching TV with nothing to do. They checked each other's badges and raised their sunglasses to look at photographs each time one of them left or re-entered the terminal. This learned behaviour of being watched reminded me of what I'd seen in Belarus in 2015. Anyway, after a lot of juggling and negotiation, we had our visa from T3, having ridden there in José's golf cart in the humid conditions. Back at T5, the officials looked at our passes and faces again and finally cleared us through Immigration and Customs.

José put us in a taxi for the 30-minute ride to our hotel and I calculated that it had taken three hours from landing to our hotel door! Matthew had arranged our stay at The Hotel

Nacional de Cuba, which is the most famous hotel in Cuba. While the Internet was worse than the pre-smartphone era, the hotel was grand, colonial and wonderfully dated; it was certainly a vibrant and beautiful experience to be recommended.

We booked on a tour to see Havana and met our guide in the morning. A visit to Revolution Square, with artwork of both Che and Fidel on the side of the big buildings, was followed by a walk around the beautiful Old City. The walk took in the various key squares with museums and art galleries all around. There was a plethora of street vendors in the adjoining roads, along with shops selling cigars and rum.

The tourist currency exchange rate made Cuba expensive for its poor facilities and service experience. However, what we did get was a chance to see 'the last communist country' teetering on the edge of irrevocable change. Our tour guide frankly acknowledged that success in social fairness was the only legacy of the 'Triumphant Revolution' of 1959 and that economic development had been meagre over the last 60 years! Clearly the USA embargo still stunted growth and both sides were to blame for that stalemate. Unemployment was low but so were wages, and our tour guide explained that social policy discouraged problem-solving and accountability. Crime was also low apparently but, with CCTV cameras on street corners and many policemen wandering about, it felt like somebody was always watching you. When the time came, we walked off the beaten track to people watch and admire the beautiful 1950's examples of American cars, now employed as taxis. We plumped for a 125cc three-wheeler to take us back to the hotel. The next day, we were planning to enter the USA at Key West and continue to Kissimmee, where Matthew had also once lived.

T5 was busy when we arrived but José whisked us airside and golf-carted us to T3 to pay the cashier in USD. There, we met Chris Williams from the *Royal Canadian Mounted Police* (RCMP) who was also there to pay his bill. We were just mounting up when Chris bounded over to DIGA to ask if he could borrow 850 USD. He would be faster to Key West and could pay us back there; so, we lent the *RCMP* money to get out of Cuba!

We were routed east, south of Havana, getting great views of the city, then north across the sea to the edge of Cuban airspace, before we continued east with Miami control. We talked to the Canadian plane as it overhauled us into Key West where it landed at the Customs square. News of our favour to the *RCMP* had preceded us when we arrived! On relocating to the *Signature Flight Support* apron, Chris was there as promised to take selfies and let us know that *RCMP* had resources should we need any help when in Canada. *Signature Flight Support* kindly waived their fees again and, as our phones automatically logged into their Wi-Fi, I signalled to Eddie our imminent departure and we cleared our messages quickly. One email that I'd received was the good news of the *FAI* ratification of my three Africa records (fastest to fly from London to Stellenbosch, Stellenbosch to London and the London to Stellenbosch return routing).

We took off in a decidedly buoyant mood and flew east down the gorgeous Keys scenery to Marathon, before turning north direct to Kissimmee. We were soon flying over the Everglades: uninhabitable, swampy grasses and waterways yet home to numerous rare and endangered species like the manatee, American crocodile and the elusive Florida panther. It remained flat and low-lying all the way to Kissimmee and we passed Florida Peninsula's fifth highest hill, Iron Mountain, at 295 feet!

The weather oscillated between rain cells and brighter spells. Approaching Kissimmee, we flew over Celebration where Matthew still had a house and we landed just as the rain arrived. Matthew had been an aeroplane flight instructor at *SunState Aviation* for about seven years and we were welcomed warmly by Steve Graham. At Matthew's apartment, we used the washing machine, sorted our administration and then dashed out for dinner with Steve and Matthew's local friends. Lori and Maria arrived later, having flown commercially from Cayman, to add to the evening's merriment.

We waved goodbye to Maria and Lori in the morning at DIGA and lifted into a lovely morning sky towards the Disney and Universal Studio complexes. The built-up areas looked new and the wooded areas in-between were still flat and often wet, with man-made lakes everywhere. We flew northwards past Orlando and Jacksonville and into Savannah for refuelling. Then onwards past Charleston, Fayetteville and into Raleigh, Durham. The scenery was more of the same: it was vast. In Raleigh, *Signature Flight Support* looked after us once again. Eddie had connected me to Tom Haines and I confirmed our meeting for the following day. Tom was Editor in Chief of the *Aircraft Owners and Pilots Association* (AOPA). *AOPA* has about 350,000 members and fights for the rights of general aviation in the USA (there is an *AOPA* UK too). Flying in the USA is easy, and Matthew and I were looking forward to talking to this very important industry body. That evening, I also juggled our routing spreadsheet to enable us to visit Tomasz in New York on our route from Frederick to Nantucket.

We had a relatively short flight northwards past Richmond and Washington DC to the Municipal Airport of Frederick. Washington is 'protected airspace' and Matthew had completed an online course to understand all the proper procedures. The scenery was much the same as the day before with the addition of the Shenandoah Hills to the west. We landed right outside the *AOPA* HQ. Tom was working on his aeroplane and came over to greet us. He had been co-pilot to Adrian Eichhorn as far as Cairo when Adrian did his *RTW* flight, supported by *G.A.S.E.* in 2016, and hence the connection. We introduced Tom to DIGA and he gave us a tour around the *APOA* hangars.

At our hotel, I agreed the route up the Hudson River and through New York to meet Tomasz at White Plains, the airport where he worked. Matthew and I were excited about flying New York city low-level. Tom kindly drove us to a restaurant that evening to meet up with Dave Tulis and his wife, Martha. Dave would be looking after us the next morning at *AOPA* HQ and coordinating the press aspects of our visit. Martha had spent time in Colombia and shared her experiences. Adrian also joined us and as we ate well, we unashamedly talked about aviation adventures all evening!

On the Monday morning, Dave gave us a tour of the *AOPA* headquarters, making us feel special with his personal introductions, and Tom gave us useful tips on flying into New York. As we mounted up at DIGA, an *AOPA* team captured pictures and video assets for their magazine and social media. This flight was all about the amazing city of New York: flying the East River and Hudson River low-level routes to see gorgeous Manhattan and circling the Statue of Liberty. The weather was perfect, and we were very excited. After a two-hour flight from Frederick, it was a hectic

20 minutes that started once we passed the Verrazano-Narrows Bridge, a double-decked suspension bridge that connects the New York City boroughs of Staten Island and Brooklyn. It is amazing how close to New York you may fly and we weren't alone. I have flown the Heli lanes of the iconic cities of London and Paris but frankly, New York was jaw-dropping, man-made scenery on an extravagant scale.

Tomasz picked us up from White Plains Airport and drove us to his house in the Bronx. We would be staying there for two nights before moving on to Nantucket: quite possibly the poshest place in the USA! Tomasz's wife and daughter were just about to leave for a holiday in Poland as Matthew and I arrived, so we had about half an hour of orientation and swapping of keys before Matthew went to meet his cousin who ran a pub in Manhattan. Tomasz himself was off to Wisconsin on Wednesday for three intensive weeks of crop spraying.

The Bronx has a certain reputation, which it probably doesn't quite deserve these days and Tomasz had seen positive change over his 14 years' living there. However, it was still essentially a scruffy area of poor quality housing, with rubbish and dog poo on the street, as I discovered on my walkabouts. On the Tuesday, we all rode the sweaty subway into Manhattan to people watch, visiting Times Square and The Explorers Club. We celebrated our friendship at a Japanese restaurant. Matthew and I agreed to let ourselves out of the flat the next morning because of Tomasz's very early departure.

Tomasz had given us enough information to blag the 'Sierra Route departure' from White Plains, which he knew well because he flew corporate helicopters there. The route took us south-westerly to Bronxville, down the Harlem

River, then on to East River Corridor and the Hudson, to the Verrazano Bridge again. We desperately wanted to fly New York again and experienced another jaw-dropping ride with the rising sun, giving us the best possible photographs of the monumental skyscraper scenery. The autopilot came in very handy at that point too! We turned east along the coast past Coney Island, Long Beach and the Hamptons, finally heading across the sea for Nantucket Island. We really couldn't believe how easy it had been to fly about New York.

We saw a few fishing boats along the way but not much else. Nantucket is a tiny, isolated island off Cape Cod, Massachusetts, and is a summer destination for New Yorkers with beautiful, dune-backed beaches. A very chatty and engaging Betsey Sanpere from the *Nantucket Flying Association* (NFA) greeted us at the airport. Formed in 2004, the *NFA* is the focal point for all general aviation on Nantucket Island, putting on a variety of promotional and fun activities for people of all ages. Eddie had introduced us and Betsey was kindly hosting our visit. She had organised an early evening 'meet and greet' at the Atlas restaurant, which laid on some great nibbles as we chatted with the various locals who came along with their children, interested in our flying adventure. Kids flattered us by wanting their *NFA* colouring books signed. The colouring book is made up of sketches of visiting aircraft and DIGA was already there, ready to be coloured in. We finished the evening with a pleasant, sociable meal, meeting a colourful character called Frank – a fireman at the airport – and a nurse from the small island hospital, amongst others.

The interior of our B&B was a decidedly unmodernised throwback to England yet with an American exterior.

Nantucket was marked by unpainted, cedar-shingled buildings, many surrounded by trimmed privets. At breakfast, I met a lady who claimed she was 'an artistic person who didn't know how to make anything work' and we started a bizarre conversation about Nantucket, weight loss and sustainable development. It was an education cut short by my excuse to join Matthew for a walk around town!

The wharfs and cobblestoned streets were lined with restaurants, high-end boutiques and steepled churches; it was busy and swelled by tourists joining the Nantucketers. We also visited the extraordinarily well-curated Whaling Museum. The wonderful side of the story wasn't the hunting of whales unsustainably, but the endeavour of these early Nantucketers, the development of their ships and their long-range sailing skills in search of whales. They were taking more risks than us to circumnavigate. Nantucket's economy nosedived when whaling dropped off in the late 19th century as whale oil lamps were replaced by fossil fuel oil lamps. Now Nantucket has reinvented itself as a tourist economy with an incredible history and has become a very popular place for the wealthy to retreat to (apparently more so after the 9/11 atrocity).

In the afternoon, we met with Betsey for a visit to the *Linda Loring Nature Foundation* (LLNF), where Seth, who had come to dinner the previous night, showed us around. The focus at the centre was on science and nature education in schools during winter, using the conservation of the unique sand plain habitat surrounding the centre. That evening, I chatted with Betsey and Frank the fireman, who loved motorbikes and flying. Frank agreed to see us off at the airport the next day before he started work.

The weather was perfect sunshine in the morning and

Frank waved us off, as promised. We flew east of Martha's Vineyard in a northerly direction, past a string of British-named places including Barnstaple, Sandwich, Plymouth, Gloucester and Portsmouth. We routed east of Boston, then over the forested landscape with sections of agriculture all the way to the St. Lawrence River, Québec. Within minutes, we had cleared Canadian formalities on the Customs square and then literally hopped over the trees to *Capitale Hélicoptère's* maintenance facility: a nice big, new hangar complex. It started to pour with rain as we landed and we got drenched while dragging DIGA into the hangar.

Christopher Stapor welcomed us and made all the introductions; Francois would work with David Cross and I on DIGA's 100-hour inspection, starting the following day. We cleaned and unpacked DIGA, I communicated logbook data to *HQ Aviation* and Pierre-Luc pulled his tool trolley up alongside DIGA, in readiness for the next day. It was a pleasant, temperate 20°C, compared with the humidity of Nantucket, and we would very soon be into the arctic north. I updated David Cross at our hotel over an early meal, before he crashed out after 20 hours' travelling!

14

The most beautiful place on earth

David and I grabbed an early taxi. It was another of those Toyota Prius hybrid electric cars; a clever, hybrid solution while electric cars become more established and the charging infrastructure expands. At *Capitale Hélicoptère*, we cracked on with the inspection activities, working quickly with François. David inspected the blades for any signs of corrosion and addressed small areas needing attention. By 3pm, all DIGA needed was a test flight and some touch-up painting the next day. With a bit of time to kill, we took the bus into Québec to see the visiting tall ships moored in the harbour. It was mobbed with Québecers and tourists enjoying a sunny weekend afternoon. David was flagging because of the jet lag, so after a quick meal and a beer almost putting him to sleep, we headed back to the hotel, feeling decidedly chilly as the sun set.

François, David and I had the local Sunday morning skies to ourselves for DIGA's short test flight. It was a brilliantly blue, clear morning with perfectly clean visibility over the city. After painting, repacking and servicing paperwork completed, DIGA was ready. David and I taxied directly to visit the Québec Aquarium, which was then just a short walk to our hotel. Messaging Lavinia and Eddie, I agreed to fix our arrival back at Wycombe Air Park for Monday

7th August, which included some contingency in case the forecast turned out worse than it looked. This date permitted press and well-wishers to plan ahead.

On Monday, we planned a double hop to Schefferville via Sept-Iles. Pierre-Luc arranged DIGA in the hangar next to other *Capitale Hélicoptère* helicopters for some group marketing photographs. After thanking David, Christopher and his team, Matthew and I lifted. We flew northwest up the St Lawrence River, avoiding the gusty bumps by flying at 4,000 feet. Below us were forests and small lakes and then the St. Lawrence River itself. As we approached the seven islands of Sept-Iles, we could see whales blowing spouts of water.

After we debugged our windscreen, we could see a big column of smoke and firefighting aircraft tackling forest fires as we left the airport. It was still bright and windy as we set off northwards. The scenery transformed slowly to sparsely forested tundra and literally hundreds of lakes. It was pretty remote and reminded us of sections of Russia and Alaska. We climbed high again to reduce the effect of the turbulence and the views were spectacular. About halfway to Schefferville, we were dodging sleety-type rain, which we could see coming for miles. As the turbulence reduced, we descended lower to see the tundra and strikingly pretty yellow moss growing between the trees.

Schefferville Airport was abandoned except for refuelling purposes, which we managed quickly before it started raining persistently from the grey sky above. Without cell coverage, we succeeded in finding transport to a homely guesthouse. Schefferville existed primarily because of the iron mines and the whole place was therefore very muddy. Unsurprisingly, we were greeted at the guesthouse by a 'no boots policy'. My broken French was the only language spoken to the cheerful French proprietor because the other guests were English-speaking Canadians. After a wonderful, home-cooked meal, and in the absence of Wi-Fi, we all chatted while watching a gorgeous orange, late evening sunset.

I awoke at 3:30am with the sunrise and the weather looked inviting for another double hop north. Again, we had the airport to ourselves as we left and we enjoyed more of the same beautiful but bleak and remote landscape scenery until we reached Kuujjuaq, the former *Hudson's Bay Company* outpost at the mouth of the Koksoak River. Donning our *Typhoon* dry suits, we were soon off again, crossing almost sheer rock with mosses and hundreds of lakes, rivers and other pools of water. The two settlements of Kangirsuk and Quaqtak both looked bleak places with their buildings up on stilts above the hard permafrost.

We launched across the Hudson Strait to Baffin Island, the fifth biggest island in the world, which we also needed to cross to reach Iqaluit. There were patches of sea fog making extraordinary patterns below us and, in the distance, with some excitement, we spotted our first free-floating iceberg. After weaving through low cloud on Baffin Island, we were soon heading across the beauty of a mirror-calm stretch of Frobisher Bay with sea ice and cloud reflections, to Iqaluit and its bright yellow control tower. At the *Frobisher Inn*, we attended to our evening regime and considered carefully our third double hop via Qikiqtarjuaq to Ilulissat in Greenland. Ilulissat closed at 5pm, and we would lose two hours travelling east. So, we needed an early start and good weather to cross some spectacular territory and then the Davis Strait.

A German couple in a small fixed wing plane were parked close to us when we reached DIGA. We were all chatting as we climbed into our dry suits; they wanted to use the runway first after its inspection, but we didn't need one anyway! After fighting off the remaining 'twin-engine mosquitoes' in the cockpit, we shut our doors and departed first. We had a very helpful tailwind and the weather looked perfect for our direct route over high mountains, before descending back to Qikiqtarjuaq at sea level.

The scenery across the Hall Peninsula was beautifully desolate, rocky and undulating, with water pools and remnants of snow. We climbed steadily with the rising ground and had incredible views of sea fog below as we reached Cumberland Sound, an arm of the Arctic Ocean. We continued climbing, anticipating the mountains ahead, and the temperature dropped to 2°C. It was a fabulous day to be flying with the arctic visibility, pack ice chunks, patches of fog and magnificent, snowy mountains, all bathed in sunshine but set against the contrasting dark rocks. We could also see straight down into the clear water below as we approached the Cumberland Peninsula, part of the Arctic Tundra Biome and the world's coldest and driest biome. When we reached 7,300 feet to clear the mountains, we were looking down on glaciers everywhere and their journey from start to dirty moraine finish, as most were in recession. Mount Thor, at 5,495 feet – with Earth's greatest drop of 4,101 feet – was close by but obscured by cloud that we were avoiding. Dropping to sea level for Qikiqtarjuaq on Broughton Island, we could see the expanse of sea ice. The runway was given in 'true' degrees because the variation between true north and magnetic north was so great (about 34°): a first for us as we landed on the dusty, gravel apron.

Two Rotors: One Planet

The weather still looked good so, after refuelling and a toilet stop, we lifted again low across Broughton Island direct for Ilulissat. We crested the col to be met by the utterly breathtaking views of the sea ice, stretching for miles out over the David Strait. We climbed to about 5,500 feet to get radio reception and enjoyed the impressive view, which lasted for about 125 nautical miles out from Canada. At about 150 nautical miles from Ilulissat, we could see Greenland and just the odd iceberg peeking out of the sea below. With 50 nautical miles to run, we spotted Disko Bay ahead, with icebergs as big as cruise ships. It was now a sunny day as we crossed the 69° of latitude north, with the Great Glacier (local name 'Jakobshavn Glacier') ahead of us. Ilulissat is known as 'Iceberg City' because the icebergs come from the mouth of the ice fjord, pushed out from time to time over the underwater moraine field by the Great Glacier about 30 miles up the fjord that carves them. As we talked to the relaxed controller at Ilulissat, we couldn't resist any longer and descended to 100 feet to fly patterns between the icebergs like excited kids. We even spotted two humpback whales in the water!

On landing, we discovered that it was actually Jørgen Søndergård in the tower. A man called Johan Høeg Hansen had been following *TJR* for some time and, when he realised that we were going to Greenland, he had kindly made an unsolicited offer of his experience of the region and an introduction to his friend, Jørgen. Jørgen said hello and invited us up after we'd de-suited and secured DIGA. He had lived in Ilulissat for about 20 years and we picked his brains for local information. Ilulissat has some wonderful scenes of Nature which we wanted to see! Jørgen offered to be our guide the following day, which looked to be another sunny one: Matthew and I were excited.

We accompanied Jørgen to the airport in the morning to reconfigure DIGA to carry the three of us, putting some equipment into Jørgen's truck. It was unusually warm at 14°C. Jørgen dealt with the flight plan and Matthew flew first, to the mouth of the Ilulissat Icefjord, one of the northernmost *UNESCO* World Heritage Sites. He then flew up the 800-metre-deep fjord, low-level over the chunks and bergs, and along the mile-wide wall of the 'Great Glacier', famous as the source of the iceberg that sunk the Titanic! It was breathtaking with all the different shapes and colours of blue water and white ice. The 10,000 feet-thick Greenland icecap flows ice to this and all other fjords. Next, Matthew flew north across the edge of the icecap towards Northern Glacier, which had an even taller cliff face wall into the sea. We flew close, up and down, taking pictures. The scale was very imposing, almost ineffable.

Then Matthew flew the walls and crossed the fjords of several more glaciers, heading north to Eqi, another imposing glacier wall. From Camp Victor on the hillside overlooking Eqi, tourists come to watch ice crashing into the sea at regular intervals. Matthew flew us back and forth across this wall, giving us front row seats as we felt the rumble of the glacier calving beneath us. We then landed at Camp Victor for lunch and could hear the ice crack like thunder when it broke off five kilometres away. It was overwhelmingly striking.

Then it was my turn. I flew close by a couple more glacier walls and then we headed back south towards Ilulissat, flying low down the fjords. I was looking for an iceberg suitable to land on: Jørgen had seen it done here before by people making an advert for *Breitling* watches. A perfect candidate presented itself in Disko Bay; it was huge and relatively flat on top. I circled, we checked it out and, according to Jørgen's experience, it was stable. We set all our videos running and I checked the wind direction before making the approach. I settled DIGA down gently, keeping the engine running while Jørgen and Matthew got out to take photographs. Then Matthew looked after DIGA while Jørgen and I took some more photos before lifting carefully again. Feeling rather pleased with ourselves, we headed back to fly around the really big, stranded icebergs at the mouth of the Icefjord, before landing back at Ilulissat. Wow – we certainly didn't get to do *that* every day!

We prepared DIGA for the following day and met Jens Biilamann who ran *Ilulissat Tours*, providing pleasure flights out of Ilulissat and Nuuk. Jørgen introduced us and we agreed to meet up with Jens in Nuuk in a few days' time. That evening, we sat out on Jørgen's veranda, eulogising our amazing experience with views of the stranded icebergs and the Icefjord as a backdrop. We'd had a fantastic day with good weather, amongst the most extraordinary glaciers and icebergs that Nature has to offer. Ilulissat was surely the most beautiful place on earth and I vowed to return soon.

Our next stop was Qasigiannguit, only 29 nautical miles south, to finally meet up with Mikael Strandberg. Mikael is a Swedish explorer extraordinaire, sometime tourist guide and wonderful character. Mark Evans of *Outward Bound Oman* had introduced us, and I had Mikael to thank for our re-routing through Ilulissat. DIGA was soon looping round over beautiful Qasigiannguit, with its brightly-coloured, elevated houses, inviting hills and scenery, idyllic bay with icebergs and boats, and sled dogs. Mikael intended to spend a year in Qasigiannguit with his young family, documenting their experience in 'Man with a Family'.

Mikael greeted us as we landed with his video camera running. He was a delightfully extroverted, witty man, very interested in others and with many stories of his own adventures. He had cycled the length of the Americas and from the top of Europe down to Cape Town, as well as walking across deserts and Siberia in winter. He was a hardy, self-sufficient person and we hit it off instantly. Qasigiannguit was down to only 1,000 residents now that the shrimp factory had closed. Mikael, his wife Pamela, an anthropologist, and their two young children (aged seven and five) had only just arrived the day before us! In that time, they had revived a tiny, old wooden house belonging to Svend Hardenberg who we would also be meeting in Nuuk the next day. We slept on the floor and the toilet was a poo-in-a-bag arrangement! It was a great experience for us all and incredibly hospitable of Mikael and Pamela. We enjoyed wide-ranging discussions, met local people and nosed around the community. We had arrived in the middle of their 12-week summer. In the Arctic, the 'white nights' are beautiful, with great, long twilight sunsets and sunrises made even better by fine weather with a smattering of high cloud reflecting light and magic colours. However, for the rest of the year, Qasigiannguit would be cold, harsh and cut-off. None of the towns in Greenland are connected by road, only air or boat as the weather permits!

Both Matthew and Mikael liked football and so that discussion continued over breakfast before we wished the Strandberg family the very best and took photographs at DIGA in the sunshine with their Explorers Club flag. As the Strandbergs waved us off from the helipad, the water was calm with a mirror finish and we set off low across the bay, in between the icebergs. We climbed over the hills and headed south over picturesque fjords, lakes of differing glacial-melt blues and the mighty Greenland landscape. We climbed without turbulence to 8,000 feet to clear the icecap before cruise descending into Nuuk, giving our position calls in latitude and longitude coordinates and using our *Satphone* for regular 'operations normal' calls.

Nuuk was another friendly airport serving the capital and population of 18,000 and a base for the red Dash-8 commercial aircraft of *Greenland Air*. Arriving at our hotel, we bumped into Brian and Sylvia Foster, who we knew were circumnavigating westward with handling from *G.A.S.E.* Matthew decided to go out with them for a burger while I accepted Svend and Julie Hardenberg's invitation to dinner. The hotel Wi-Fi was good enough to set my backlog of photographs and videos uploading, which would give Eddie lots of material for his next Facebook post. I took a taxi to the 'red house' and I thoroughly enjoyed seeing the world through Svend and Julie's eyes for an evening. Julie had an arts degree and worked on many innovative projects in Greenland and abroad. Svend had a commercial background and worked to develop viable start-up companies in Greenland, attracting investment for them. We had a delicious meal and an interesting discussion about what Greenland needed to do to become independent and sustainable. The Hardenbergs were proud Greenlanders.

At breakfast on our rest day, I met the Fosters. They had sold up their business and left the UK for South Africa where Brian had assembled the aeroplane they were now flying. It sounded like they had suffered terrible weather along the way, which made me feel very fortunate. Brian was also the proud owner of an old Allouette III helicopter in civilian colours; Roy Holden and I had both last ridden in these in Rhodesia.

I had time to catch up on my administration and social media, and persuaded Matthew to join me later for a barbeque with Jens and Bente Biilamann. Jens is a colourful Dane who'd been living in Greenland for over 20 years and was married to Bente, a characterful Greenlander. Through their living room window, we could see the motorboats racing home from their summer houses after the weekend, and the low-level fog rolling in, as the sun set to twilight behind the hills on the other side of the Sound. It was beautiful. They ran *Ilulissat Tours* and both flew the Dash-8 for *Greenland Air*. Jens also had an old Russian Antonov II, based in Denmark, which they used regularly. Jens had all sorts of business ideas and I was sure we would meet again.

Our planned route was to fly south to Narsarsuaq and then north up the east coast to Kulusuk, taking in more of the Arctic panorama. This route was also the most sensible option to avoid whiteout, freezing and other dangerous weather-related problems. However, the weather remained excellent and Jens assured us that the next day would be cloudless: perfect conditions for a direct crossing from Nuuk to Kulusuk Island, over the Greenland ice cap. Very few people get the opportunity to fly a helicopter across this ice cap and we didn't need much persuasion to join that small group!

Jens and Bente took us to the airport and confirmed the weather for us. Jens also gave us the coordinates of DYE 3, an abandoned USA early warning system airbase, left over from the Cold War. It was on our route at an altitude of 8,000 feet on the ice cap and he wanted us to reconnoitre it. After selfies with DIGA, we took off.

From Nuuk to Kulusuk, the ground rises from and falls to sea level through a mid-ice cap altitude of about 9,000 feet. We climbed, digesting the gorgeous views and the ice cap approaching ahead. The different strands of glacier fed the long fjord's fingers with huge icebergs and pack ice and the azure-blue water was electric. The edge of the ice cap was glacial flow, with cracks like the back of a scaly animal. Continuing on, there was more snow on top of the ice. Flying at 9,500 feet, everything was clear ahead and the now hazy blue and white horizon was like a curved dinner plate. We couldn't discern whether the white ground ahead was cloud or snow; even in these perfect conditions the contrast was an issue and any bad weather would've been lethal. The temperature was a balmy 4°C. I thought to myself that this white desert was possibly the most beautiful desert of them all.

DYE 3 looked like an oil rig sunk into the snow with a dome on top; its dark colour against the snow created a good contrast, which helped us to see it. It was really too bright and almost impossible to read our cameras. We approached and tried to land in several places but couldn't judge how far we might sink in, so we settled for photographs. Nearing the edge of the ice cap and heading for sea level, we appreciated the ice cap transition in reverse order. For the last 40 nautical miles to Kulusuk, we were low-level across the ink-blue sea, with broken pack ice and colossal, azure blue-bottomed icebergs. It is the desktop background I now see daily on my computer!

Kulusuk Airport is a small dirt strip on an island with one friendly hotel close by, overlooking an iceberg-filled bay. We joined about 20 chatty tourists who had no idea what we had been up to. I had time to reflect that evening: this

Greenland sector had been a wonderful part of *TJR*. The people we had met had all been so friendly, generous and helpful, and it had been made 'perfect' with good weather, the freedom of the flying administration and being able to see the breathtaking Arctic panoramas from our helicopter platform. I reaffirmed my vow to return with DIGA as early as summer 2018.

At breakfast, I confirmed that the weather was perfect for our single biggest flight across water to Reykjavik, Iceland. I got talking to John who had worked at the hotel for three months. He was a bus driver in Denmark before he retired and had since travelled the world inexpensively through about 60 countries. It was very interesting to hear his thoughts on life. We lifted from Kulusuk above a beautiful sea fog with icebergs poking through and looking back, we had our last spectacular sights of Greenland. We flew VFR on top at 3,000 feet for most of the way across the Denmark Strait and Eddie confirmed the weather was clear at Reykjavik and a mild 14°C when we arrived in our *Typhoon* suits.

Iceland is the world's eighteenth largest island and Europe's second largest, after Great Britain. We landed and cleared Customs formally for the first time in a while, refuelled and then walked to our hotel directly opposite. With excellent Wi-Fi and back on my own UK phone contract, my communications were running at full speed and I completed my administration and upload regime. Robin Doten, who we had met through Robert DeLaurentis in San Diego, messaged to say that she was also in Reykjavik that night. She had been touring in Europe and had hooked up with her companion, Noah, to see Iceland before returning to California. We four agreed to meet and spent a few hours chatting away at a tourist bar in town. Robin had travelled widely, gathering experiences to bring her closer to Nature and other cultures. When I suggested that I was looking for crew for my third journey, she was interested.

I used Wednesday to see Reykjavik while chasing the Iceland *CAA* for permission to use Hornafjordur on the southeast of the island as our point of exit to the Faroe Islands. Permission finally arrived at 9am on Thursday morning. We could see DIGA from our hotel and it didn't take long to get ready. We lifted low-level to the southeast across green, lava fields, over smelly, sulphurous thermal power stations, big flood plains and winding rivers. It was beautiful, volcanic scenery but a dull day, although the sun was trying to come out. We passed Selfoss and continued following the southern coast road.

To our left (the north), we could now only see the bottom of the mountains and glaciers because of the low cloud covering. The scenery was rich, dark volcanic soil with plugs of volcanic rock stabbing up out of the plain, and all the shades of green represented in the vegetation and cultivation. The weather deteriorated and it started to drizzle and become foggy as we crawled along the coast at 400 feet – a tactic we hadn't employed since Alaska. Eddie messaged to tell us that what we couldn't see was Hvannadalshnúkur, the highest mountain in Iceland, whose peak is part of the rim of a super volcano called Öræfajökull and Iceland's most active. By now, we were in the worst foggy conditions of the whole *RTW* journey at 250 feet, although we could always have landed if we'd really needed to. Fortunately, within 15 minutes, we came through the worst of it and, as the weather improved steadily, we passed the southern tip of the Hvannadalshnúkur ice cap and the Iceberg Lagoon, before landing at Hornafjordur. Geiri, the controller, reminded me of Gado in Agadez; he was a multi-job man and he chatted away as he processed our papers. A policeman interviewed us before we could leave for Vagar Airport.

The weather at Vagar was forecast good and we could see that it was better in our direction of travel. With our dry suits on again, we climbed to about 1,000 feet heading directly over the sea, flying southwest towards the Faroe Island of Vagar. We saw one very big whale blowing at the surface. We had to dodge some rain and fog patches and, with Eddie watching our tracker, we could eventually see the Faroe Islands with their spectacular cloud blankets. We flew up the fjord with its notorious windy and turbulent welcome and we were handled efficiently before securing DIGA. The 18 islands have a population of about 50,000 people, with 20,000 of those living in the capital, Torshavn. A young student airport employee very kindly offered to give us a lift to our hotel in Torshavn, taking the trouble to show us the dramatic scenery of Vagar and Streymoy on the way.

Matthew and I checked the weather thoroughly for our last, big cold water crossing to Scotland. It was cloudy but an improvement on the previous day and with a really good tailwind. We then enjoyed the Streymoy and Vagar scenery, again noticing many more of the grass-roofed buildings as we returned to the airport. I called Drew of *Far North Aviation* at Wick to confirm the weather there and Adrienne arranged our accommodation at Ackergill Tower, a castle built in the early 16th century. Departing Vagar, we flew southeast between the beautiful islands of Sandoy and Suduroy and past smaller islands with sheep grazing on ridiculously steep slopes. There were little settlements only reachable by boat and some, only by helicopter. Soon the strengthening tailwind swept us past the Orkney Islands and we could see the Old Man of Hoy, a 449-foot red sandstone sea stack popular with climbers, before we coasted into Scotland.

At Wick Airport, we received a warm welcome. Drew refuelled DIGA and Adrienne dealt with our administration, releasing us for the short two-minute hop to Ackergill Tower. The castle was grand and we joined other guests for an evening meal. After that, I still had my chores to complete, including laundry and my administrative regime and I also made time to think through what I might say to the press, when asked.

On Saturday, our plan was a double hop to Northampton via Bagby. Eddie had booked us into the Aviator Hotel at Sywell Airport where we would standoff for our guaranteed arrival at 11am at Wycombe Air Park on the Monday morning.

I enjoyed scrambled eggs and black pudding for breakfast at the castle before we took off in drizzle, routing direct, west of Aberdeen, east of Edinburgh and west of Newcastle. It was windy and turbulent, with a pushy tailwind. We thought nothing of routing across the sea, having become desensitised to the risk and knowing that we had all the beacons, cold weather gear and G.A.S.E. tracking us. While the UK was very green below, it was no longer pristine forest either and we both commented on the orderly cultivation and replanted forests. I had memorised Bagby to Sywell because I had used the route for training and testing equipment for Africa and RTW and we passed untouched right down the middle of big, moody rain clouds en route. A local photographer, Paul Crotty, later gave me some stunning pictures of DIGA arriving against that dark, tempestuous sky.

Friends in the UK following our tracker now assumed that we were home and started to congratulate us on social media. It was quite emotional for us both, but we still had the weekend to prepare for the final 30-minute flight on Monday. Sywell Airport wasn't as spectacular viewing as Avignon where I had paused on the Africa journey, but Matthew and I celebrated my African *FAI* records at dinner. I had ample preparation time for thank you emails, reflections on what I would improve for next time, social media and press duties.

On Monday morning, I was interviewed very early on the radio by BBC 3 Counties and I would follow that with a Nick Coffer interview on the Tuesday in their studio. I hoped that talking about the *TJR* project would increase exposure and grow the charitable donations. I packed everything, breakfasted and checked out in plenty of time. It was a dull day with low cloud, but we judged it to be of no real concern. I had no nerves for this 'domestic flight' and I was looking forward to seeing everybody, being home, getting a better diet, restarting my training regime and bizarrely, being able to enjoy the photographs on a big computer screen.

I thought we would have a nice leisurely 10 minutes before lifting as we took photographs but as we mounted up, I couldn't find my video cameras. Oops, I must have left them in my room. I hurriedly retraced my steps and found them on a low shelf out of sight – phew! We completed one last check-walk around DIGA and even though Wycombe Air Park was expecting us, I called ahead anyway. En route, we had to avoid some very low cloud at Westcott but Wycombe was still confirming an ample cloud base of 900 feet and we touched down to a crowd of family and friends in light drizzle. We had completed the first equatorial, antipodal circumnavigation by helicopter. It had been a monumental effort by our extended team, and Matthew and I felt like we had achieved something.

I could see Peter Drissell, who had helped with our India permission, and Nigel Winser, my sustainable development mentor; Ruth and Tom from *Helicopter Services*; and David Cross who had personally prepared, inspected and serviced DIGA to handle these journeys. I would go on trusting David with my life and benefitting from his extensive experience of Robinson helicopters. It was a great turn out. We dismounted from the *TJR* configuration for the last time on the *RTW* 2017. There was a 'Welcome Home' banner, hugs, handshakes and photographs, then everybody headed for the warmth of the coffee shop out of the drizzle. We chatted to well-wishers and time passed all too quickly. Before we knew it, people were heading back to work and it was just Lavinia, Leon and me left at the *Helicopter Services* offices. I returned Thingy to Leon for safe keeping; Thingy had done his job for a second journey. While I got my *FAI* documentation signed by *ATC*, Leon hangared DIGA.

15

Plenty of time

Matthew and I returned from our antipodal circumnavigation on 7th August 2017, having landed in 41 countries, to complete a journey of about 32,000 nautical miles in 121 days. About 16 months to plan my next departure seemed sufficient. Surprisingly, I didn't feel tired, possibly because I had shared the workload with Matthew and the autopilot! Sharing and telling people what we had done, researching sustainable development some more and preparing for the next journey around Latin America became my full-time job once again. I had so many people to thank and a lot to do. The *RTW* journey had been life-changing for me: you can't see so much of the world like it is, researching the facts and not be affected by it. My personal journey had started towards driving an electric car, becoming more plant-based and eating less meat. Once again, home life seemed boring compared to the adrenalin and excitement of the journey but I settled back in slowly and began working to get my fitness back.

After a quick once-over at *HQ Aviation*, DIGA was immediately back working for *Helicopter Services* with about 60 hours to go until her next scheduled service. I debriefed Leon on my flying experiences, especially the autopilot, and he introduced me to Felipe Nascimento who had started his commercial pilot licence course at *Helicopter*

Services while I had been away. I organised a meeting with my mentor, Nigel Winser, for the end of August and started sorting my digital assets ready to update the website with presentations and a short video. I also planned to produce a poster and coffee table book as I had done for Africa. It was great to look back at every picture and feel the memories it triggered.

However, I needed to determine my next routing quickly so that I could assess the weather each day for the flying I would be doing in one year's time. I felt that it was important to understand the rain of the Amazon and the wind of Patagonia. This would give me just three months to establish the principal logistics so that I could watch the weather as if I were flying the route from November to February. I knew that I wasn't going to be able to fly from London during a Greenland summer (high northern latitude) or park DIGA in the USA somewhere in order to fly the Patagonia summer (high southern latitude) because DIGA couldn't get that much time off work! In theory, shipping her to the *Robinson Helicopter Company* (RHC) in California made sense, until I compared that with the much cheaper shipping cost to the east coast of South America.

I considered an anti-clockwise route but at this time, servicing requirements and my absolute desire to fly up the Amazon dictated a 'fly clockwise' decision, in spite of the prevailing headwinds in the Caribbean and Patagonia. Working with Eddie and Ahmed, I stitched together a route clockwise around South America from São Paulo, looping up the Amazon to Tefé, south to Port Velho and via Bolivia and Paraguay, back to São Paulo. I wanted to fly into Angel Falls in Venezuela, so I researched and planned that route, but I had options for avoiding Venezuela if the political uncertainty continued to make it unsafe.

The draft route wasn't perfect, but it was good enough to let me assess the weather religiously for four months as if I were flying each leg, one year ahead of when I would actually be doing it. The Amazon weather worried me: diurnally, my weather apps would just turn blue with rain and I had memories of getting stuck in Calabar and Douala for eight days just trying to cross 200 miles. I would really have a problem progressing 1,500 miles if it were that bad in the Amazon! However, my weather simulations seemed to give short flying opportunities, mostly in the morning. Once again, it was talking to local pilots later that convinced me it could be done safely.

The *HeliSAS* autopilot from *Genesys* had proved to be a revelation. It had made all the difference and Matthew and I used it for portions of most flights. It specifically made light work of conditions where the horizon was poor, increasing safety margins; it was definitely a workload reducer too and could possibly be a lifesaver. With the stabilisation on and a heading set, the autopilot could also be trimmed for a controlled ascent or descent. Matthew and I saw marginal VFR conditions flying into Cairo International, atrocious desert haze conditions across Saudi Arabia at FL075 and difficult visibility approaching the cloudy, smoggy cities of Dhaka, Chittagong, Manila and Kaohsiung. We also relied on *HeliSAS* in the misty, rainy conditions that we faced in Malaysia, Indonesia, the west coast of Alaska, Canada and the Faroe Islands. I discussed with Leon that the correct balance to strike was to be flying within your VFR limits and not the limits of the autopilot. The autopilot did not know whether we were maintaining visual flying or not! I honoured my commitment to Jamie Luster of *Genesys* and wrote the product endorsement, feeling well-qualified to do so, contrasting my Africa and *RTW* experiences.

Comfortable with the performance of the autopilot, I had already accepted that the final journey would be back to solo piloting and I discussed this with Leon and my wife, Lavinia. However, I was still open to the idea of a crew member to share the experience with, whose role would be photography and social media. Since I had already flown with a male crew member, I decided to look for a female crew member, or just go solo. I asked around. I had serendipitously met Robin Doten twice on *TJR's RTW* journey. So, we talked, and we were both interested in making it work. This journey of a lifetime matched her free spirit and she was savvy with social media and also spoke some Spanish.

Robin agreed to come to London for a couple of weeks and meet Lavinia at the end of September. When she arrived, the two weeks passed quickly. I was able to explain the *TJR* project in detail, talk through my plans for the *Latin America* (LATAM) journey, define our roles and talk through what the daily regime might be like. I wanted to be damn sure that Robin would still be friends with me after sitting in DIGA over the jungle for months on end! I gave her some flying lessons to familiarise her with the workings of a helicopter; we talked through the mission equipment and emergency aspects; we visited Maraid at *Costwold* to measure up for clothing sizes; and we joined a weekend trip to Wales with a group of *HQ Aviation* customers.

I also took Robin to meet my two best friends, Howard Linton, who I had met at university, and Martin Grieder, who I had met about 10 years later. I valued their opinion: if they felt that Robin could handle the rigour of a journey with me, then I would be comfortable. I think we generally satisfied ourselves that we could work together as a team. Robin still needed to win the support and approval of her boyfriend and we agreed to meet one day at the end of October 2017 while he and Robin took a holiday in Europe.

I met Felipe Nascimento at *Helicopter Services*. He was from Brazil, spoke both Portuguese and Spanish and was now living in the UK and working for the *UK CAA Safety Group*. Like others at *Helicopter Services*, he had followed our *InReach* track on the big office screen. He and Leon had seen Matthew and I waiting in Panama while trying to find a low-level route into Colombia to our antipode at Neiva. Felipe had ended up helping Leon with translations from Spanish when they had thought we were in trouble there! He was an ex-Navy helicopter pilot and had many friends and contemporaries still flying in Brazil. Felipe was enthused by the *TJR* project and interested in crewing but didn't have the time to devote to it. However, he offered to help me and introduced me to other Brazilian, military helicopter pilots who provided crucial advice on how to fly the Amazon safely, which in turn led to sensible route changes.

Tim Tucker kindly introduced me to the well-established *RHC* dealers in South America who he knew personally through delivering safety courses there and he said I could use his name. With his help, I engaged Marco Audi of *HBR* in Saõ Paulo, Willie Tufro of *Hangar Uno* in Buenos Aires and Sergio Nuño of *Arrayán Aeromar Helicópteros* in Santiago. I also had options in Rio de Janeiro and Guayaquil if necessary while I juggled my routing.

I was looking forward to my mentoring session with Nigel; our discussions were always so inspiring. My previous life as a management consultant meant that I had been able to work alongside bright people and since retiring, interaction with Nigel and my sustainable development research was a good substitute. I shared with him some of my *RTW* experiences and best photographs, before we planned 'future backwards' from the departure date of the *LATAM* journey. I would make applications to join the *Royal Geographical Society, The Explorers Club* in New York and to become a Fellow of the *Institution of Mechanical Engineers*. I also had time to research a better understanding of sustainable development and to anticipate my own presentation on the subject, based on my experiences, specifically anticipating gaps to be closed on this third journey. Nigel pinged off re-energising emails to Steve Jones (*Antarctic Logistics & Expeditions*), Andrew Mitchell (*Global Canopy*) and John Ingram (food security expert at *Oxford University*), all of whom I'd met at tea a while back. I would follow them up now.

Nigel introduced me to Marcelo de Andrade, Chairman of *Pro-Natura* in Brazil. Their friendship dated back to the late 70's/early 80's when they were doing expeditions and Marcelo used the *RGS* facilities as his office. Nigel also introduced me to Neil Laughton of the *Scientific Exploration Society* (SES) who suggested that I consider joining *SES* too. I left Nigel's house buzzing with ideas.

I received suggestions and input from Mikael Strandberg, the explorer, who I'd met in Greenland via Mark Evans. When Steve Brooks returned my call, he summarised his experience of flying in South America, warned of the scale of administration to expect and advised on the local currency requirements and weather. His book, '*Due South – Through Tropics and Polar Extremes*', had good descriptions and photographs of his route, which I could also refer to.

I called Marcelo de Andrade of *Pro-Natura* who turned out to be extremely connected in conservation circles in South America. *Pro-Natura* was tackling the social, economic and environmental problems that faced rural communities in over 40 countries in the developing world. *Pro-Natura* had demonstrated that the vicious cycle of rural poverty, unsustainable agricultural practices, deforestation and accelerating climate change could be reversed. Marcelo suggested a brilliant schedule for Brazil in the Mato Grosso region where I could witness how the land had been degraded from the Amazon forest. I juggled my routing around again. He also very helpfully introduced me to José Koechlin, founder of *Inkaterra* in Peru, and Claudio Hirsch of the *National Park Foundation of Argentina.*

I talked to Claudio Hirsch whose foundation was set up to support the *National Parks Administration of Argentina.* He suggested an optimal routing in Argentina to take in the stunning national parks and also set about getting me the necessary permissions to fly low in the parks, which was a long, bureaucratic process. Claudio had also supported Laura Crawford Williams, whose book, '*Wildlife in Wild Lands*', arrived before Christmas 2018. It was full of magnificent pictures of Patagonia and represented a wonderful record and dedication to the late Doug Tompkins, who was regarded as one of the most ambitious and successful conservationists in history. Doug and his widow, Kris, were two key names in the conservation movement in Chile and Argentina, and the parks and conservation areas they had been instrumental in creating were of international importance and great success stories. Claudio knew Kris and would later introduce me to her in an attempt to set up a meeting.

Two Rotors: One Planet

I emailed José (Joe) Koechlin of *Inkaterra* and received a swift and positive response. *Inkaterra* had pioneered ecotourism and sustainable development in Peru with sites in the Amazon, the High Andes and on the coastal desert. They were committed to scientific research as a basis for conservation, education and the wellbeing of local communities. Joe kindly developed visit suggestions with emails back and forth. He then introduced me to Gabriel, based in Lima, which resulted in me bending my Amazonian route into Puerto Maldonado in Peru from Brazil, then down the length of Paraguay and back to the Mato Gross region into Brazil.

Robin and I were both able to meet with Steve Jones at the beginning of October 2017. Because of his job with *Antarctic Logistics* and his experiences helping *Operation Raleigh* expeditions, Steve knew a lot about expeditioning in South America, its history and lots of points of interest. We poured over his detailed maps and he emailed me a comprehensive 'brain dump', country by country, which was brilliant intelligence for us! Robin and I weaved in as much of Steve's advice about interesting spots as we could. He also suggested that I should try to meet Kris Tompkins.

Steve also introduced me to Olaf Wuendrich. Olaf ran *ColibriVentura*, which organised, guided and supported logistical tours, expeditions and special projects in the lesser-known areas of Patagonia and the Aysén region of Chile. Olaf had excellent connections with authorities, national park people, local support, transport for drum fuelling and more. Talking back and forth, Olaf helped with more points of interest, advice on routing up the west coast across the Southern Icecap (in Chile), warnings about the windy and rainy weather to expect and places to keep in mind for safety stops. Olaf also introduced me to a charity called *Teletón* in Coyhaique, which was a perfect fit because of its support to integrate disabled children. Getting hold of Olaf and *Teletón* always proved difficult though, with long delays between communications.

I arranged to meet Jennifer Murray to ask her advice for flying South America. We met in London for lunch and I proudly accepted a signed copy of her book, '*Now Solo: One Woman's Record-breaking Flight Around the World*'. She was a legend and it would have been wonderful for Robin to have met her too but sadly, the dates didn't fit. Jennifer understood the challenges of long-range flying better than I did, and it was very interesting to compare notes enthusiastically. She had made many contacts in South America and one key introduction she made for me was to Gérard and Margi Moss. Gérard was a pilot, environmentalist, explorer and Earthrounder, born in Switzerland and a naturalised Brazilian. As Jennifer and I wished each other well, she left me with a parting observation: "You have to be prepared to die to do what we do!" Indeed, it was always a possible outcome, and Nigel, Lavinia and I had spoken of the arrangements in the unlikely eventuality of such bad news, with reporters standing on the doorstep.

Before Christmas 2017, I was in contact with Gérard. We got on well and he was incredibly helpful. With his environmental projects, he had flown all over Brazil and so was able to look at my routing and make suggestions for cheaper, smaller airports and aeroclubs, which were still a prominent feature of general aviation in South America. He knew the Amazonian weather intimately, having flown about 1,500 hours gathering scientific data for the *Flying Rivers Project*, landing his scientifically-equipped float plane just about everywhere! He was fluent in Portuguese and understood all of the administrative issues that I would face. Gérard and Margi insisted that we add Brasilia to the route and stay with them for a few days. Soon my route had incorporated all of his suggestions of airports and places to stay and I had become more confident that my plans would work.

I met up with Andrew Mitchell at the *RGS*. We had a fascinating discussion and once again, I was like a sponge, soaking up his lifetime of knowledge. Since he founded the think tank now called *Global Canopy* at Oxford in 2001, Andrew had focussed on the inclusion of forests in the *2015 Paris Climate Agreement*, reducing the impact of global supply chains on this 'natural capital' and on designing innovative, public-private finance instruments, such as green bonds for climate-smart agriculture. He gave me ideas to research for my improved sustainable development presentation and my website explanation of the amount of carbon released as a result of my personal lifestyle.

Andrew introduced me to Dane Gobin of *Iwokrama* in Guyana. I read up on the science behind the importance of the coastal forests and *Iwokrama* was a unique example of sustainable development in such an ecosystem. I made contact with Dane and with Carol Marcus, who helped organise an amazing schedule involving Georgetown, flying into the Iwokrama River Lodge and meeting a local community. I needed to get special permission from the Guyana *CAA* to make the internal flights and *Iwokrama* kindly helped me make the appropriate connections.

Andrew also introduced me to *Ecosphere+* who specialise in supporting forest conservation in critical, tropical ecosystems around the world through climate finance.

Talking to Lucy Arndt, we discovered that my carbon offset purchase with *Ecosphere+* could go towards addressing the drivers of deforestation in the Amazon through a project they were supporting. It worked with local communities to develop more sustainable livelihoods and protect the *Tambopata-Bahuaja Biodiversity Reserve*, in Puerto Maldonado in Peru. I could visit the project based in Puerto Maldonado, which was a fantastic routing coincidence.

I also took Andrew's advice to address my CO^2 footprint with a button right on the front page of my *TJR* website and explain my travel situation in the context of carbon-offsetting linked to the importance of forests. It felt good to finally understand the size of the aviation problem, relative to other contributors to climate change like production, energy generation, agriculture and food. I had used *Climatecare* to offset my Africa and *RTW* journeys and I would use *Ecosphere+* to offset by *LATAM* journey.

I called John Ingram, Food Systems Programme Leader for the *Environmental Change Institute, University of Oxford.* 32,000 miles had passed under my belt since we had last met at Nigel's for tea. I explained that, passing over the Arab states, it seemed unbelievable that anything could grow. Then, looking at the widespread subsistence farming on degraded land right across India (as we flew), with nothing planted until we got to Bangladesh, it was a wonder that they could feed so many. Asia seemed to prefer palm oil trees and the deforestation and destruction was shocking, while Japan was unbelievably organised with rice paddies and forest. I needed to understand the issues of food security, land degradation and desertification much better. John talked me through his own work and steered me to the work of David Tilman and Michael Clark (*Food,*

Agriculture & the Environment: Can we Feed the World & Save the Earth?). I found a good few of their published papers, which provided fascinating reading, alongside John's presentations and publications.

I also emailed Kris Tompkins to establish that she was happy to meet if we could get our schedules to cross in Chile.

On 17th November 2017, Mike Green was unusually about 10 minutes late returning from an instructional flight. We learned the incredibly sad news that he had perished in a mid-air collision. It was a bolt out of the blue and hit the *Helicopter Services* staff hard, Leon and Ruth particularly so. Mike was an instructor with *Helicopter Services*, based at Wycombe Air Park and one of Leon and Ruth's best friends. He was also our friend and colleague who, as a senior instructor and examiner, helped and mentored so many pilots throughout the industry during his long and distinguished career. It was almost impossible to remain upbeat after such tragic and unexpected news, but Mike would have wanted us all to carry on as normal and keep flying.

The valuable input from Andrew Mitchell (*Global Canopy*) and John Ingram (food security) had resulted in a much-improved sustainable development presentation. I conveyed the challenge of sustainable development as a mix of climate change, use of land and pollution, through novel entities such as plastic. I had now, finally, grasped the link between all the drivers and understood the numbers provided in *IPCC* reports from their scientific research. My sustainable development presentation now positioned the challenge using these facts, which underpinned the need for people to act responsibly and live within Earth's means. Then the remainder of my presentation had a positive spin, highlighting what could be done by governments, companies and individuals. If I were a young engineer starting out on a career today, this world would be such an exciting time to try and solve problems that really mattered.

My second epiphany (from the work of Tilman and Clarke) was that we use more than 55% of our available agricultural land to feed mainly red meat to about two billion earthlings, where it constitutes only 20% of their calorific consumption. This is unsustainable on so many levels. My research into food and agriculture convinced me to eat less meat and become more vegetarian, which I never thought would happen to me so quickly. My daughter was also now following with interest what was consuming my time and was forming her own views on climate change, quickly becoming pescatarian.

With the blessing of Robin's boyfriend, Robin and I planned to meet up at the end of April 2018 to continue the flying lessons and to get Robin kitted out in time for a return trip to Greenland that I was planning for June/July. This would be followed by Spanish lessons at a school in Salamanca.

On 26th January 2018, Kenya lost one of its greatest ambassadors for wildlife conservation, Willie Roberts. Willie was instrumental in founding the conservancy movement in Kenya. He set up the first wildlife conservancy, saving the greater Mara from being carved up for farming, laying down a clear path for success in community conservancies in Kenya and an example and an inspiration for others to follow. Willie had also introduced the white rhino to the area. I sent my most sincere condolences to Sue Roberts, his widow. My heart went out to Sue, her family and the *Sirikoi* family. Lavinia and I had so enjoyed the company of such a very special man.

Also in January, I was contacted by Ruben Dias who had been following our *RTW* journey; he was planning a similar trip with Mischa Gelb and asked if I would help. They lived in Vancouver, both were pilots and Mischa ran his own helicopter training company. I was always happy to help a fellow aviator, especially one attempting to fly long range. I provided the first of a series of 'brain dump' emails. Ruben flew over to meet me, with his son Diogo, a couple of weeks later and I learnt that they wanted to take off in May in an R66, which didn't leave much time. Anyway, they were able to crawl all over DIGA and I showed them my equipment and where it was situated. They were also going to be supported by *G.A.S.E.* and I explained the modus operandi. Many more messages went back and forth between us. Their 'EPIC' tour, as it became branded, began on 1st May 2018 and it was great to follow their *InReach* satellite track and catch up with their vlogs. We welcomed them to *Helicopter Services* at Wycombe Air Park on 6th and 7th June as they passed through.

On 7th August 2018, I congratulated them: "Hello Ruben and Mischa, from someone who knows what it takes to dream of, organise and execute such a feat, congratulations on your antipodal circumnavigation of Earth. What a fantastic achievement, which you can dine off for quite some time." Ruben and Mischa responded: "Yes, we did it and we owe a lot to you. We will never forget your unconditional support, your long list of critical suggestions and recommendations and the continuous cheering for us. You are truly a great airman and most importantly, a good friend."

Ruben and Mischa became the second helicopter pilots to fly an equatorial, antipodal circumnavigation of Earth.

They also landed at the twinned cities of Palembang in Indonesia and Neiva in Colombia on opposite sides of the globe and did it faster than Matthew and I had done on *TJR*.

I explained to Ruben that when I flew *RTW* eastbound through antipodes in 2017, I had been in discussion with the *Helicopter Club of Great Britain* (HCGB) to be sure that I filled in all the relevant *FAI* documents en route for the subsequent record submission. We used the same *FAI Sorting Code Section (SC9 5.3.7)* as we had done for Africa, identifying the antipodes as the two control points.

However, after submission and much discussion, this approach was rejected by the *FAI* who concluded that they didn't have a '*Speed around the world through antipodes*' category. With the *FAI's* help, we instead submitted a five-record claim under SC9 5.3.7 to protect the accomplishment, which was ratified, while the *HCGB* proposed a new category specifically for '*Speed around the world through antipodes (Eastbound and Westbound)*' to the *FAI*. The new category was ratified by the *FAI* in about March 2019 and published as *SC9 5.3.8.*

With these unusual circumstances, I explained to Ruben that I was trying to claim the record retrospectively, believing that I was the first person to have achieved this feat. However, the *FAI* rules don't accept retrospective claims either and I was stumped, until they kindly provided a letter vouching for the achievement, which I could use to satisfy the *Guinness World Record* requirements.

At the end of January, I met with James Ketchell at White Waltham airfield. He was a young, serial adventurer who made his living through inspirational speaking. James had become the first and only person to have successfully summited Mount Everest, rowed solo across the Atlantic

Ocean and cycled 18,000 miles unsupported around the world, all of which had been dubbed 'The Ultimate Triathlon' by the press. James had completed numerous other smaller, but significant adventures too. His website said it all really and I had a signed copy of his book. He was a really personable guy.

James told me that his next challenge would be to fly an autogyro around the world. He had asked *G.A.S.E.* to help him but Eddie thought he might be a nightmare to work with, having only 50 hours of local flying experience under his belt. James had no idea yet, but he would learn, I told Eddie, and that was where I could help. I needed to instil in James a 'need to know about aviation stuff that would keep him alive' mindset, and to give him options on solutions to challenges he would face before even getting to the start line. Basically, a crash course in everything I thought I had learnt applied to his open cockpit autogyro. Fortunately, he didn't only take advice from me!

I took James flying with me every time I could so he could practice his radio work and I also introduced him to people who had helped me. James had already written and published a book and he introduced me to Pru Gayton, a freelance copywriter, who had edited his book. I watched James talk, raise sponsorship and get ready month by month. He bounced ideas off me and I helped if I could. He, in turn, watched me prepare with Robin for the Greenland trip and then for Latin America. He followed Greenland on the tracker and would go on to follow our *LATAM* journey, messaging me with questions en route. James was especially keen and needed to become a weatherman using the same apps that I was using. It's too easy to just look at the local sky instead of following the forecasts over a number of days. It was the weather that could kill him, I kept reminding him!

Robin arrived for her second two-week stay at the end of April. We were able to get some more flying lessons in and go through more of the preparation details and kitting out. Because she was American, we had to be especially careful that we established her visa requirements correctly, which were different to mine, to avoid any unintentional hiccups. We also covered the (now familiar to me) insurances, emergency number registrations, malaria pill-taking analysis, crew badges, routing discussions, crew documentation preparation, to name a few. We also made arrangements for the equipment and cold-water gear for Greenland, which we would need in Latin America too and finally, we booked our Spanish language course. Once again, the time flew by.

With each journey, there were pieces of equipment that I didn't use. I was grateful for not having had to use the emergency stuff, of course, but even in the clothing department, I still didn't get the balance right. *RTW* had not been as cold as it could have been. Anyway, all the systems and items of equipment worked, which was the key thing. I was also just thinking about fine-tuning for the final journey. There were lots of smaller, proactive tasks I could work on. For example, media wise, I could anticipate the return press and have the website page ready to switch – that sort of thing. The daily mounting and dismounting of cameras and uploading was naturally time-consuming, but I thought I might be able to speed that up a little too. I had ideas for little pockets and pouches here and there, after talking to *Aircovers*, and with a few more brackets on the helicopter, it could be a 'well adapted office space'. I intended to encapsulate key data on A5 cards to have to hand, which would survive the humidity better than paper. I was an engineer after all and I looked to simplify, speed up and continuously improve.

Felipe Nascimento introduced me to his buddy, Lieutenant Commander Bruno Martins, Operations Section of the command of 9° Naval District (Manaus). I provided Bruno with my first routing through the Amazon and he used his knowledge and systems to give me alternatives, flying the river routes. His 'brain dump', translated by Felipe, was extensive and extremely helpful. It included *Search and Rescue* (SAR) advice and many tricks of the trade including the use of *InReach* beacons, which I already relied upon. Bruno explained how to fly the weather and what to be aware of, money requirements, personal safety considerations, equipment to be carried and 'protection for the helicopter', for example, from hail. Before we set off, I had all of Bruno's contacts in my phone and on my *SAR* details with *G.A.S.E.* and the authorities: one call and the Brazilian Navy would know I needed help. I was very grateful for these solid inputs given so generously.

Felipe also introduced me to Jessica Henderson who had over 40,000 followers on her Instagram account. She helped me with a professional review of the *TJR* website in the first quarter of 2018. This was perfect timing for me as I was able to refresh my website while adding the *RTW* assets.

Siobhan Gill, my doctor in the UK, also discovered that there was a vaccine against Dengue fever available in Brazil and manufactured in France. Her research showed that it was a temperature-dependent vaccine and was only provided in Brazil. The mosquito that spreads Dengue bites during the day; if you contract it a second time, it can apparently be worse, and I had a high chance of catching it again in the Amazon. Felipe introduced me to a doctor in Brazil who could have helped me but in the end, a course of three injections, given six months apart in Brazil, proved impossible to make happen within my timescales.

From the moment I had set eyes on Ilulissat in July the previous year, and then enjoyed the stunning beauty of the rest of Greenland with Matthew as we completed our *RTW* journey, I had wanted to go back. I had made some great friends in Greenland and Ilulissat was probably the nicest place on earth. I was also hoping to catch up with Mikael Strandberg, his wife Pam and their children, who would be tying up their year-long stay in Qasigiannguit and their 'Man with a Family' documentary. I wanted to give Mikael a ride in DIGA and perhaps get some great footage of the area for him. So, in January 2018, I announced my intention to return in the summer, made arrangements and agreed to meet my family in Ilulissat. Jørgen, who worked in *ATC* in Ilulissat, knew we were coming, as did Svend and Julie Hardenberg and Jens and Bente Biilamann in Nuuk.

Sadly, Mikael's daughter had developed an eye condition which thankfully, was recognised early, but there was a distinct possibility that the family would not be in Qasigiannguit as originally hoped. There was much uncertainty and his little girl was indeed undergoing surgical treatment and we were going to miss one another.

Robin arrived from California and we packed DIGA. We had all the systems in place as if we would be leaving for Latin America. We routed via Wick, the Faroe Islands, Egilsstadir and Reykjavik on Iceland to Kulusuk on the west cost of Greenland. We had our mix of weather but enjoyed stunning views of the Faroe Islands with their cloud blankets and the mesmeric beauty of the volcanic activity of Iceland. In Kulusuk, we met up with Joel and Isabelle Giradot and Erik and Florence Odin, two French couples flying Cessna 182s to Kulusuk. We combined to check the weather and waited for a suitable crossing of the icecap directly to Ilulissat, which was our original intention. Toughing out the fog and the misty rain, we visited Tassilak by boat together and had a look at massive icebergs from water level. Both French couples were good fun.

The freezing levels were forecast to remain too low for an icecap crossing and we instead took the first break in the weather to go around the coast via Narsarsuaq, Nuuk and then on to Ilulissat. The weather south was poor and we had a tailwind of 50 knots. Robin took it all in her stride and we were working well as a team to get the best photographs. Robin was also getting the hang of the mounting/dismounting and start-up/shutdown processes with DIGA and also getting into and out of our *Typhoon* dry suits on a stony apron! From Narsarsuaq heading north, we absorbed the beautiful contrast of sea fog filling the fjords below with the white glaciers and sea ice against the dark rocks, and the brilliant white icecap in the distance. It was once again absolutely beautiful and a good reason for being alive.

Lavinia, Hannah and Fraser had already made it to Greenland, found their way around Ilulissat and met up with Jørgen. The French couples arrived and were able to stay with Fleming, who was a local character and pilot on the *SAR* helicopters. Jørgen, Robin and I scouted a neat route past all the local glacier walls, including the Great Glacier and the Dead Glacier and we located and landed on a suitable iceberg out in Disko Bay. Robin and Jørgen took some fabulous pictures. Swooping back to Ilulissat Airport, I picked up my family to make the same circuit. I got the feeling that they liked it and they each have their picture of being on an iceberg! We enjoyed a night at Fleming's bar and with the French couples, some 'twilight downer' (rather than sundowner) beers on Jørgen's deck, with the iceberg-filled Disko Bay as our backdrop – it was past 12 midnight! Jørgen's neighbours had Robin and me over for a barbeque and that was the first time I had tried seal meat. It was a wonderful time and too soon we were routing south, overflying Qasigiannguit to Nuuk to stay with Svend and Julie. We managed a local flight with them and a spot of fishing, then we waited for the weather to improve for our reverse journey home. We were gifted sunny weather to Narsarsuaq, Kulusuk and into Reykjavik. The views were beautiful; with benign wind conditions, I was able to fly close to the mountain peaks. There was a moment of poor weather en route to the Faroe Islands but soon we were safely back home. If we needed it, this was final proof that Robin was ready and we were satisfied that we could work together well.

Within a few days, Robin and I were off to the intense heat of Salamanca to sit in a classroom full of kids and learn some basic Spanish. Robin was in a more advanced class than me but I was able to get my head around the basics of pronunciation, numbers and dates, which would prove helpful later.

By the beginning of August, with significant input from key contributors, I had my visits and routing largely established. Like *RTW*, the maintenance was tricky because the distances required two stops and DIGA also needed a rebuild after shipping. Looking at the possible *RHC* maintenance centres in Rio de Janeiro, Sao Paulo, Buenos Aires, Santiago and Guyaquil, it still seemed that a good place to start and finish the journey would be in the Guianas – either Georgetown, Guyana or Paramaribo, Suriname or Cayenne, French Guiana. It also made sense to me to enter the Amazon with DIGA recently serviced.

However, with only 14 weeks to go, I was still frustratingly waiting to get a straight answer on the logistics and Customs arrangements for shipping DIGA. When I investigated maintenance companies to rebuild DIGA, both Guyana and Suriname required a ridiculous Customs import bond exceeding $100,000. French Guiana was a department of France and therefore technically in Europe for shipping, but the maintenance company in Cayenne refused my request for help. I went around in bloody circles before I found a great company, *MSJ Shipping*, and an excellent rebuild centre in West Palm Beach, *RotorTech*, suggested by David Cross. On reflection, shipping to the USA cost less, needed only a small bond payment and put DIGA in the hands of people who had experience of shipping and rebuilding helicopters. I wasn't sure why it had taken me so long to figure that out! So, while I should have been practicing my Spanish calmly, I was instead in a mad rush to organise shipping to the USA, add the Caribbean and Central America legs to my routing, readjust the service points and communicate the routing dates to my visits and hospitality stops.

Finally, after much planning and countless changes, my third epic journey was now on track. Robin and I would fly around Latin America from West Palm Beach to Puerto Williams and return. Iwokrama in Guyana would now be our first visit, which made it easy to fix that important date and we would enter Brazil at Macapá. I dropped off a packed DIGA at *HQ Aviation* on 30th October 2018. She was then taken down to big pieces, boxed, containered and sailed from London Gateway on 6th November. It had taken a lot of hard work from Martin Suddards and Ali of *MSJ Shipping* to make all this happen.

I enjoyed one last mentoring session with Nigel, this time to map my future backwards for the goals I would set myself for three years beyond the final journey. We discussed and set goals for communicating what I would have seen and what expeditions might be next. This would help refocus me on my return in March 2019. I also made my last visit to *Helicopter Services* and the staff wished me good luck. Leon once again passed Thingy to me and wished me well.

During the last week of November, Lavinia joined David Cross and me in West Palm Beach to reassemble DIGA at *RotorTech*. Art Apicella, the Operations Manager at *RotorTech*, made us welcome and introduced us to Paul, an engineer who hailed from South Africa. Paul had Robinson helicopter experience and would assist us with DIGA's rebuild. Walter, the owner, chatted to us while we waited for the container to be delivered and the crane to arrive. Everybody was welcoming, friendly and chatty and the large hanger was full of helicopters undergoing maintenance. It was Monday 26th November and we would be setting off the following Sunday.

I had already watched the rebuild process of a brand-new machine at *HQ Aviation*, so this would be my second rebuild. David had done it many times and *RotorTech* had all the tools we would need, positioned in an empty bay. The container was dropped to the ground by the crane. In the UK, all of this would be done by one driver in a Hiab truck and trailer. The boxes carrying the rotor blades and the gearbox were unloaded and then DIGA's hull was rolled out. We kept all the boxes for the return journey and unloaded DIGA. We reunited the gearbox with the hull and made all the connections, reattached the tail empennage and reconnected the rotor blades. After oils and checks, we started DIGA and checked her over. After a compressor wash and a few adjustments, David and I test flew her out towards Lake Okeechobee. I organised some photographs with the whole *RotorTech* team who had by now looked at my *TJR* website and realised what I was preparing for!

On Wednesday, I dropped David off with friends at Orlando Executive Airport and then recovered back to West Palm Beach to pack DIGA and meet up with Robin. We made sure that we were all sorted and still had a few days left to look around. I watched the weather, prepared my PLOGs and flight plans ahead and sorted my eAPIS for our exit from the USA. I also had my *FAI* paperwork certified by *Air Traffic Control*. Dana Bunch, an *FAA* officer, was familiar with the process and would sign me out and back. He wished me luck. Finally, Robin and I were packed and ready for what promised to be the most amazing experience.

16

20% of our oxygen from the Amazon rainforest

On Sunday 2nd December, Lavinia drove us round to *RotorTech* and Art kindly let us in, stored our suitcases and helped me push DIGA out. I made sure we had all the requisite pictures and after several hugs, kisses and well wishes, Robin and I climbed aboard. It was hot and humid, and DIGA was heavy. I went through my now familiar start-up routine, establishing the *InReach* tracking and its two-way communications with our indispensable virtual team at *G.A.S.E.* We lifted at 8am and started down the chain of Caribbean islands with good weather and stunning views, planning to overnight on islands new to me including Turks & Caicos, Puerto Rico and Barbados.

With a steady headwind, we overflew Nassau and refuelled at Exuma in the Bahamas. We were treated to the spectacular sights of cays, beaches, private dwellings, small marinas, big boats, little airstrips and flat, swirling islands. The hue of the brilliant, blue-coloured waters changed with depth and the pure, white sand dazzled below. It made for breathtaking viewing, albeit hot and humid. We landed for the evening in Providenciales, Turks & Caicos to a rum punch welcome at Immigration and Customs. That evening, we processed our photographs; Robin wrote a great Facebook post and I used *Rocket Route* for my flight plans and eAPIS into Puerto Rico (a US territory).

On Monday morning, we lifted with the sun in our faces and climbed to 7,500 feet to find the least headwind and get radio reception. We worked Miami Centre until the eastern end of Hispaniola (Dominican Republic and Haiti) and then San Juan control. DIGA was searched in San Juan and our *TJR* clothing patches, business cards and website helped explain to the US Customs why we were carrying wads of different South American currencies! With excellent Wi-Fi, we knocked off our social media and administrative regime, allowing plenty of time to go out for an evening meal. So far so good.

With efficient handling, we departed on time, climbing to 1,000 feet to stay below the scattered clouds and avoiding the sporadic light rain showers. We flew direct to St John's on the island of Antigua, passing between the Virgin Islands and St Croix, then south of St Maarten and north of St Kitts where Matthew and I had landed the previous year. Our wooden, beaded seat mats that you often see on car seats in hot countries were doing the job of keeping our bottoms cooler in the humid conditions!

Departing St John's with fuel, we flew over English Harbour where James Ketchell had landed after rowing across the Atlantic. We overflew Guadeloupe and passed Dominica, Martinique and St Lucia, heading directly for Barbados. Flying south southwest almost eliminated the headwind component of the trade winds. We saw a lot of the brown weed called sargassum on the surface of the water. It's an environmental problem with warming sea temperature and fertiliser nitrate pollution making it a growing menace. On a beach, it's a smelly nightmare to clean up.

We were delayed and messed about by an obsessive

Bradley Adams Airport controller during our approach to Bridgetown. In our defence, one of the commercial jet pilots asked of the controller why all the drama, especially if 'the helicopter' was VFR, low and clear of the active runway! But finally, we were on the ground on 'island time', amongst the delightful Barbadian folks with their wonderful accents and infectious personalities. As Robin and I prepared for the next day to enter Guyana, we enjoyed the mix of our dilapidated accommodation and gregarious hosts in their holiday atmosphere, eating great sea food while listening to the crashing waves.

Our departure for Guyana was seamless by contrast with our arrival into Bridgetown. We elected to fly direct at 6,000 feet for better visibility and cooler temperatures but we had to dodge the bigger CB cloud stacks. With about 100 nautical miles left, we were forced to descend below the thickening cloud base. Here, it was much hotter and more humid with a very hazy horizon comprising mist, cloud and light rain from time to time; perhaps not surprising for our latitude of 7° north. Soon, we were flying over the greener and muddier waters emanating from the enormous estuary of the Rio Essequibo. We coasted into South America, crossing the Demerara River into Georgetown and landed at Ogle Airport. We thought we were leaving the Caribbean behind, but Guyana felt like, sounded like and thought of itself as part of the Caribbean islands.

Peter Ferreira from *Air Services* was expecting us. He introduced us to the pilot, Akeem Stoll, who would guide us into the jungle. We also met the owner of *Air Services* and the President of the *Guyana Marine Conservation Society*, Annette Arjoon-Martins. We discussed her conservation work while she kindly dropped us at our hotel. Robin and

I were now on the most biodiverse continent in the world with over two million plant and animal species.

Dane Gobin, the CEO of *Iwokrama International Centre*, an organisation for rainforest conservation and development, picked us up for dinner at 6pm in a Toyota Land Cruiser. Granted, it was already a big vehicle, but the doors felt incredibly heavy on the slight slope and the glass was really thick; it was a five-tonne, armour-plated car with diplomatic plates. I'd never seen one before and Dane explained that he just felt safe in it! Over a tasty vegetarian meal, we discussed Guyana, its new-found oil wealth and sustainable development issues, including the forest, conservation, climate change, as well as the connecting road to Brazil and Iwokrama – our reason for being here. *Iwokrama International Centre* manages the forest in central Guyana, showing how tropical forests can be conserved and used sustainably for ecological, social and economic benefits to communities. Then Dane showed us Georgetown at night while driving us back to our hotel.

We used Thursday to prepare for spending three nights at Iwokrama River Lodge before returning to Georgetown, to fly to Suriname on the Monday. Back at *Air Services*, Akeem helped me finalise routes, coordinates and fuel calculations, giving him what he needed for filing the necessary paperwork for our jungle flying. Robin and I reconfigured DIGA to carry three people, storing all of our cold weather equipment, then I emailed Eddie our local schedule of flights.

Akeem took us to meet the Director of Aviation Safety at the Guyana *CAA* offices in town. Captain Christopher Kirkcaldy needed to brief us, check me out and meet Akeem. I had been corresponding with him to get my 'conditional permission' to fly into the jungle. That settled, Akeem dropped us at the *Iwokrama* offices where we met Carol Ann and Raquel. Raquel described the *Iwokrama* story and Carol Ann kindly organised our itinerary with the Iwokrama River Lodge manager.

We were ready for our flight into the jungle the following day and free to attend to our end of day regime using the hotel Wi-Fi. Akeem was excited to be joining us on our trip and we wanted to involve him as a team member. We chose dinner at our hotel, which catered for the diverse cultural mix of Guyana, with a huge range of mouth-watering offerings.

We lifted first thing in light rain for a 90-minute flight, low-level, directly across the forest canopy over the rolling hills south southwest. Leaving the environs of Georgetown, we were soon over pristine, steaming forest, which was a first for me: nowhere to land! The lodge was perched on the Essequibo River in a beautiful setting and we flew over the Fairview village runway and circled to take pictures before landing.

Mike, the manager of the lodge, introduced us to the eco-lodge and its conservation and research activities, also describing the sustainable logging activities. He was frank about needing higher occupancy and the practical issues faced by poor, local people earning money for the first time: do you 'spend or invest'? We agreed that even governments didn't get that right – just look at the different approach the UK and Norway had taken to their oil dividend.

Our guide, Tichie, was approachable and knowledgeable and we were like sponges learning from him on our excursions. After settling into our accommodation, the one-hour road trip to our canopy walk was an exciting drive down part of the red, muddy dirt road carved through the forest from Georgetown to the Brazilian border, which continued to Manaus. On our walk, we saw notable trees including the bullet tree (which produces latex); iconic birds including red-billed toucans, red and green macaws and scarlet macaws; and interesting animals, including bullet and leaf cutter ants. We noticed that all the forest trees had some plant exploiting them to climb up to reach the light. The undergrowth was dense and damp when we walked through it.

We enjoyed the wildlife awakening and the cool of the early morning on our boat trip up the Essequibo River to hike up Turtle Mountain. The resident black caiman glided chillingly easily through the water! The forest was full of life, but not all laid out in front of us like the African savannah. Here, we had to wait, listen and look intently. Tichie was an excellent guide, adding capuchin and spider monkeys and a channel-billed toucan to our list of sightings. He also pointed out a boba palm tree, which can 'walk' its root-like legs over time to move slowly to get better light. Wow! While the words 'forest' and 'jungle' are used interchangeably, there is an essential difference: 'jungle' is impenetrable sections of a whole 'forest'.

After lunch, we met with Mike's rangers, local people developed and trained by *Iwokrama*. Rangers use their traditional knowledge of the forest and their contacts to work with and facilitate the scientific researchers. They patrol the park and carry out baseline measurements throughout the year that support the independent audits validating *Iwokrama's* eco credentials. Akeem and I prepared DIGA to take some staff and rangers for a quick flight from our lodge. We had offered Mike and Tichie this opportunity the previous day and they both bit my arm off! I flew, Akeem marshalled professionally, and Robin was on the ground to capture the emotions before and after. The whole place got involved and let's just say, they were *very* excited!

The head teacher from the local school came to say hello and we organised a surprise for his pupils the next day. At 4pm, Tichie boated us up to the rapids near the ferry crossing of the Essequibo River to look at rock carvings, thought to be thousands of years old. Ashore, Akeem finally got to play with our drone against a backdrop of vultures, flocks of green parrots and local kids swimming enthusiastically in the rapids.

On Sunday morning, we said goodbye to our fabulous hosts, lifted, circled and hopped over to Fairview runway, which was essentially just a dirt track. We approached the school pupils and their families waiting behind the fence, hovered for them and then landed to exchange simple gifts. It was beautiful to see their smiling faces. Then we set course southwest towards Annai, picking our way through the hills under the low clouds until we could see the natural transition from forest to savannah, while Akeem enjoyed a bit of R66 flying.

We circled the football field and landed. The helicopter attracted attention and soon we were surrounded by the village leaders and their families. They said that they felt blessed but crikey, we felt humbled! All the people we met were from the Mucushi tribe, living in Wowetta village, a total of 410 people. Robin captured pictures, Akeem looked after DIGA and pretty much every child wanted to sit in her for a photograph. I was invited over to the newly-built Benab, which was a traditional, round building used for public meetings. We enjoyed a good discussion on every subject, from carbon offsets to tourism and football. They were articulate, matching their traditional knowledge with science, and confident of their community representation at government and with Guyana's policy on sustainable development. They benefited directly with money received for using the forest sustainably and indirectly through the training and experience they gained, an invaluable asset. Three of the leaders were previously Iwokrama rangers. Developing tourism was their priority and I found these discussions humbling.

We set off north from Wowetta back across the forest, with Akeem guiding us to Mahdia to refuel. We saw nothing but forest, low cloud and the scars of gold mining by small miners who had created nasty erosion using mercury, which poisons the ground. From Mahdia, we detoured west, climbing up to 2,000 feet to Kaieteur Falls, flying down the river out over the lip of these spectacular falls and down the gorge now northwest, directly back to Ogle Airport. The industrial-scale gold mining scars showed destruction and pollution on an horrific scale.

We said our farewells to Akeem and readied DIGA for the following day. Our taster in the forests of Guyana had opened our eyes on so many levels and prepared us for getting the best out of the forest to come. We pounded the hotel Wi-Fi, uploading pictures, posting on social media and preparing for the few days ahead.

Even with the help of *Air Services*, the formalities for leaving Guyana took two hours. Looking at the normal weather build up by lunchtimes, I resolved to start early in the mornings through the Amazon. We flew coastwise to the small country of Suriname. It was pancake-flat with rice paddies (we think) almost all the way, with small strings of tin-roofed houses. The shore was muddy, tidal and flat, and the sea was brown from the water emanating from all the rivers.

Soon we were inbound to a tiny, little runway of Zorg en Hoop Airport in the middle of Paramaribo. Stuart, Zael and Vishaal from *Pegasus* met us at Customs and Jerome welcomed us when we repositioned to *Pegasus*. I had corresponded with Jerome and Vishaal over the previous months when Suriname had potentially been my shipping and rebuild point for DIGA. So, it was satisfying to finally meet them. They fuelled, hangared and cleaned DIGA.

Robin and I made time to meet Andy Bijkerk of *MAF* at his hangar. Keith Ketchum of *MAF* had introduced us and Andy had kindly offered to be our host. Andy explained that there were three pilots who flew doctors out to clinics and brought people into the hospitals. *MAF* had been very helpful to me on all three of my journeys. Back at *Pegasus*, Jo-Ann kindly helped me with flight planning and general declarations for the two flights the next day, before we retired to our hotel at about 4pm.

It rained hard during the night and the persistent rain still greeted us in the morning. As Stuart drove us into *Pegasus* early, we joked about the local published weather reports, which couldn't be right! Fortunately, DIGA was in the *Pegasus* hangar. I delayed both flight plans on *Rocket Route* by one hour, until it became obvious that we should again delay Paramaribo to Cayenne by another hour and cancel the Cayenne to Macapá routing altogether.

We tucked into the box breakfasts that our hotel had provided and drank more coffee as others arrived for work. By 9:30am, it was obvious that we weren't going anywhere. The following day looked better, so I cancelled the final flight plan. Eddie and *G.A.S.E.* took over to delay logistics by one day ahead. I was just hoping that the weather wasn't going to be impassable like this in the Amazon.

Pegasus, and indeed Suriname, was a very friendly place. The language was Dutch and English, which took me back to my Afrikaans school days. We were enjoying good company, even if it meant a shortened stay at the Uakari Floating Lodge in Tefé. By 12:30pm, the runway edges were like a swimming pool. Robin sorted a Facebook post and I had my own administration to do, so we spent the afternoon at our hotel, ready for a rerun the next day.

With Stuart's help, we bade *Pegasus* farewell and took off at 7:30am, crossing the Suriname River direct for Cayenne in French Guiana. We were soon over forest with little sign of people and flew a 'sandwich flight' between mist over the forest rising to 300 feet and overcast cloud above us at about 1,500 feet above mean sea level. While the horizon always looked like the mist was meeting the clouds, the sun shining through in places gave me confidence that the route was passable. We were about 20 nautical miles inland.

As we crossed the border at the Maroni River and changed to Cayenne control, low cloud began to appear, and marginal VFR conditions developed with intermittent shafts of sunlight and the forest directly below. We passed north of the Petit-Saut Lake on the Sinnamary River, taking pictures of the dam. More substantial cumulous clouds were gathering and, on our approach to Cayenne, we had to avoid rain and could see menacing CBs approaching the airport.

French military helicopters were doing circuits as we landed on the apron. I took shelter in the fuel truck as the heavens opened for 15 minutes before DIGA could be refuelled. Our handler, Patrick, welcomed us in French and we dealt with the formalities in his office in Euros and with good Internet.

We assessed the weather and Eddie offered local hotel options. I didn't want to fly over impenetrable forest with cumulous storms. Macapá was VFR but *Windy* suggested that the first third of the journey would be dodging clouds. I decided to fly as I could follow the coast if I had to.

We climbed higher and higher out of Cayenne over the low cloud, flying in between the much taller CBs, VFR on top. At one stage, the auto pilot dropped out because I'd let our speed drop below the minimum limit in a steep climb. We were over the jungle, talking to Cayenne and then no-one. Eventually we were through the cumulous weather and under a stable cloud base at 2,000 feet with improving visibility, as forecast.

Crossing the River Oiapoque, which marks the French Guiana–Brazil border, we were over a beautiful, swamp landscape with many shades of green and few people. Forested sections represented higher ground and we could see burnt patches within the forest. With the weather improving, we descended and with 1½ hours to go, we turned south direct to Macapá and made up some time. It was now 25°C and very humid. We could see dirt roads and small groups of houses with much more evidence of deforestation by individuals to crop inefficiently on small plots. About 60 nautical miles north of Macapá, we saw our first tarmac road and below us, the purpose of deforestation was to plant trees for making paper. It was all new to us and we had loads of questions.

Finally, we were rewarded with a view of the north channel of the mighty Amazon River. Wow: DIGA had travelled!

Half of Macapá was in the Northern Hemisphere and the following day we would be in the Southern Hemisphere, staying there for most of our journey. We had gone from English-speaking to Dutch to French. Brazil would be Portuguese-speaking, before Spanish all the way home.

Macapá was a biggish airport but relatively quiet. We landed away on an empty apron and were greeted by a friendly pilot, Roger. He provided translation for our handler and a string of other officials and a fueller. There were the usual Immigration and Customs formalities which included an interview with the police, all conducted at the airport. The friendly policeman was amazed at our intended routing up the Amazon to Tabatinga via Santarém and Manaus, and he gave us tourist tips.

Our entry into Brazil required the completion of a temporary import/export document linked electronically to our permit (the AVANAC number, which Ahmed had arranged). Our handler accompanied us to get this temporary document at the *Recita Federales* offices in town where the local office staff translated, in return for stories of our *TJR* adventure! We were just in time to pick up the paperwork before they closed at 6pm and, while all the bureaucracy seemed ridiculous, we couldn't file the flight plans without it.

We taxied back to our hotel on the river side and popped out to catch the sunset and take a few pictures of the mighty Amazon River, before eating at a rather spartan, riverside restaurant. Back at the hotel, we had a lot to do as a result of our double hop and many experiences.

We were up at 5:30am for our usual morning regime, including exercise. At the airport, our handler was now also using Google Translate and Roger was kindly on hand again to translate and explain. Roger phoned in our flight plan to Santarém and I quickly learnt more about the Brazilian system. Normally foreign aircraft must file by telephone in Portuguese (oh yes!); locals all use the military system for filing plans; foreign aircraft may only file to English-speaking airports; one had 45 minutes grace to get airborne; or 30 minutes grace to delay it! Practically, this meant that we were 'flying the administration' before even thinking about flying the challenging diurnal weather of the Amazon. The system frustrated local pilots just as much as it would us. I would need to make a pilot or *ATC* friend for each flight plan, which was going to be fun!

We took off at 8:30am to fly south southwest across the forest, north of the river to meet it at Almeirim and then fly direct to Santarém over the meandering Amazon. Leaving Macapá, the many joining waterways were home to individual houses on stilts at the water's edge, accessed only by boat. To reach Almeirim, we had to climb to 3,200 feet above a carpet of cloud, with only brief glimpses of the lush, green forest or wetland below and river to our left.

Crossing the Rio Jari marked our passage from Amapá state to Pará state and the clouds dissipated at 1,500 feet. We descended below to boundless views of the forest and the converging Amazon River. Almeirim was a small town with a reddish, dirt track airport, individual houses on the tributaries, power lines, deforestation and plantation trees, again for paper production. This part of the Amazon was colossal with big tankers and container ships navigating its muddy brown waters and, apart from a few 500-feet high ridge hills, the topography was flat to the horizon. We started to see domesticated animals: small herds of Indo-Brazilian white cattle and a zebu breed developed in Brall from Gir, Kankrej and Ongole cattle. We also saw white birds (possibly egrets or herons) at ground level and soaring vultures – a potential hazard!

The land between the streams and to the side of the river was extremely flat and green, with occasional remote, waterfront, stilted houses, which we guessed probably had no running water or electricity. It was very pretty from our viewpoint in DIGA. The scene continued to unfold, and the clouds burnt off to be replaced in the distance by cumulous build-up and distant rain. We passed south of Monte Alegre, still flying above the Amazon River. Approaching Santarém, housing, farming and land clearing became more marked. We saw the beginning of the crystal-clear water of the Tapajos River, which joined the Amazon from the southwest. The two rivers don't actually mix for many miles.

On landing in Santarém, we were welcomed by our handler and Alexander, who translated for us. After *WFS* refuelling, we secured DIGA against the inevitable rain later. It was a 30-minute taxi ride to our hotel in the city with a population of about 300,000. With good hotel room electrics and Wi-Fi, we polished off our photograph upload for Eddie, in time to walk around from about 5:30pm getting pictures of the Tapajos River. Santarém was bustling and full of small shops bursting onto the pavements, which themselves had big drop-offs to smelly, street-side culverts. We ate at an open-air restaurant overlooking the river and left before the evening's dancing started. Armed with bottles of fresh water, I completed my diary and flight plan, while Robin wrote her Facebook post. I now had my MKI eyeball calibrated for looking at the weather that *Windy* was forecasting and I was keeping a regular watch.

We heard rain for most of the night and headed back

to the airport by 7:30am to go through formalities and monitor the weather. *Windy* confirmed that a big weather cell had passed over and was heading towards Manaus and falling away to the south during the day. I used the delay to communicate with *G.A.S.E.* about Bolivia and with Lavinia about Peru. We were still just one day behind our proposed arrival in Tefé, where we had planned to stay for four nights. Even now, I decided to pinch more days from Tefé's itinerary to deploy later and ensure that we could leave Brazil on a weekday because it was important to keep to my commitments in Peru.

Anderson from *ATC* happily assisted with my flight plan in English and explained the specific way the 'route' should be defined. He understood my challenge and said that we *could* fly low-level along the Amazon River if we had to. The weather in Santarém and Manaus was improving. We lifted at 11am, flying westwards immediately over the Tapajos River with its lovely white, sandy beaches and then low over a forest section, monitoring Amazonica control. We saw signs of deforestation which we now knew was usually to steal the wood. When the police came, the culprits apparently burnt everything. About 100 nautical miles west of Santarém, we saw the Amazon River to our right as we converged with its huge, winding veins and crossed into the state of Amazonas.

There were sporadic towns and settlements along the Amazon, with surprisingly good 4G connectivity. There was more human activity on the northern side of the river with a road network emanating from Manaus. It was 24°C and humid, which was bearable with all the vents open but immediately oppressive with the vents closed against the occasional rain showers. Ahead, we were reassured to see the dark weather cell moving off to our left (to the south). We had a good tailwind component and the weather at DIGA remained reasonable, while to the north, there was the familiar build-up of isolated CBs that we could avoid.

It was a beautiful panorama: loads of very green wetlands, muddy brown water everywhere, more white birds below and vultures around, 'waterfront housing' and white cattle with their tracks criss-crossing the greenery. Manaus Approach, based at Edwardo Gomes International Airport, controlled us into the small, non-radio airport called Flores, situated right in the city and giving us great views all around. With a population of about three million, Manaus is located on the north bank of the Rio Negro, which merges with the Solimões (Upper Amazon to the border with Peru), to form the Amazon River. Once again, due to differences in temperature, speed and density, these two rivers flowed side by side before merging.

We landed outside the aviation training institute in Manaus, *Aeroclub do Amazonas*, and then the fun began. After a search, I located Heitor of *Pioneiro, BR Aviation* who explained that *WFS* didn't supply here or at Tefé, but that he could provide fuel, and on my credit card too! He also confirmed fuel availability at Tabatinga. Heitor spoke great English and introduced us to Agusto and Saulo, two commercial pilots flying all around the reddish dirt strip airports. They were delighted to help! Heitor provided the coffee, Saulo chatted with Robin and Agusto took me through the flight plan preparation to both Tefé and Tabitinga. He then phoned them in for me and I gleaned more about the local flying conditions. We exchanged contact details and since Augusto had DIGA's details, he insisted that I should call him any time for delaying, renewing or filing new flight plans. He was a gentleman true to his word.

We secured DIGA then met Hélio, the Superintendente of the *Aeroclube do Amazonas*, while paying our landing fee. There, Cassiano overheard us talking and kindly drove us to our hotel. We discovered that he was Portuguese, had been a conscripted soldier in Mozambique and had lived in Brazil for the last 30 years, working for Honda in Manaus. Finally, we were having dinner in time to sort out our evening regime, while watching the weather on *Windy*.

Our flight the following day depended on us leaving Flores (Manaus) as soon as the weather improved enough to get the best en route conditions and arrive at Tefé before the CBs took hold there. With Augusto helping administratively, we took off from the *Aeroclube do Amazonas* in light rain over Manaus at 1,000 feet.

As the Rio Solimões flowed majestically, we again enjoyed our routing over forest, wetland and endless tributaries which fed the Amazon. Mist rising from the recently soaked forest looked like plumes of smoke rising from fires. We struggled through about 30 minutes of rain in marginal VFR conditions while sweating with the vents closed. When it cleared, we could see the now-familiar isolated CBs building ahead. We were gifted views of more beautiful forest and river panoramas and additional evidence of deforestation by individuals who seemed to have electricity pylons running to their deforested plots.

We were the only ones at Tefé but Heitor's fuel was available quickly. We were soon through to the cool shade of the airport hall. After a few anxious minutes waiting, Carol, from the Floating Uakari Lodge arrived, smiling. It was Saturday and she had kindly organised our water transport that day and back the following afternoon, with a hotel for our Monday morning departure to Tabatinga.

The Uakari Floating Lodge was managed by the communities from the *Mamirauá Sustainable Development Reserve* and *Institute*. *Mamirauá* is the biggest protected, flooded forest in the world and situated in the *Central Amazon Conservation Complex* (a *UNESCO* World Heritage Site), which itself is part of the *Amazon Biosphere Reserve*. Carol explained that only 4% of Brazilian Amazon consists of freshwater swamp forest and that the *Mamirauá Reserve* plays an important role to protect this ecosystem. The white Uakari monkey, with its brilliant red face, lives only here, and *Mamirauá* was created to protect its home range.

Our boat ride was fast and we initially passed all the floating Tefé services for the river such as fuel stations, food stops and even houses. Then we were whizzing up one of the smaller tributaries seeing the stilted riverside houses close-up and dodging the forest debris, including logs floating downstream. After an hour, we arrived at the Uakari Floating Lodge to a warm greeting and orientation before taking a guided canoe ride, paddling along the edge of the river. We saw many bird species, cruising caimans, squirrel monkeys and we heard howler monkeys in the jungle, but no sloths yet! Then it was back for a lovely dinner before a short night walk. It was really hot and sticky but we went to sleep in our floating lodge behind our mosquito-screened, open windows, totally immersed in the sound of the forest and river surrounding us.

The rain at night made a pleasing sound and we woke to the noises of the forest. We were educated with traditional Brazilian food for breakfast, eating all together with the other guests and hosting staff. When I came to pay, my credit card seemed to be blocked: this was possibly one unusual place too far for Barclaycard! I needed to call them but that would have to wait for 4G reception.

We boated to a forest walk the next morning. We learnt that the whole area would get another six metres of water from a mixture of rains and then the snow melt of the Andes. This annual flooding made this a special biome. We could see the high-water mark on all the trees way above our heads. Underfoot there was spongy, muddy leaf matter and the damp, buttressed roots and gnarled, hanging roots made for creepy scenes. Bird and bug song thronged above us in the trees. Macaws, parrots, toucans, capuchin and squirrel monkeys, a very pretty bird called a cigana and woodpeckers all delighted us, as did grey dolphins in the water. Unfortunately, there was no sighting of the rare uakari monkey. Bizarrely, a couple of the trees sounded like they were sucking up water, a bit like a bubbling brook but with no obvious water flow.

We said goodbye to our Uakari hosts and guides before our late afternoon return boat. About 500 metres from the Tefé dock, the motor conked out! I had cell coverage, so I called Barclaycard while it was quiet, but the replacement boat arrived so fast that I found myself climbing from one bobbing boat to another on the Amazon River, while trying to continue my conversation, against the new boat's engine noise! Luckily it all turned out well and we spent a pleasant evening back at our hotel.

We had breakfast at the tenth-floor restaurant and could see all the vultures which had taken up their city-cleaning positions. Again, we were the only people at the airport and the approachable *ATC* folks organised our flight plan and were happy for us to route over Uakari to get our aerial photographs.

We had a long flight following the river westwards to the tri-border town of Tabatinga, which had a road border with Colombia and a river border with Peru. At Tabatinga, we were 700 nautical miles from the Pacific. Robin and I had come a long way west just below the Equator, almost 1,400 nautical miles from the Atlantic, into the world's largest tropical rainforest. So far, we had been very lucky with the weather!

This flight was under an overcast sky with a base of about 1,200 feet and we flew low again all the way, above the familiar scenes, eating our apples and sipping our hydration tabulated water. Rivers were definitely the arteries of life out here, but it was getting more remote now and we were often flying for miles over nothing but pristine forest. We saw more palm tree-like forest in wetter areas and could often make out pairs of macaws in flight. Our windscreen had collected a lot of biodiversity and we photographed the gradations of generations of oxbow lakes as the river moved and the forest reclaimed the soil. But sadly, every river and every road brought access and deforestation; even out here, Eddie was able to Facebook message me intermittently.

Respecting Peruvian and Colombian airspace, we landed at Tabatinga International Airport; it was small and we secured DIGA quickly. The English-speaking *ATC* helped post our flight plan for 9am the next day to get us away to Rio Branco before the forecast mid-afternoon thunderstorm activity. An airport employee whose shift was ending offered us a lift to the Takana Hotel, which Eddie had booked for us. It had some Wi-Fi bandwidth and intermittent electrical power but otherwise, it was agreeable accommodation. The hotel was colourfully painted and decorated with animal carvings and ethnic items from the indigenous Takana people. Service was typically Portuguese: all smiles but very leisurely!

We immediately tackled our normal regime, adding laundry into the mix. Revisiting the weather forecast regularly, it seemed prudent to take off at 7am, which meant an early start, setting our phone alarms for 4:45am.

It had been another great day flying the Amazon River but I was looking forward to reaching Peru and our rendezvous with hosts *Inkaterra* and my family for Christmas. We had time for a quick walk around the block in the dark with motorbikes bumping their way down the dirt tracks! Taking our lives in our hands, we crossed the main 'dual carriageway,' heaving with motorbikes and three-wheeler traffic, to nose around the shops and see what brands and substitutes there were. The place was bustling with people doing their evening shopping. Then we ate as early as we could at the hotel before getting to bed.

It rained very heavily during the night, hammering the tin roof and splashing loudly on the pavements. Up at 4:45am, my weather assessment showed that a huge cell passing slowly over Tabatinga northeast to southwest would join up with the predicted rain everywhere from about lunchtime. I decided it was a no-fly day and popped down to let the hotel know that we would be staying another night, only to find the 24/7 reception abandoned! I went back at 5:45am to cancel the taxi: still abandoned. Reception rang at 6:45am to see if we wanted our taxi when I discovered the correct local time – the state of Amazonas had changed local time by an hour without promulgating that to the world. Oh well, one less mistake for us to make the following day *and* we had time to ask Augusto to delay our flight plan and still be the first at breakfast!

Breakfast was a popular local attraction and the restaurant was full of businesspeople, families and also a table of policemen. I messaged Ahmed who was having no luck in locating a local handler in Rio Branco to help us reverse out of the temporary import/export document and close down our AVANAC number. We had been told it was important to do this electronically because we wanted to re-enter Brazil from Bolivia in January. We decided to play it by ear in Rio Branco!

Robin spent time on our social media whilst I sorted our administration and of course, we watched the weather. We were prepared for an early start on Wednesday 19th December. I really needed to get out of Rio Branco to Peru on the Friday. No panic just yet. I updated *Inkaterra* who would be hosting us in Peru. Our flight the next day would be the longest flight in the Amazon yet, leaving the main rivers and cutting across the forest. Towards Rio Branco, we were likely to see more roads and development in the forest.

Reception gave me directions to the Colombian border and a safe restaurant. At 5:30pm, when it was cooler and dry, we walked 15 minutes down the kamikaze dual carriageway absorbing the fumes, smells and sights, then we crossed the open border with Colombia. The businesses seemed more industrial than the colourful mix of schools, shops, stalls and restaurants on the Brazilian side. We walked back to the tiny, local São Jorge restaurant and bagged the table next to the big fan, while people watching the dual carriageway and drinking a beer. As the sun set, the traffic and street life increased with various eateries coming alive with entertainment. Our meal of chicken pieces, rice and vegetables was delicious, fast and great value at 11 USD for everything, including the tip.

We arrived at Tabatinga Airport *ATC* at 7am, just as it started to rain persistently again. Cheyenne, the meteorologist, and one *ATC* officer, both charming, gave us access to all the forecasts and flight planning assistance that we needed in their broken English.

On the apron, there was a military *SAR* Blackhawk helicopter. It had rescued the pilot of a downed aeroplane who had taken off from Eirunepé and crashed in the forest four days ago! The Blackhawk pilots joined us in *ATC's* air-conditioned offices while others packed their gear into the helicopter. They were checking forecasts, like us, and hoping to get back to Tefé but the sky was bursting and the rain came and went. Captain Lucas had 800 Amazon flying hours and he planned for 120 knots over the ground and usually flew VFR like us. This was rainforest and so the weather had to be perfect.

Cheyenne popped outside with her umbrella to make observations for her hourly airport weather report. We both delayed our flight plans again and by lunchtime, everybody agreed to call time. Cheyenne's mum kindly gave us a lift back to the Takana Hotel. The forecast looked better for the next day and since we'd missed breakfast and lunch, we ate mid-afternoon at the São Jorge, people watching again. Back online later, Claudio Hirsch, from the *National Park Foundation of Argentina*, had emailed me the brilliant news that our permit to fly DIGA in the national parks of Argentina had finally been signed. I was grateful for his assistance however, right now, we needed two days of good weather!

In the morning we had a good breakfast, arriving by 7:30am at *ATC* and in good time to prepare for our 9am departures, alongside the Blackhawk team, who helped us with the translations. We both had a morning weather window before the inevitable heavy rain later and we would certainly see the typical isolated, towering CBs building and joining up as we arrived in Rio Branco around lunchtime. However, compared with Calabar, Nigeria and then Douala, Cameroon, we had only lost two days to rain delay in the Amazon, so we were lucky.

Just as we were ready to leave, we were informed of the requirement to present ourselves at the police station in town first. Frustratingly, we could have done this any time. So back and forth we taxied, luckily without any delays, in time to wave to the Blackhawk already taking off. With bills paid, hands shaken, selfies taken and a warm goodbye from our *ATC* friends, I pressed the start button; my heart sank as DIGA failed to start. Calmly and patiently retrying, the turbine burst into life on my fourth attempt, activating our flight plan just in time. Neither David Cross, myself or Rolls-Royce had any idea why this happened.

We flew low at about 500 feet over the canopy under a low cloud base. Bruno Martins had suggested the safest route over three points of civilisation. But with the tailwind and good visibility, I opted for south southwest, direct across the pristine forest, to make up time. We traversed numerous squiggly, muddy rivers including huge tributaries making their thousand-mile plus journeys to Tefé and Manaus. Eddie watched our progress and supplied a smorgasbord of geographical information.

We sweated with the vents closed during light rain and avoided the huge, isolated, towering CBs, which we could see raining for miles around the flat, undulating landscape. We enjoyed the variety and detail of the trees and vines from our low altitude. Robin and I knew what was down there from our Iwokrama and Uakari forest walks. Beautiful macaw pairs and vultures also made their way across the forest and we photographed the overgrown oxbow lake features again.

Crossing into Acre State and approaching the Rio Branco (400,000 population), we witnessed man's deforesting activities, a proliferation of settlements, dirt roads, cattle grazing and finally suburbs. Our approach was delayed, avoiding a CB unloading at the airport and after landing, another menacing, towering CB deluged the airport apron with cupful-sized drops. DIGA was a lone, red spectacle at the edge of the apron against the green forest and biblical sky. Finally, fuelled and secure, the crew of another *SAR* Blackhawk came over to DIGA. 1st Lieutenant Tales Pimenta spoke English with an American accent. The guys wanted to see an R66 and in return, they kindly showed me around their impressive machine. They had rejected flying due to the weather and were heading for a stopover too.

Robin and I located necessary airport officers to talk to and Tales approached, offering to translate. Apparently, we needed to go to the *Recita Federales* in town the following day (Friday 21st December), which was only open between 8am and 1pm, to get the temporary import/export document stamped for exit and the AVANAC permit closed electronically. This airport wasn't a standard point of exit for general aviation flights and we needed to apply retrospectively (normally done 48 hours in advance) and then just hope! This information wasn't obvious at the time of my logistics planning in the UK. Additionally, Rio Branco was only open for international flights from 7am until 12pm. Then of course, we would still need to file our flight plan by telephone in Portuguese, settle payments, pass by the police and so on. Basically, we just had to fly the administration and hope Mother Nature would provide the specific weather window that we needed.

We exchanged a Brazil *SAR* badge for a couple of *TJR* pins and left with Tales' best wishes and phone number, before taxi-ing the nine miles into the city. Our hotel was modern and with breakfast starting at 6am, we'd be well fuelled for the challenge. We polished off our evening regime and I updated my *Inkaterra* contact who was meeting us in Puerto Maldonado the next day.

17

Llanos de Moxos

In the morning, we door stepped the *Recita Federales* office and found two Customs officers. Using Google Translate, we pleaded to use the best weather that day so that we could see our family at Christmas, and they found a way to help. We thanked another friendly man in the street who ordered us an Uber back to the airport where the Wi-Fi actually accepted my *Rocket Route* flight plan. It took all of two hours, but we were processed and airborne by 10:45am.

The forest and squiggly river panorama were familiar but the scale of deforestation for grazing the white Indo-Brazilian cattle breed was shocking. It was lush and green-looking but not pristine. We flew over a huge, new road-making initiative carved out of the forest. The CBs were building but the weather held for our short flight southwest across a section of Bolivia and into Peru.

Soon we were talking to Puerto Maldonado tower, traversing the winding Madre de Dios River. *WFS* fuel was delivered from ground tanks, then we covered DIGA and went through Immigration and Customs, to be greeted by the delightful *Inkaterra* hosts who were waiting patiently. We were now in control of catching our commercial flight to Cusco to see the high Andes and spend a brief Christmas with my family, climbing Machu Picchu. Success and relief in equal measure!

Two Rotors: One Planet

Sandra chatted to us about how *Inkaterra* had been pioneering ecotourism and sustainable development in Peru since 1975. Soon, she had us riding a longboat 15 kilometres on the Madre de Dios River to the Reserve Amazonica for our first night's stay. It absolutely poured with rain on the journey. We would next have cell or Wi-Fi when passing through Puerto Maldonado on Sunday 23rd December.

The Reserve Amazonica was a wonderful *Inkaterra* experience in one of the world's most remote and extraordinary tropical environments. The Peruvian menu was magnificent, and our perimeter walk revealed a small group of sleeping monkeys, a family of agoutis (giant, lovable rodents) and my first sighting of a sloth, albeit a dot high up in a tree! We completed our evening regime and captured some sunset pictures before a night boat ride. Our guides were authentic, friendly and enlightening.

Our accommodation was designed perfectly to immerse us in the night chorus of critters and the dawn chorus of birds. It was Mother Nature at her most breathtaking. The following day, we took a boat ride to hike the trail to Lake Sandoval, an old oxbow lake. The trail was muddy from the rain and the forest particularly humid. We saw saddleback tamarin and squirrel monkeys, as well as brown cappuchin monkeys, considered intelligent because they use tools.

Then we paddled canoes into Lake Sandoval, down a forest channel, spotting the family of eight, nearly extinct, giant river otters who were all squealing and barking as they caught and ate fish whilst lounging on their backs. This wetland ecosystem with its palm trees is the most CO_2-effective of all forest ecosystems. Robin and I had seen a lot of it from the air without realising. Lake Sandoval also contained piranhas and arapaimas, which are the largest freshwater fish with both gills and lungs to breathe in the low oxygenated water conditions. We could hear the loud, whooping call of howler monkeys in the distance again.

After lunch, we joined another boat ride in the heavy rain to take a canopy walk. High in the canopy, we could see the forest steaming but in terms of wildlife, unfortunately only a small toucan due to the adverse weather conditions. Then the boat took us to another *Inkaterra* property. We were welcomed at Hacienda Concepcion and enjoyed more superb service, great food and a nice evening of discussion with an Australian couple. We retired early to experience the evening's unstinting critter chorus.

The next day, we were off to Puerto Maldonado by boat with a bag of our warmer clothing. Apparently, the huge Golden Gate lookalike bridge was part of the international, transcontinental highway in Peru and Brazil, called the Trans-oceanic highway. We could see DIGA covered safely as we boarded our 40-minute commercial flight to Cusco (at 10,500 feet) where Lavinia, Hannah and Fraser were already waiting for us in the agreeable weather of the high Andes.

Our *Inkaterra* guide enthralled us with stories as our minivan drove to the 120-mile long by one-mile wide Sacred Valley and we visited Pisac. The steep-sided hills were all utilised and the sun glinting off tin roofs reminded me of the high western part of Rwanda as I flew from Goma. Along the road, the newer brick and concrete buildings with their terracotta-coloured, tiled roofs all looked a bit higgledy piggledy and unfinished. The 'terraced look' was part geology and part human terracing.

The Pisac Ruins were located high above the valley floor and the modern colonial town of Pisac and its ruins are considered to be one of the finest remaining Inca archeologic sites in Peru. The arrival of the Spanish Conquistadors saw the Inca population decimated from 11 to one million through wars and disease. Nonetheless, modern Peru, with a population of 31 million, is proud of this history and its ethnic social heritage is possibly the strongest in the South American continent. We were met with a warm welcome at *Inkaterra's* Hacienda Urubamba for an overnight stop.

Dressed in warmer clothing, another guide picked up the Inca story while driving us to Ollantaytambo to catch the train to Machu Picchu. The red, plastic flags signalled local, corn-based beer bars along our route! The train climbed high, initially following the Inca trail, which my daughter Hannah had previously walked. I was seated next to a 15,000-hour ex-US Army helicopter pilot and we juggled silent viewing of the iconic mountain scenery with pilot talk as we ascended to the cloud forest.

Once we were settled into *Inkaterra's* Machu Picchu Pueblo Hotel, we relaxed for the afternoon. As it was Christmas Eve, we appreciated Peruvian hospitality, music and food. A trio playing traditional pipes also rendered Hotel California and Smoke on the Water. Before dinner, we toasted a rich culture, good company and a perfect end to our 2018.

Christmas Day didn't feel like it at all! We were up early and off, gasping at the enormity of the granite geology of the mountains as we bussed to the entrance and started our climb of the 1,600 steps. Unfortunately, the mist stayed with us and our views from the top were limited but our tour around the ruins was fascinating. Built in the 15th century, Machu Picchu was used by the Incas as a refuge from the Spanish empire in the 16th century and the Spanish never actually saw it. It was inscribed as a *UNESCO* World Heritage Site in 1983.

We all travelled back to Cusco together. It had been a long, tiring day at high altitude. Robin and I were due to head back to Puerto Maldonado the following day while my family would continue their holiday.

We were dressed for Puerto Maldonado and freezing, as we waited at Cusco airport for our flight. From our Airbus A320, I had a different perspective on the weather that we normally flew below, which gave me confidence. Sandra from *Inkaterra* met us at the airport. She helpfully made the final arrangement telephone calls to the *Tambopata-Bahuaja* project folks for my 3pm visit. *Ecosphere+* had put me in touch with *Aider*, their delivery partner here.

Sandra also confirmed that Immigration and Customs were in the town and not open as it was Boxing Day, which meant door stepping them at 8am the next day, abandoning an early departure for our intended double hop in Bolivia. *G.A.S.E.* also confirmed another challenge: somehow my AVANAC number had not actually been shut down by the *Recita Federales* in Rio Branco and they were now on holiday. Robin and I then returned to the Hacienda Conception before I would have lunch, then dash back.

At 3pm on Boxing Day, I met Vanessa Hilares and Sandra Anccasi at their modest *Aider* office. Sandra from *Inkaterra* chaperoned and translated, although Sandra Anccasi spoke wonderful English anyway. Here, it was *Aider's* critical work that enabled local people to realise sustainable development in *Tambopata-Bahuaja*. It was important for me to understand the passion they had for their work with farmers on the drivers of deforestation and the application of carbon credits to protect the rainforest. The projections of deforestation due to gold mining were absolutely horrifying. Vanessa made a brilliant presentation and I expressed my sincere appreciation for a great discussion. Sandra and I said goodbye and caught a three-wheeler scooter taxi back to the port for my boat back to Hacienda Conception.

The dawn chorus triggered our morning regime and we were first in the queue at the Immigration offices at 8am, with Sandra representing our case politely. The airport insisted that I fly exactly the route stated on my permit, which I had experienced before in the DRC. My Peru permit said we were exiting southwest to Trinidad but Bolivia had asked us to kindly enter using Cobija on their northern border with Brazil, before proceeding to Trinidad. Ahmed immediately applied for a new permit, I gave Sandra 12 USD to pay into the airport's local bank account and we were finally airborne at 11:45am. However, the CBs were not isolated now and a complete blanket of rain forced us to land short of Cobija in an opportune forest clearing to wait it out.

Cobija couldn't have been more welcoming and an English-speaking pilot helped us turn around in only 45 minutes. With the weather actually improving to the southwest and a good tailwind, we could make Trinidad before sunset. There were still some monster isolated CBs about but none that would affect us.

Initially, the landscape was flat and forested with pockets of development and cattle farming. We knew that more palm trees meant it was wetter underfoot. Crossing the Rio Madidi, we were treated to a vista of much bigger, grassy flood plains. This scenery reminded me a lot of the Okavango delta in Botswana, except the animals here were domesticated cows. Eddie communicated that we were over the tropical savannah ecoregion of northern Bolivia called the Llanos de Moxos, with extensive remains of pre-Colombian agricultural society spread all over it. We descended to 450 feet, seeing grassy wetland with cow tracks for miles, punctuated by little outcrops of trees and lakes or small rivers. It was unquestionably the most beautiful wetland I have ever seen.

At Trinidad, we were greeted warmly by an official called Herlan who chatted while examining all my documents. After fuelling and securing DIGA, he helped us to a taxi and promised to assist in the morning. At our modest hotel, we sorted ourselves out, communicated with *G.A.S.E.* and slept soundly.

The next day, we were headed to Santa Cruz, a big city of 2.6 million people. We'd have a tailwind for this short flight but it would be sporty flying with 18 gusting 30 knots. Santa Cruz was Instrument Meteorological Conditions with the weather forecast to improve for our arrival. Herlan kindly walked me through all the airport departments and we took off in the sunshine, excited to reacquaint ourselves with the Moxos Plains and get some more photographs.

The mixture of wetlands, little water courses, lakes, clumps of palm trees and forest unfolded below us in an infinite variety of greens, some with the shadow of a cloud and others with the sun shining through. It was as flat as a pancake and the variety of textures and colours were so beautiful. There were occasional cattle farms with associated, isolated buildings. The Moxos Plains stretched nearly all the way to Santa Cruz and we were flying low above ground level, climbing steadily as the ground did. As we approached Santa Cruz, roads, vehicles and farms were interspersed with the remaining patches of forest.

Landing at Santa Cruz, we could see the big, skyscrapered city about eight miles away. The general aviation apron was a long way from the large international terminal but Saulo, working for the airport, handled us efficiently. I told him that we planned to fly back into Brazil to Cuiabá the following day and contrast the deforested Mato Grosso region of Brazil with the forested Amazonica region we had seen while following the river.

Eddie booked us into the airport hotel for a quick getaway the next day and Ahmed communicated that he was finally able to apply for a new entry permit, taking 24 hours! I let Saulo know that we would delay a day and leave on Sunday.

Cuiabá was the capital of Mato Grosso state where Marcelo de Andrade, Chairman of *Pro-Natura*, had kindly arranged meetings for me with local officials over the new year period. *Pro-Natura* provided viable economic alternatives to people struggling to make a living from imperilled environments. After that, we would fly to Brasilia to meet Gérard and Margi Moss who had helped enormously with the route planning, before continuing via Rio de Janeiro to São Paulo for DIGA's first service. With the sun fading, we were able to fit in a swim at the hotel pool at sunset.

I woke to a lovely response to Robin's latest Facebook post but also to the shattering news from Ahmed that Cuiabá was no longer a point of entry. Apparently, many recent status changes by the Brazil *CAA* hadn't yet been promulgated through their official websites and documents, which *G.A.S.E.* relied upon. This was a logistical nightmare! I reached out to Gérard Moss who had excellent knowledge of flying in Brazil. Fluent in Portuguese, he was certainly the person to help. So, a fraught 12 hours of messaging, emails and WhatsApp calls ensued, between us and airports and officials, while juggling time zones and office hours, during a long weekend before New Year.

Looking of out the hotel window, I was consoled only by the fact that the weather was unflyable anyway. Robin and I squeezed in exercise, meals and our chores. We were in a nice hotel with very good Wi-Fi, so it could have been worse!

With many heads, we finally had a solution: Corumbá to the east southeast and just over the border in Brazil from Puerto Suárez in Bolivia would replace Cuiabá. It was Saturday 29th December 2018. Subject to weather, it seemed we could fly to Corumbá on Wednesday 2nd January 2019 to re-enter Brazil properly with a handler and officials available for the temporary import of DIGA. On Thursday 3rd January, we would double hop to Brasilia. It sunk in that I was losing the important meetings in Cuiabá; I had some urgent emails to write to keep the *Pro Natura* folks informed and make my apologies.

We awoke to unflyable weather on Sunday too, but it didn't make me feel any better. Ahmed updated us as the paperwork fell into place at his end. We still had to apply for a new exit permit from Bolivia because we were about to overstay the original permit and we had changed the Brazil entry airport from Cuiabá to Corumba. That could only be done on Tuesday with the holiday closures.

Robin researched excursions to the salt flats but that wasn't going to happen at such short notice and I tackled my administration and chased actions. We met hotel guests at the pool in the afternoon – at least the rain was warm!

On New Year's Eve, the weather was also unflyable but the forecast for our flight to Corumba and then our double hop to Brasilia was looking good. Robin identified a local park where we could see 'Victoria Amazonica': these are giant lilies, nine feet in diameter, normally found in the oxbow lakes we had overflown. The park said it was open but it wasn't! However, we enjoyed an entertaining taxi ride with our American-accented, Bolivian taxi driver across Santa Cruz. In his opinion, Bolivia was not as lawless as it had been!

Friends to the east celebrated New Year before us and we didn't feel so bad going to bed at 10pm.

On Tuesday, all the logistics finally matured and I was able to relax a little. Robin and I prepared for an early departure the following day. I lined up the logistics with *HBR* and David Cross for DIGA's service in São Paulo and was also conveniently able to arrange the use of the *HBR* helipad in a city called Belo Horizonte for refuelling, en route to Rio de Janeiro.

Saulo met us with paperwork in hand and we thanked Oscar, the boss of the Santa Cruz Airport, who had also been so helpful. Then we hopped in the van, alongside the Customs sniffer dog, to ride to DIGA. The low cloud was lifting as we flew east southeast, crossing the Rio Grande, a big, mostly sandy riverbed. It was strikingly flat to the horizon with trees bordering rectangular, farmed fields and later mixed with rectangular forest patches. Tin-roofed houses lined the separating roads.

It was again bumpy with a good 15 knot tailwind component. Eddie messaged that we would cross the northern section of a massive freshwater conservation reserve called Banados del Izozog (Baths of Izozog) attracting many rare species. We converged slowly with a very long hill feature to the left of our track (north) flying over short, scrubby forest and a mixture of winding rivers and oxbows lakes. The hill feature fizzled out but the parallel railway line and road crossed beneath us and looped towards Puerto Suárez out ahead. There were isolated farms and we crossed arrow-straight, dirt roads heading south into the distance.

We routed directly overhead Puerto Suárez, crossing the border into Brazil with the 3,000 feet hills to the south of Corumba and farming to the southwest. We were over the area called Border Lagoons with blue water and open, green grasslands and palm trees. Our handler, Emerson, met us with Google Translate as our only common language. He confirmed that we were on the edge of the famous Pantanal, the world's largest, tropical wetland area, lying mainly within the Brazilian states of Mato Grosso do Sul and Mato Grosso, and extending into northeast Paraguay and southeast Bolivia.

We were trusted to pay for DIGA's fuel in local currency the next day. Emerson then drove us to the border post with Bolivia to clear Customs, before crossing the border into Puerto Suarez, to change USD on the street where the practice was legal. After an ice-cream, we went to the *Recita Federales* offices in Corumba to complete our temporary import/export document linked electronically to our new AVANAC number. The officer also advised us that our point of exit in Curitiba should be Alfonso Penna because the *Recita Federales* was conveniently based at that airport. Emerson's English-speaking boss could handle us there too.

Emerson then helped us check in at our hotel. Robin and I ploughed through our administration, leaving time to search for a restaurant by walking around the block until we found the only lively place to be.

The next morning was a perfectly clear-blue sky and the first since our Florida take-off 33 days ago! Barra do Garças, our refuelling stop, was currently foggy but forecast to clear.

Emerson agreed to take us to the Crista Rei do Pantanal on the hill above Corumba to view the city over the beautiful Pantanal on the way to the airport. I was on the phone to a Rio National *ATC* controller who helped me file two flight plans using English: one to Barra and a second to Piquet, our final destination in Brasilia.

Emerson waved us off, flying east northeast across Mato Grosso do Sul. This was the rainy season when the rivers of the Pantanal overflow their banks and flood the adjacent lowlands, forming shallow lakes and innumerable swamps and marshes and leaving island-like areas of higher ground. The blue and green textures looked dazzling in the sunshine. White cows roamed over the grassland areas and we witnessed man's deforestation around the drier edges.

We crossed into Mato Grosso state and climbed above the highlands. They looked like a series of table mountains. The tops were flat and farmed while the sides were gullied and forested with rivers between; it looked like cattle farming in the large valleys. The ground then fell away slowly to the Barra do Garças, an elevation of 1,000 feet.

We were doing our best to avoid glare in our photographs by using our black towels, which was a particular problem when flying east. With 4G available sporadically, Gérard told me that he had encouraged Barra do Garças to have the fuel truck standing by, ready to take credit card payment. We were the only movement there and resumed our journey within 45 minutes.

We flew eastward, entering Goiás state and climbed slowly to Brasilia, elevation 3,500 feet on the central plateau of Brazil. The scenery was mostly irregular-shaped fields, interspersed with farms, cattle and vestiges of forest consigned to the edges of fields and hill tops. It was pretty

Latin America
The Journey

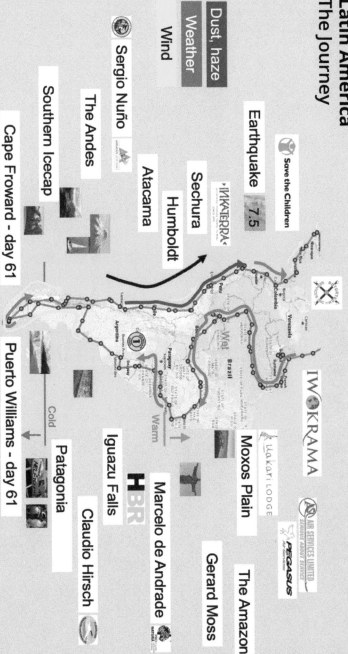

Weather

Dust, haze

Wind

Earthquake

7.5

Save the Children

INKATERRA

Sergio Nuño

The Andes

Southern Icecap

Cape Froward - day 61

Atacama

Humboldt

Sechura

Puerto Williams - day 61

Patagonia

Iguazu Falls

HBR

Claudio Hirsch

Marcelo de Andrade

Moxos Plain

Uakari LODGE

IWOKRAMA

Gerard Moss

The Amazon

AIR SERVICES LIMITED
SERIOUS ABOUT SERVICE

PEGASUS

Cold

Warm

Wet

Amazon River en route to Manaus – Brazil

CBs joining up north west of Rio Branco – Brazil

Reassembling DIGA at RotorTech, West Palm Beach

Beautiful Llanos de Moxos. Beni – Bolivia

Gérard Moss and me,
Piquet Airport – Brasilia

Sergio Nuño, Robin, Sandra
and me, Montes Apalta Estate
winery restaurant – Chile

Robin, customs dog and me, Guyaquil – Ecuador

Robin and kids for Arbol STC visit Cali – Colombia

Phenominal Península Valdés – Argentina

Isla Martillo Penguin Colony, Ushuaia – Argentina

Victor Cove near Arica – Chile

Leon Smith, me and my wife Lavinia with the Britannia Trophy

and reminded me a bit of a less deforested UK. The weather was still good, and control vectored us south around Brasilia. It was a huge, spreading city of 2½ million people and seemed to have many organised satellite suburbs. Eddie messaged us that Brasilia was built to look like an aircraft from above!

We landed at Piquet, a small, private airport belonging to a famous F1 racing driver, on the southwest outskirts. We were greeted by Geraldo Piquet, Gérard and Margi Moss and their guests, Ninian and Anna, who were visiting from São Paulo over New Year. After group photographs, we pushed DIGA into one of the hangars. We were then excitedly shown around the various flying machines in the private hangars. It was the most warm and friendly of welcomes to fellow travellers.

Gérard drove us to his house and we settled in to share their relaxing home, abandoning our normal regime until 'amanhã'. We enjoyed a lovely, relaxing evening in conversation with some extraordinary new friends.

We spent Friday and Saturday with Gérard, Margi, Ninian and Anna, unashamedly talking about flying experiences and sustainable development. Gérard was an accomplished pilot and twice an Earthrounder, as well as being the first person to do it in a motor glider. Gérard and Margi Moss are well-known for their environmental work to protect the Amazon forest and evaluate the quality of its water and air – specifically, the *Flying Rivers* research project [https://en.wikipedia.org/wiki/Gérard_Moss]. The *Flying Rivers* project involved 1,500 hours spent in a specially-equipped flying boat. Gérard's knowledge of flying (especially in Brazil) and his assistance so far had already proved invaluable to me.

I sorted my administration ahead to fly via Belo Horizonte to Rio de Janeiro and São Paulo, preparing flight plans and PLOGs. Robin and I also had the luxury of using a washing machine.

Gérard took us all sightseeing around Brasilia. We drove up the 'body of the plane' and under the 'wing spar' and past all the parliament and ministry buildings. It was pleasantly warm and we took the obligatory photograph at the parliament building that says we have been to Brasilia! Late on Friday, Ninian and Anna caught their return flight to São Paulo.

On Saturday, Gérard and I met with Geraldo and his friends at Piquet Airport to talk aviation, *Three Journeys Round* and the *Flying Rivers* project, before joining Margi and Robin and another pilot for a buffet lunch. I chose a delicious, traditional Brazilian selection, guided by Margi. Our final dinner out was a pleasant precursor to a non-alcoholic beer with Gérard back home, discussing sustainable development, including his next 'planting a million trees' project.

Geraldo and Gérard helped me get DIGA out and then Geraldo called in my two flight plans in Portuguese. As we bade farewell, Gérard suggested that I request a flyby of the most famous Christ the Redeemer statue when entering Rio de Janeiro. I started DIGA, established *InReach* communications with Eddie, lifted and cleared to the southwest. We flew over vast, cultivated fields with rivers and forested portions, which later became a bit drier with dirt roads following the hill ridge and trees lining the watercourses.

Belo Horizonte looked big with its six million population and we were soon being controlled inside the flying corridors over the city, to land at 3,700 feet altitude at the *HBR* heliport for refuelling. It was a small facility with four big helipads right on our GPS coordinates.

Gérard confirmed by WhatsApp that we needed to be hangared at our destination, Jacarepagua Airport in Rio de Janeiro, and he kindly made arrangements. Flying south was bumpy with thermal activity and we climbed to 5,000 feet to clear the hills around Belo Horizonte with the ground about 3,500 above mean sea level. It was farmed, rolling hills with irregular-shaped forest all the way. The weather was building, as expected.

We were controlled down the flight corridors to the sea and then turned to our left (northeast) along Barra da Tijuca beach. I requested a fly past but it was denied due to cloud and so we turned for an immediate landing at Jacarepagua. With efficient handling, we were soon at our hotel. Rio was a serious holiday destination full of great services, so we cleared our administration, ready for a city tour and meeting with Marcelo de Andrade the next day.

Except for the smoggy haze from Rio's metropolis, it was a gorgeous day from our hotel window. We took an Uber to Leblon Beach and hopped on a Rio tour bus. Our tour guide amused us as we cruised down Leblon, Ipanema and Copacabana beaches to Sugarloaf Mountain. Downtown, we saw the Portuguese-influenced architecture with narrow, cobbled streets, graffiti everywhere and the rich, lovely cultural mix of Portuguese, local Indians and African people. We passed favelas and then the biggest football stadium in Brazil, the Maracanã.

The different metropolitan areas of Rio were nestled between the steep hills and, while Rio's population was six million, the sprawling metropolis was 13 million people.

After the tour, we took the metro three stops back to Copacabana. The four-kilometre long beach was thronged with people, vendors, beach volleyball and places to drink. It was 37°C and the array of body types and minute swimsuits would have mortified even a doctor!

In the evening, we met Marcelo de Andrade and chatted at a popular 'after beach' restaurant. His son and nephew were with him and we were later joined by his wife. Marcelo had been inspired to start *Pro-Natura* in Brazil, which very quickly extended its reach to projects in 42 countries in the developing world, tackling the social, economic and environmental problems that rural communities face. He was a serial entrepreneur and also ran a fund focussed on sustainable development investments. We certainly agreed that mankind was destroying Earth's capacity to support it – how dumb was that! If you had the choice to do something different, why wouldn't you?

Marcelo was very well-connected in conservation in South America and I was pleased to finally have met this inspirational man who had introduced me to Jose Koechlin of *Inkaterra* in Peru and Claudio Hirsch of the *National Park Foundation of Argentina*. It was an energising meeting for me.

At Jacarepagua, I needed to pay my dues before Euzebio, a local, English-speaking pilot, kindly helped me plan my helicopter routing to the *HBR* heliport across the metropolis of São Paulo (population 22 million). He then called in my flight plan in Portuguese. Immediately on take-off, I requested a Christ the Redeemer statue fly past, which was granted, after which we descended with great views of Rio to rejoin the corridor offshore flying east southeast. The radio was busy work and the white beaches, steep forested mountains and islands made for beautiful viewing down the coast.

Eddie updated us with snippets of information. At about the latitude of the Tropic of Capricorn, we turned west, climbed to 3,900 feet to get up over the forested mountains and picked up the corridor from Romeo to São Paulo. To the right of our track (north), we photographed the incredibly beautiful and tortuous lake on the Paraibuna River.

Soon, we could see the huge build-up of the cityscape fingers of the metropolis of São Paulo in the flat areas between the hills. Then we were low over the city, which reminded me of the metropolis of Osaka and Kyoto in Japan. It was stunning.

I was excited as we approached one of the largest heliports in the world: *HBR* heliport serves Saõ Paulo where helicopters are used for both convenience and safety. *HBR* looked after hundreds of helicopters in Saõ Paulo and had been recommended to me by Tim Tucker. It was an efficient operation with many years of experience. I had communicated with Raphael Audi whose father, Marco Audi, was the owner and had himself been flying helicopters since 1978.

Smilie marshalled DIGA on one of the 19 helipads. She was moved into the maintenance hangar while Flavia welcomed us into the striking client reception area where we were greeted by Eduardo, Operations Director, and Rafael, Head of Maintenance, of *Robinson* helicopters. *HBR* was a fully *EASA*-compliant facility and Rafael knew David Cross of *HQ Aviation* who didn't need to join us for this 100-hour inspection. I asked Rafael if he would inspect DIGA's blades first. Isaque would be my contact. Anna, who we had met in Brasilia at the Moss' house, arrived to whisk Robin away to see São Paulo. It was a great start to a Tuesday afternoon, and we planned to be leaving on Thursday.

Isaque took me over to talk to Rafael at DIGA and introduced me to Marco Audi who was there ahead of us. We were chatting pleasantries when Rafael called down from his ladder to say that one rotor blade was delaminating at its outer end. There was a defining silence as that bombshell sunk into my brain: this could be an expensive, mission-crippling delay!

OK, I thought and looked at Marco. I said, "We need to source a matching pair of rotor blades, understand the cost and delay, and then subsequent events can unfold." Marco, also a problem-solver, smiled back and said, "Indeed, better to have found this out on the ground and also better here, in *HBR's* wonderful facility!" It was going to be an anxious couple of days of toing and froing across time zones, clarifying specifications, sourcing the rotor blades, negotiating prices and logistics.

Marco, Eduardo and I all left the office late and Eduardo offered me a lift to my hotel where I met Alexandre while having dinner. He was a pilot from Rio with a helicopter at *HBR* in for its service. He recognised me from earlier in the day and it was good to have someone to talk to that evening.

I rode with Alexandre back to *HBR* on both Wednesday and Thursday, having breakfast and dinner with him before he returned to Rio. I based myself in the offices near Isaque and Marco, who had moved on to Californian time to work with *RHC*. My catch-up meetings with him were usually late.

I used my time to sketch out the what-if scenarios and flush out time-dependent issues that would trigger dates. For example, DIGA's importation documentation would need renewing in 20 days. I kept David Cross and Leon up-to-date too and I used any spare time for my thank you emails and administration.

I nosed around the excellent facilities for pilots and the hundreds of customer helicopters hangared at the heliport. Everything was geared to servicing customers, helicopters and pilots. I fell into all three categories and received incredible attention from a great team. I met Raphael Audi, Marco's son, who arrived and introduced himself. Rafael updated us that DIGA's normal 100-hour service was complete, except for the blades.

Talking to Marco, we hatched a plan. Logistically, we could use a new pair of blades already at *HBR* with permission of the owner who would then take the blades that would be ordered for DIGA. Rafael would work on the blade swap between Friday and Monday, then we could complete the blade balancing, test fights and all the aviation paperwork on the Tuesday. The target departure date was now Wednesday 16th January. I felt mightily relieved to have a timeline for leaving and very grateful that it was only a six-day delay. This was a fantastic result and only made possible by the generous support of the *Robinson Helicopter Company* and *HBR*.

Robin needed to know the plan because Anna and Ninian wanted to head out to their farm on Friday through to Sunday and I was also invited. I called Ninian to say please count me in. I took an Uber to my hotel and updated *Helicopter Services, HQ Aviation, G.A.S.E., WFS* and everyone downstream of São Paulo. I could now relax a little and enjoy an immersion into Brazilian homelife for the weekend.

18

The Patagonia Steppe

Ninian drove me to his farm the next day, stopping for breakfast en route. It took about three hours heading northwest out of São Paulo towards Joanópolis. It was nice and sunny after the previous night's thunder and lightning spectacle from my hotel window.

The farm was wonderful and isolated; 36 hectares of land on a lake with gatehouse, little church, outbuildings, hangar, grass runway, swimming pool, five horses and a huge, colonial-style house with gorgeous views of the lake. This was a great lifestyle project involving reforestation and his animal release programme away from Ninian's city work.

I settled in and relaxed by the pool and on the veranda until Robin and Anna arrived later with Anna's son, Luca. Ninian served up some caipirinhas before we all went down to the lake for a swim. It was spaghetti for dinner, and we sat and chatted amongst the splendid flora and fauna, all watching the weather change.

Having slept like a log, I got up early to photograph the sunrise, exercise by the pool and soak up the morning chorus of birdsong. It was still and sunny and a couple of big ground birds, called seriema, were squawking loudly. They live in grasslands, savannah, dry woodland and open forests of Brazil, Bolivia, Argentina, Paraguay and Uruguay. Ninian said that when he reforests here, the trees can grow up to a metre per year, depending on the variety. The conditions were perfect. After breakfast, Robin and I swam right across the lake and then back, to help Anna get her new pedal canoe working on the water.

In the afternoon, we all drove to a local Brazilian barbecue in a nearby town called Atibaia. The kids were swimming in the pool while the adults were talking, drinking and eating. These were Anna's friends and apparently, this was an example of a typical Saturday. It was open-hearted and intoxicating, with more caipirinhas for the adults. Women in Brazil are never topless, but they wear what amounts to dental floss on the bottom half, leaving little to the imagination – somewhat ironic!

We braved a huge downpour on our way home which made driving conditions dangerous and unpleasant. We went straight to visit Ninian's son, William, and his three guests who were staying at the house that William had built on the farm's property. They were all very lively individuals in their late twenties, enjoying their own barbecue and campfire. William's girlfriend, Paula, was vegan and completing a Masters in sustainable development. She and I had an interesting discussion about what we eat and how that affects the climate.

I repeated my early morning routine on Sunday and got talking to Anna about conservation matters. Her first son, Piero, was a lawyer studying in Milan on a *UN* sustainable development course. Robin and Luca returned from their lake swim and the main house filled, as William and his guests came up for breakfast. It was a wonderful routine for this family every second weekend.

Mid-morning, we all went down to the lake for a swim together. There I met Mig, one of Ninian's neighbours, who had sailed over from his house. He had successfully managed to get local, carefully chosen vegetation and trees to re-grow in the zone between the high and low watermark of the lake, his area of conservation research.

With the decision made that we would head back to São Paulo, leaving at about 8pm to avoid the main traffic, we had time to relax, sort our photographs and for me to write my diary. Robin would travel back and stay with Anna again.

Early on Monday morning, I was back at *HBR*. In the maintenance hangar, Rafael was on track with *DIGA* and I used my time to plan ahead, talking to *G.A.S.E.* and *WFS*. Marco Audi organised some of his contacts to support us in Buenos Aires. Tim Tucker had also introduced me to Wille Tufro of *Hangar Uno* and Edelio Mella, who ran four helicopters in Ushuaia. Local knowledge and support were the best ways to stay safe.

The next day, my Uber taxi driver chatted away in the English he'd learnt from passengers. He was a nurse at a big German hospital in São Paulo, taking care of elderly patients and so we had something in common to talk about.

I answered my daughter's question, messaging her that we would be moving again the following day, heading to Paraguay and Uruguay briefly before entering Argentina and heading to the cooler south.

Rafael signalled that he had completed the static balancing of the blades. I was going to fly with him for the dynamic balancing requirements. This would involve running the helicopter on the ground, progressing to hovering, then to short flights as he made any necessary adjustments. A local pilot called Juca helped me with the radio work and also filed my flight plan for the next day. After five short flights over the favelas, we had the rotor blades balanced perfectly.

The light was fading as the support team packed all the equipment away and hangared DIGA. The job was done.

Rafael went off to complete the mountain of paperwork and I thanked Marco Audi for his assistance. Marco helped me get an Uber and I hopped into his Range Rover to drive down to the gatehouse. It was late and *HBR* was a secure facility on an industrial estate. Marco waited and wound down his window. I noticed that his car was bullet proof: wow! That was the second one I had seen on this journey. He took personal security very seriously and, while I hadn't seen any violence, the police were certainly all heavily armed.

Early on Wednesday, Robin met me at *HBR*. Flavia arranged for DIGA to be moved into a prominent position on the helipads for group photographs with the *HBR* workforce in the sunshine. I thanked everybody for their support and after the final selfies, we were ready to go. We flew southwest at about 4,000 feet over the forested hills and we could see the scenic coast and various bays and lagoons to our left. We were controlled direct to the apron at Afonso Pena Airport, our point of exit from Curitiba in Brazil to Cuidad del Esta in Paraguay. Benefiting from the same handler as Corumba, we made a perfect administrative exit, proving finally that it could be done!

We received permission to lift just as an enormous CB was spreading over Curitiba. It was just starting to rain and the storm front was gusty and bumpy as we climbed, turning to the west to get remarkable pictures of the storm to our right of track (north). We were cleared for 500 feet above ground level across Paraná state. For miles, we saw lush, green, forested rolling hills with farms and roads. The cultivation was mostly mechanised with some small holdings, cattle and lakes dotted here and there. It was beautifully green. The Iguaçu River meandered beneath us and to the south of our westerly track. We passed over yet another beautiful lake that had a long, squiggly shoreline because of the varied rolling nature of the hills.

My request to overfly the Iguaçu Falls was granted at 4,000 feet and from that altitude, the falls looked both big and small at the same time! From there, we descended direct to Guarani International, serving Cuidad del Esta in Paraguay over the tri-border with Argentina and Brazil. We could see the Friendship Bridge connecting the Brazilian city of Foz do Iguaçu to Ciudad del Este.

It was 36°C at Guarani and we were soon processed at this small airport and in a taxi for the 30-minute drive to our hotel. The roads were chaotic with sleeping policemen to protect crossroads on the 'motorway'. Four policemen managed the traffic at each crossroad with pedestrians, motorbikes and dust everywhere. We were staying two nights here and would now remain on the same time zone (GMT-3 hours) all the way round South America to Panama.

After an excellent breakfast, Robin and I had decided on a short tour to the Salto del Monday Falls in Paraguay. We were at the confluence of the Iguazu River and the Paraná River, which was the second longest in South America, next to the Amazon, and flowed into the Rio de la Plata (also known as River Plate). Our taxi driver, Silvia, guided us as Robin practiced her Spanish. It would be Spanish all the way to Florida now. The 85-metre drop of the falls was impressive, and the walkway and lift were right on the edge, giving views top to bottom, close up to the thundering sound effects and often in the spray. It was humid with lush growth everywhere.

Returning to the hotel, we must have been right under a CB as it was discharged with no warning. Since the streets didn't have any underground drainage, the roadside rivers carved right through the fruit and vegetable markets, washing wooden crates, bags and produce down the street in the muddy water.

Back at our hotel, I sorted the next day's departure by email and called Willie Tufro of *Hangar Uno* to coordinate our meeting with him at San Fernando, the small airport in Buenos Aires. Then we had time for a walk around the city streets, which were a real contrast of smartish shops, dirty roads and rubbish on the streets. However, we could buy an ice-cream with a credit card!

We arrived early at Guarani Airport for our double hop via Artigas to Montevideo in Uruguay. Artigas didn't publish a weather report and *Windy* was showing that a big storm cell would cross west to east slowly over Artigas. So, it was a waiting game at the small airport café. I drank a Fanta, which took me back to my childhood and we used the Wi-Fi. I delayed our flight first by 1½ hours, then another hour, until I was satisfied. We would have a tailwind to start with, turning to a headwind as we skirted the western side of the clockwise-turning weather system on our journey south.

The northeast arm of Argentina separates the south region of Brazil from Paraguay and we would touch four countries in just one day, to fly from Paraguay across Argentina and Brazil to Uruguay. Flying south southwest, we were over mixed farming and forested areas for miles. Starting out fine, our weather would become widespread light rain with mixed cloud layers.

We crossed the Paraná River again and entered Argentinian airspace. Here, the ground was hilly and the clouds were really low and misty. I was at 200 feet above ground level, searching out my pillar box view to advance safely. Once beyond that, we flew over low, flat ground with good horizontal visibility and entered Brazil, crossing the meandering Rio Uruguai a couple of times. The ground looked sodden everywhere and the rivers were filled with the recent rains. Now our views were an endless panorama of beautiful farming scenes: cattle, farmsteads, dirt roads, little irrigation channels and forested patches, with frequent shafts of sunlight. Crossing the Ibicul River, we could see that it had recently burst its banks, flooding the surrounding fields. The ground climbed slowly until we were finally landing at Artigas (elevation 420 feet) in Uruguay. Here, the forecast to Montevideo was improving.

We experienced a hospitable turnaround at Artigas. The English-speaking Customs officer handled everything while we chatted to the operations gentleman who had flown helicopters in Africa. A group of kids was assembling to see us take off for our domestic flight south, across Uruguay to Carrasco International Airport in Montevideo.

I flew as low as possible under the 30-knot headwind to minimise its effect. The landscape was immediately different from Brazil, characterised by gently rolling land with an average elevation of about 383 feet. It was really green and essentially pasture for cattle and sheep. We saw our first gaucho on his horse, although others had motorbikes. We also saw rheas, horses and endless little streams flowing fast with rocks and rapids, reminiscent of the salmon rivers in Scotland.

We crossed Lago Rincon del Bonete, the largest body

of water in Uruguay, which was formed by the damming of the Rio Negro. By now, the weather cell was well off to the east of us and we were progressing south towards fine weather, albeit still with a stiff headwind. Claudio Hirsch messaged that he would also be in Buenos Aires on Sunday and would meet us at the airport. Montevideo control directed us straight on to the apron at Carrasco and we were met and handled efficiently in English. We secured DIGA and took an Uber to our B&B-style hotel on the beach front, organised by Eddie. Kite surfers were squeezing their last runs in the now beautiful, setting sun. The weather looked perfect for experiencing Montevideo the following day.

Montevideo is about the same latitude as Cape Town, South Africa and now we finally had a fresh climate, after an arduous 48 days in the sweaty Amazon region. We needed to dig out some warmer clothes for our walkabout. Montevideo is a modern, progressive city and during our sightseeing tour, we searched out the famous 150-year-old Mercado del Puerto, which is a festival of meat. We sampled the delicious cuisine using our Spanish and forefingers!

We walked and walked, enjoying the exercise and forming an impression that Uruguay was a very pleasant country. Still, the police on the streets were heavily armed and there were CCTV cameras everywhere. That evening, 'A Long Road to Freedom' was on TV. It's a 2013 biographical film of the remarkable life of South African revolutionary, president and world icon, Nelson Mandela, and an excellent bit of movie drama history for me. "There can be no keener revelation of a society's soul than the way in which it treats its children." I can see and hear him saying it even now.

Two Rotors: One Planet

On day 50, we flew up the northern coast of the Rio de la Plata, which is the estuary formed by the confluence of the Uruguay and Paraná rivers. It's the widest river in the world with the city of Buenos Aires (population three million) sitting along the southern coast. We crossed into Argentina at Isla Martin Garcia and flew southeast to San Fernando Airport, situated in the north of Buenos Aires.

The connectivity in South America was very good and I messaged our estimated time of arrival. Willie Tufro greeted us, walking us through Immigration and Customs and getting DIGA down to *Hangar Uno*. Willie was a charming character and showed us around the well-branded and very impressive *Hangar Uno* jet, aeroplane and helicopter hangars, as well as its training and simulator facilities. He'd had a *Robinson Helicopter* dealership for over 30 years. Matthias, an instructor, translated my basic flying Spanish crib card, which I did indeed rely on later.

Claudio Hirsch then arrived. Claudio and Willie hadn't seen one another for about 25 years and they chatted energetically. Willie himself was off on holiday and wished us all the best for enjoying Argentina. *Hangar Uno* would sort our domestic departure in two days. Claudio then took us out for a typical Argentinian lunch of meat and local beer. We chatted about what we might see and he suggested that it was a bit like Iceland but with more wetlands! In the very south, there would be snow even on the low hills. Then there would be the contrast between the drier west in Argentina and the wetter, colder forest of Chile. It all sounded enticing. It was appropriate to be able to thank him personally for all his advice and national park permissions. Claudio then bade us farewell at our hotel where Robin and I cleared our chores so that we could make the best of the next day's sightseeing.

It was a perfect, blue-sky day and after breakfast, our Uber whisked us to Palermo down the wide, tree-lined streets, which were a mixture of low-rise shops and high-rise tenements. There, we walked around the park and pedestrian areas, people watching. Buenos Aires is known for its preserved, eclectic European architecture and rich, cultural life. We found a trendier area on the streets around Plaza Serrano and walked up and down El Salvador and Honduras streets; it seemed like evenings and weekends around here would be lively. We found a little place to eat before heading home.

Robin sorted a Facebook post while I messaged ahead to Olaf Wuendrich and *Teletón*, keeping in contact with Kris Tompkins and checking in with *Hangar Uno* for the following day. Our weather was looking good.

Our routing through Argentina would take us to Bahia Blanca, Viedma, Trelew, San Carlos de Bariloche, Esquel, El Calafate, Rio Gallegos and finally, Ushuaia. At *Hangar Uno*, we mounted up and then chatted casually until our 9am take-off time, planning to double hop to Viedma. At the last minute, the tower suddenly disallowed our flight plan because Bahia Blanca didn't speak English. Viedma Esquel and El Calafate were also only Spanish-speaking airports.

Matthias, the instructor, came to our rescue. He introduced us to Mati, his friend at *Bahia Blanca Aeroclub*. We could file a flight plan to the aeroclub and swap Robin for the bilingual Mati to make the short hop to Bahia Blanca for fuel and formalities. Then we could file a flight plan from Bahia Blanca back to the aeroclub and a second from the aeroclub to Viedma and not worry about my level of Spanish until I was inbound. Private aeroclubs were prevalent in South America and very helpful as it turned out!

We took off at 9:45am and flew down the Rio de la Plata helicopter corridor, low at first. When we climbed 2,000 feet, we were rewarded with astounding views of Buenos Aires on a sunny, cloudless day. We routed southwest direct across the main cattle, pig and chicken farming areas. We saw pools of water and lakes but it wasn't as wet or green as Uruguay. It was however beautiful and flat, not much above sea level. The roads were mostly just dirt but now and again, there was a bigger conurbation with lots of tree planting.

Mati certainly enjoyed his helicopter flight and bizarrely, Bahia Blanca tower practiced their English with me! Immediately southwest of Bahia Blanca, it was like a salt flat: dusty, hot and barren, but we were soon back to a familiar agricultural scene with a mix of cattle too. It was a lot drier now and only green when irrigated. We were excited to see a group of about 10 rheas running wild. Approaching Viedma, the ground was flat to the horizon. There was a patchwork of dry farmland with irrigation canals from the river, very few trees and still the mix of cattle hanging out near the water troughs provided. The climate was now comfortably temperate and the sky still completely cloudless.

Viedma spoke English after all and as it was a domestic flight, everybody was relaxed. ATC sorted out our coastwise flight plan to Trelew the next day so we could see the marine life of the globally significant conservation area called the Península Valdés. For the other only Spanish-speaking airports, I blagged it that my Spanish had already been accepted for Bahia Blanca and Viedma and that worked! We found our digs for the evening and after a nice walk, we settled for some street food and bottled water before our usual evening regime. People had been so helpful.

We rose to another pleasantly warm, stunningly beautiful, clear blue-sky day, which reminded me of growing up in Rhodesia. We mounted up at Viedma and took off, waving to an audience of airport staff taking pictures. We were heading southwest to the coast where I descended low-level to circle the Gulf of San Matias anti-clockwise and then tour clockwise around the Península Valdés.

The dry scrubland of San Matias reminded Robin a bit of Arizona, and the Península Valdés reminded me of my coastwise flying in South Africa, although the land was much more barren here. It was the wrong season to spot southern right whales and orcas that were known to beach themselves on the shore to capture sea lions and elephant seals. However, we did see thousands of seals, sea lions, hundreds of penguins, guanacos, rheas and all sorts of birds. The scenery and wildlife were both exceptional, making for great photographs with the odd, sudden turbulent bump to make us tighten our seat belts!

Trelew was also a pleasant administrative experience and our taxi was driving through spread-out, low-rise, tree-lined avenues under a cloudless sky. It was absolutely gorgeous and I messaged Claudio to convey what a satisfying day we had just experienced. After an early meal, we walked down to the park next to a little lake. Just like in Viedma, families were out enjoying the facilities in the long evening with the sun setting at about 9pm.

We woke to another gorgeous, clear, sunny day and had a hassle-free departure from Trelew. We were heading from sea level inland and west northwest to San Carlos de Bariloche (elevation 2,900 feet) with its Andes backdrop, situated on the southern shores of Lago Nahuel Huapi.

We climbed initially to 2,000 feet high above the dry, flat scrubland of the Patagonia Steppe with a headwind of about 20 knots. There were isolated farms with their small selection of trees, presumably fed by borehole water. We climbed again as the ground rose to an escarpment, a range of hills and then higher hills to 6,000 feet. With increased elevation, the flora became relatively greener. We spotted groups of llamas and some free-running horses. Eddie informed us that there were only two people per square kilometre out here, compared with England's 427!

At 70 nautical miles, we could make out the white, snow-capped Andes mountains rising to about 7,000 feet behind Bariloche. Landing was easy with a gusty 25 knot wind. Bariloche was a busy holiday destination and kite surfers were out in force on the lake in front of our hotel, taking full advantage of the wind. Patagonia was not only windy, but the Chilean side was also wet and windy. This was why I had scheduled generous stops here, to allow for contingency and flexibility to fly in only the best weather.

The pedestrian precinct of Bariloche could have been the street of a Swiss ski resort in summer, mixed with local traditions: a smaller version of Vail. Indeed, Bariloche historically had influential links with Chile and Puerto Montt through the mountain passes (only 120 nautical miles to the Pacific Ocean). It was very pretty and lively with a good choice of food.

Earlier, I had been contacted by the local firefighting aircrew based at their own small airport, right next to Bariloche. Emiliano had been following *TJR* and kindly offered to meet me for breakfast to discuss if he could help in any way. He organised our local area flight and insisted that we keep DIGA in their hangar with the firefighting aircraft and set off from there to Esquel the next day, which would be easier. We ended up shortening our local flight around Lago Nahuel Huapi because it turned out to be uncomfortably bumpy at 30 knots, gusting 48 knots and rather too close to the mountains. We landed at the firefighting base and compared aircraft and notes enthusiastically with the aircrew, before enjoying a meal and their generous company and local knowledge. It was an unusual use of our day and a welcome break in their vigil. Emiliano dropped us at our hotel on his way home that evening.

Fabulously clear skies and a negligible wind greeted our short morning flight to Esquel. We said goodbye to the firefighters and Emiliano's young son, Fran, who had drawn a picture of DIGA and come to see us off. It was smooth flying south at an altitude of 7,500 feet and utterly gorgeous, with the edge of the Andes to our right and the Patagonia Steppe to our left.

I used my Spanish crib card to land at Esquel and we were soon off flying south in flawless conditions for a longer flight to El Calafate. We saw sheep, llamas and cattle as we crossed escarpments and valleys running west to east to the coast. It was scrubland and what looked like salt pans too, basically a cold, desert climate. We monitored Balmaceda's frequency and passed Lago Buenos Aires at the foothills of the Andes, which was a gorgeous, glacial-blue colour.

We identified Volcán Arenales rising to 11,000 feet, then we were treated to striking, lenticular cloud formations developing high above. It was a clear sign of strong winds over the mountains and ahead. Emiliano said that glider altitude records had been set by the *Perlan Project* at El Calafate, exploiting this phenomenon. As predicted, the north westerly wind really picked up and our ride became uncomfortably turbulent.

We recognised Mount Fitz Roy and passed Lago Viedma, fed by glacial melt from the Southern Patagonian Ice Field in our continuing, real-time geography lesson. It was now 2°C cold outside the helicopter. We descended in turbulent conditions, crossing Lago Argentino to land on the aeroclub apron at El Calafate Airport. We gathered more warm clothing and tied DIGA down firmly against the howling, gusty wind. *ATC* helped me file two flight plans for Monday to Reo Gallegos and then on to Ushuaia, subject of course to the fickle weather. Robin and I walked the busy tourist main street, dressed warmly, to find a place to eat before retiring to our hotel. We booked a trip the following day to the Perito Morena glacier inside Los Glaciares National Park, which is a World Heritage Site.

On Sunday morning, I monitored the forecast and called Edelio Melia, who was based in Ushuaia, for his local opinion. I also anticipated my drum refuelling logistics in Chile for Puerto Natales and possibly another in Coyhaique, depending on the weather and any headwinds.

Then we joined our bus to the Perito Moreno Glacier, seeing the grassy scrubland vegetation of the Patagonian Steppe close up. Four colossal condors from the vulture family soared above; they kept the Steppe clean.

We stopped at a viewpoint then joined a boat to get a closer look. Finally, we walked the trails in front of Perito Moreno, listening to the cracking and grumbling of the ice as it moved. Astonishingly, this glacier moved one to two metres per day and the loss off the front was in balance with the massive deposition of snow forming the ice. Over 80% of the Southern Patagonian Ice Field is in Chile, creating about 50 major glaciers.

The cause of the glaciers at this low altitude and latitude was the wind from the Pacific and the 2,500-metre high Andes. The wind rises and cools adiabatically, providing precipitation and snow mostly on the Chilean side. This generates cold forests, glaciers and five metres of rain on the Chilean side, 400 millimetres on the Argentinian side and a rain shadow in the middle of the Steppe, hence the desert there.

Back at the hotel, John and Sasha Pattinson of *Aircovers* messaged us with the progress of their son, Loris, who was sailing a boat up the east coast of Chile to Puerto Montt.

That morning, rain at El Calafate was forecast to pass and it was clear to our first stop at Rio Gallegos with 30 knots. Then 25 knots of wind at Ushuaia was forecast with some rain but due to improve the later we left it. I thought it might be tricky and would reconsider at Rio Gallegos. We were pushed by a tailwind southeast across the flat Patagonia Steppe once again. It was a sunny 5°C outside and warm enough in the cockpit. We could see the Atlantic Ocean, and both the river and the town of Rio Gallegos. There, we called Edelio again to confirm Ushuaia's weather and the best approach.

We took off in 26 gusting 38 knots from Rio Gallegos to a congratulatory cheer from the tower, then flew down the Atlantic coast and across the Magellan Strait, crossing into Tierra del Fuego. We then headed west over the low Andes under the clouds and down low into the Beagle Channel, before finally heading north to Ushuaia. The weather was really changeable, from rain to snow pellets, to sunshine. It was rather like Scotland but with a much stiffer wind. Ushuaia is the only Argentinian town west of the Andes and it is twinned with Nuuk, the capital of Greenland. We were welcomed by *Heli Ushuaia* and Nico hangared DIGA with their four R44s at the ex-naval base. After some discussion, Edelio dropped us at our hotel.

On the first of two days in Ushuaia, it was beautifully calm. Edelio introduced me to Melvyn Becerra who was another long-range helicopter pilot living in Santiago. We had a great discussion about tactics on various journeys and Melvyn advised on the best scenic routes through Chile. I checked *Windy* and the forecasts looked good.

Heli Ushuaia arranged an afternoon visit to Isla Martillo to see the penguin colony. Robin finished a Facebook post and we joined the bus ride. At one point, we could see Puerto Williams across the Beagle Channel where they fish the famous king crab. The first stop was a wonderful museum and explanation of the sea creatures of Tierra del Fuego. Then, by zodiac, we visited the majestic gentoo and magellanic penguins nesting on the island. There were two lost king penguins as well. It didn't rain on us, but the bleak sky created a menacing backdrop for our photography.

Back in Ushuaia, we joined Pat and Denise, who we'd met in the zodiac, for a meal and discussion about travelling. Denise worked for the *Environmental Protection Agency* in the US and had had some interesting and varied assignments all over the US. We agreed that Argentinians were wonderfully friendly people, excited to share their country's magical experiences.

The next day, Edelio also introduced me to Óscar Muñoz

at the *Club Aero Cerro Sombrero* in Punta Arenas, who would welcome us the following day and hangar DIGA against the elements. I took advice from *Heli Ushuaia* and worked with Ahmed to get our permits to enter Chile. With his local knowledge, Nico helped me plan both good and poor weather routes. If I could, I wanted to fly round Cape Horn, but our destination was Punta Arenas. Cape Horn, which is the most southerly island off South America, is the same latitude south as Edinburgh is north – about 56°. We'd experienced rain, snow pellets and sunshine in a single day! We enjoyed a final round of picture-taking in Ushuaia before again sorting our evening chores at our cosy hotel.

19

The longest country in the world

After saying goodbye to *Heli Ushuaia*, we repositioned from the ex-naval base to complete exit formalities at Ushuaia International Airport. It was day 61 and raining lightly with a cloud base at 1,800 feet covering the surrounding mountains. Thankfully, the wind was calm as we flew 20 minutes south to enter Chile at Puerto Williams.

Kristian on the tower welcomed us and happily completed my *FAI* paperwork. I wasn't able to get permission to round Cape Horn that day and because I wanted to use the good weather further north, I wasn't prepared to wait. However, Cape Froward, which is the southernmost point of the mainland of South America, was permitted, since the restricted area wasn't active.

So, we set off low-level up the Beagle Channel using the shipping lanes, past the glaciers and taking short cuts under the clouds over land where we could. Light, misty rain came and went. The scenery was wonderful with grassy hills that rose up to the mountains and glaciers that came down to meet the sea. We were able to circle the metallic Cross of the Seas on the top of the hill at Cape Froward and then, flying up the Magellan Strait, the sky cleared completely but the wind appeared with a vengeance. It was 19 gusting 29 knots when we landed at Punta Arenas.

Óscar, a meteorologist at the airport, welcomed us, sorted formalities and organised drum refuelling at Puerto Natales, which didn't have its own fuel. With others from the *Club Aero Cerro Sombrero*, we squeezed DIGA into their hangar before getting down to sharing stories. Marcos suggested a scenic route to Natales for us on Saturday and agreed to drive the drum to Natales on Sunday for refuelling.

Óscar confirmed that we could expect good weather for about the next five days as a result of the big, high pressure system off the west coast of Chile. The club had a friendly atmosphere and we were made to feel particularly welcome. That evening, I finally managed to enjoy my first meal of king crab!

On Friday, we planned to just rest, and Robin created another great Facebook post while I tackled my administration, including the previous day's logbooks. Our forward routing was Puerto Natales to Coyhaique, via Balmaceda to Puerto Montt, spending two nights at each location. Then on to Santiago via Concepción for DIGA's second service. If we were lucky enough to have perfect weather on Monday, I wanted to fly to Balmaceda, routing directly over the Southern Patagonian Ice Field. Melvyn had suggested it would be extraordinary if it was possible.

Óscar kindly drove us back to the airport and we carefully jiggled DIGA out of the hangar. Robin took celebratory pictures and we took off, averaging only 65 knots over the ground because of an enormous headwind. Our scenic route was also misty and turbulent, so I had to message Marcos to put a bit more fuel in the drum for Sunday! Natales was surrounded by picturesque mountains; with the wind finally calming and the sky clearing beautifully, it was an unusually warm 15°C when we landed there. I sorted my flight plan and the refuelling arrangements with the chatty *ATC* guys before we headed into town.

Eddie had arranged a friendly hostel which had the heating on, even though the temperature was now 20°C outside. We had time to walk around, buy some more grazing supplies and book a tour for the following day. I chose a morning trip to local caves to fit in with my refuelling duty and Robin chose a whole day trip to Torres del Paine National Park. Puerto Natales was the base for excursions to this world-renowned park whose main feature was an impressive and unique rock formation known as 'Torres del Paine'. I managed some stunning sunset photographs of Natales from our hostel before bedtime.

On Sunday, the high-pressure system delivered sunny, windless conditions and only wispy, high cloud. This was exactly what we needed the next day too.

Robin joined her trip early and later I joined mine, to the three caves of Cueva del mylodón. The mylodón was a large, ancient relative of the modern-day sloth weighing in at about a tonne. When the first inhabitants arrived in the southernmost tip of South America, human beings had completed the occupation of all the world's continents except Antarctica, having migrated out of Africa.

I was dropped off at the airport to meet Marcos and we drum-fuelled DIGA. Then I sorted chores at the hostel, grabbed a second king crab dinner and was back before Robin who arrived, tired, after a long day, with some exceptional photographs of Torres del Paine.

Day 65 was calm and clear, and the scene was set for our ultimate flying moment from Puerto Natales over the Southern Ice Cap to Balmaceda.

We flew to Torres del Paine which was breathtakingly

beautiful. We then headed up the Grey Glacier to the west of it, climbing to 6,500 feet and just skimming the ice-capped snow. We were wearing shorts; it was 16°C and warm in the sunny cabin as we gazed at stunning glaciers, fjords and azure-blue water pools. We flew over the largest glacier (Pio XI), which is one of the few glaciers that is growing, then off the ice cap and over Cochrane. We had the snowy Andes to the left of our track (west) and the magnificence of the Snake River below us. Right of track, we could see the flat Patagonia Steppe of Argentina extending eastwards to the Atlantic. It made for exquisite viewing.

We flew on over Lago General Carrera with its gorgeous, glacial melt colour. We then climbed to 8,500 feet over two desert-looking mountain ranges to reduce the turbulence, before descending into Balmaceda which lies to the east of the Andes. It was 20 gusting 30 knots and 34°C!

After refuelling, we flew west low-level for the short distance up the green, farmed valleys to Coyhaique. The Aysén region of Chile is absolutely beautiful but less often visited because there are no direct flights. The formalities were easy and we taxied to our hotel in the town, kicked off our evening regime and then took a walk, finding a TexMex place to satisfy Robin's penchant!

We had a good breakfast after getting up late at 7am. I attended to routing changes needed in Peru by messaging *G.A.S.E.* and *WFS*. I again contacted Kris Tompkins who confirmed that she would leave Puerto Montt before we arrived; so close, but sadly there would be no meeting. I coordinated with Sasha Patterson to overfly Loris in his yacht the next day, which would be the most remarkable coincidence of all of the *TJR* journeys. I also made arrangements to meet Melvyn in Santiago and emailed

Save the Children (STC) in Colombia. It was a maelstrom of communication activity.

Then we went out to find *Teletón*, which focused on the rehabilitation and integration of disabled children and young people throughout Chile, based in 14 locations. However, thus far, my efforts to recontact them after a promising initial communication (offering a helicopter ride) had failed. Anyway, *Teletón* were here in town, according to the hotel reception, and we took a taxi only to find their offices seemingly abandoned. I couldn't get an answer, sadly. Surrounded by the mountains of the Simpson River National Reserve, Coyhaique is a centre for backpackers and our driver suggested a scenic walk on the Rio Simpson instead.

In the afternoon, we arranged a short drive with a couple of engaging locals to visit Lago Elezalde, through nice farming country with all the beautiful, steep-sided mountains and geology around. Normally, the rainfall in Puerto Montt was significant but the high-pressure system was still maintaining our great weather. After a bite to eat, we prepared for the following day and were pleased to see that Robin's Southern Ice Cap Facebook post had attracted lots of positive comments.

The plan was to fly down the Rio Simpson valley towards Puerto Aysén and follow the inlet out to the sea, then rendezvous with Loris who had timed his departure from Puerto Aguirre. The clouds were back on top of the mountains in Coyhaique and the morning was fresh at 14°C. However, there wasn't any fog and mist forecast.

At first, the valley was tight with steep, forested walls. It was gorgeous flying and very scenic. A flat valley floor widened out progressively as we headed towards Puerto

Aysén. It became an inlet, which widened further as we headed west to the sea. There were many fisheries being tended to and boat operations up and down the inlet. The cloud was now high and broken but it was unfortunately hazy, the cause of which we understood better later on. It was also colder at 11°C and all around us, the forest reached the water's edge.

Ahead, about three nautical miles north northeast of Puerto Aguirre, we identified Loris' 31-feet long yacht with a yellow canoe on the bow. We circled and hovered alongside, getting pictures. We could see Loris with his camera, so we waved frantically and then set off north to Puerto Montt.

We were entirely over water up the Gulf of Corcovado with a headwind component for the first half of the journey. Reflections and haze made photography challenging. However, the geology was awesome with big, strong, steep, forested hills and beaches made from the same rock. There were hundreds of beautiful inlets and bays, uninhabited as far as the eye could see. We were treated to a string of volcanoes including Volcán Michinmahuida, at about 8,000 feet, with the clouds probably hiding more. Further on, we could see even bigger volcanoes poking above the cloud layer.

Getting close to Puerto Montt, the land was well farmed with fisheries in the bay. Our landing and formalities were hassle-free: no fuss, no handlers, no fees. I filed for Friday's flight to Concepción. Two National Forest Corporation (CONAF) firefighting helicopters landed next to DIGA to refuel. Talking to the crews, I met Lluis who had actually trained at *Helicopter Services*. We were enjoying the feeling that Chile was a friendly, safe place.

At our hotel, I dealt with my administration duties in their restaurant. Situated on the tenth floor, it had breathtaking views of the Gulf of Corcovado, the surrounding Andes and a couple of monstrous, conical volcanoes. The sky was totally clear now with a beautiful setting sun. In Argentina, the Steppe was a huge area while here in Chile, the flat area between the sea and the mountains was often only a thin strip. Puerto Montt (population 250,000) was the biggest town we'd seen since Buenos Aires and attracted many tourists, which we intended to be the following day. That evening, I enjoyed a conger eel steak for dinner, reflecting on how lucky we'd been with the weather in a normally wet and demanding place to fly.

First thing in the morning, I booked an afternoon tour to a prominent, conical volcano called Volcán Osorno. Chile has approximately 2,000 volcanoes, about 90 of which are active. After breakfast with the tenth-floor view and the sun streaming in, I checked that I had understood Melvyn's advice for flying the VFR approach to Santiago's smaller airport at the foothills of the Andes, Eulogio Sánchez. I also planned his suggested route to Concepción to enjoy the best Los Lagos region.

When our guide, Fernando, stopped in Puerto Varas to pick up more tourists, we caught our first glimpse of Volcán Osorno, which is famous for looking like Mount Fuji across Logo Llanquihue. It was a picturesque scene. Puerto Varas, also known as 'the city of roses,' was a bright, pretty town on the edge of the lake with a population of about 40,000. When we reached the base of a tiny ski station, Robin and I elected to take the chair lifts up. The views all around were brilliant and we could see Cerro Tronador (11,450 feet) on the eastern border with Argentina, which we'd seen from Bariloche too. On the way home, we chatted with a couple of Australians, also travelling around Argentina and Chile.

At the airport, firefighters were gathered around a massive tarpaulin water pool waiting for firefighting aircraft to land. We weren't rushed but they were pleased that we would be moving DIGA out of their way!

We climbed above the inversion layer to 3,500 feet and above the thin layer of broken clouds to get the best view down, and also to see the Andes right of track as we headed north. Thanks to Melvyn, we flew via the Los Lagos region of Chile to Villarrica, taking in a string of beautiful lakes and volcanoes, including the striking Volcán Villarrica, which was still smoking. We recognised Lago Llanquihue and Osorno from the previous day and the most active volcano in Chile, Volcán Llaima Volcano (10,253 feet), which last erupted in 2008.

The ground was initially all farmed with many fields and forest rows. At Villarrica, we turned towards Concepción on the coast and the second largest city in Chile (population one million). The weather remained good but the dust, haze and smoke from fires characterised the horizon. The ground below was now parched farmland. Bushfire smoke was contained by the inversion layer and flowed like a river over ground features. We continued over Rio Bio Bio, the second widest river in Chile, to land at Concepción.

We were refuelled from the ground fuelling system used for commercial jets and soon we were climbing back up to 3,500 feet to find a tailwind. The ground was initially hilly below with managed forests and then many more conurbations as we progressed across parched, farmed fields and vineyards cultivated for the Chilean wine industry. The scenery reminded me a little of that south of Rome. Snow-capped, conical volcanoes protruded frequently above the general mountain range. We converged gradually with the Andes and its skirt of smoke, haze and, I suspected, smog, on reaching Santiago (population seven million). Following the Pan-American Highway north, it was an awesome VFR approach to Eulogio Sánchez, Santiago's smaller airport at the foothills of the Andes.

Sergio Nuño marshalled us to the helipad and welcomed us warmly, with Melvyn running over to greet us too. We all chatted happily, following DIGA as she was towed around to the *Aeromar* hangar for her service. Melvyn was an incredibly warm-hearted person who loved flying his R44 a long way; I was glad to be able to thank him personally for all his help. His hangar was conveniently directly opposite *Aeromar*. I made arrangements with Sergio before he dropped us at our hotel on his way home.

The next day, we flew with Sergio and his partner, Sandra, to the Montes Apalta Estate winery restaurant for lunch; Robin instantly hit it off with Sandra. Sergio explained that the smog we could see was caused by the cold Humboldt sea current which produced the fog that mixes with the dust and fire smoke.

We enjoyed a fabulous seafood lunch and a tour of the wine cellar. Sergio was a lovely character and a great storyteller. It turned out that he had worked as an understudy for David Attenborough at the *BBC* for about five years and returned to Chile to make his own distinguished career in conservation adventure films and documentaries. He was extremely well-connected and a well-known TV personality, regarded as the 'Attenborough of Chile'. Flying back to Eulogio Sánchez and once more over the expansive north of Santiago, Sergio pointed out the tallest building in South America at about 80 storeys and built in an earthquake zone!

On Sunday morning, I was juggling logistics and variables for shipping DIGA back to the UK, which all depended on firm dates. David arrived from the UK and we had lunch together to discuss DIGA's service requirements for Monday.

Sergio took us all on a city tour in the afternoon and as we drove, we explored Santiago and Chilean history through his memories and life stories. It was interesting to understand the 'communist era', the 'military coup and rule period' and then the 'democratic period' (the last 30 years). Sergio's father had been a Colonel in the army at the time of the coup and Chile had turned around from communist rule to be the economic success it is today.

Sergio's love of helicopters developed from a need to see and share Nature during his conservation programme-making and that developed into a lasting relationship with the *Robinson Helicopter Company*. We had much in common to debate and celebrate and enjoyed boundless discussions. We both agreed that, while people could shape government policy, government policy would make the changes happen.

While David and I were raring to start DIGA's service, a normal, Spanish-style late start to the day seemed on everybody else's minds. Robin had made plans to explore Santiago with Sandra. David looked over DIGA before she was cleaned and then we began the inspection, working with *Aeromar*. David shared his knowledge in various discussions and Melvyn popped across to say goodbye once again, before flying off to Villarrica with his wife.

On Tuesday, we completed the inspection with a short test flight to the south of Santiago and released DIGA back to service for my 55 hours' flying back to Florida. David then helped Sergio balance the main rotor blades on a new R44 while I repacked DIGA. However, they abandoned the test flying until the following day when ominous, dark clouds threatened a storm with the mountain backdrop.

David, Robin, Sergio, Sandra and I ate at our hotel restaurant that evening and Sergio recounted more enthralling adventures as a filmmaker, quizzing David about *Robinson* helicopters.

I reflected again how enjoyable it was to be in the company of South Americans, all excited to share their countries' magical beauty and experiences. Chile was as easy to fly in as the UK or USA, while Argentina did have the 'Spanish-only airports' to work around; otherwise, both were fantastic flying experiences.

We dragged ourselves into the world the next day, having stayed up a bit too late for our body clocks. At the airport, we prepared and thanked Sergio for his company, kindness and hospitality: we were saying goodbye to a friend. David would use his last day to help Sergio and the *Aeromar* team.

Sergio's advice was to fly a route north of Santiago, find a valley to get closer to the coast and to follow that all the way. So, we flew up the coast in single day hops, stopping in La Serena, Antofagasta and finally Arica, our point of exit into Peru. Between La Serena and Arica, our challenge came from the dust haze off the Atacama Desert and fog caused by the cold Humboldt current. This didn't make for the best photographs but it was spectacular landscape nonetheless!

Sometimes there were flat sections close to the sea where isolated towns could get a foothold. The different brown colours of the sand with white, frothy waves on the rocks and the different greens and blues of the sea, next to the pencil-black stripe of the road, made for striking scenery.

This section reminded me of Oman. There were verdant valleys flowing east to west for rivers from the Andes issuing to the sea. We watched birds dive bomb shoals of fish.

We could often see the Pan-American Highway until it disappeared into the higher plains behind the mountains whose rocky cliffs descended to the sea. It was remote and spectacular. There were towns along the highway and dirt roads wiggling their way into the valleys and mountains behind. Chile is the world's longest country at 4,270 kilometres (38° of latitude).

It was Lobby-Fi at La Serena Hotel situated on the beach, which we rationalised as good exercise going up and down to our room before our proper evening walk down the impressive beach. The town wasn't affluent but it was as well-developed as we had seen elsewhere in Chile.

Using the free airport Wi-Fi, I decided with David Cross and Art Apicella that I could work with Paul of *RotorTech* to disassemble DIGA for return shipping, saving David a journey. We could talk on the phone if necessary.

Leaving La Serena, we climbed up over the hills to avoid the immediate sea fog, before hugging the coast again. Passing Taital, we were offshore heading direct to Antofagasta, with the mountains rising from the sea. We kept up our scan to see if we could add to the two whales we had already seen.

We crossed the Tropic of Capricorn and flew low-level around Antofagasta Bay and into the airport, before taxiing 16 miles back to our hotel. It was a rough and ready port town but beautiful in the sunshine; although desert, it was pleasantly cooled by the effect of the Humboldt current. We sorted our chores and had time for a walk to the local shops for more grazing foodstuffs.

Two Rotors: One Planet

On leaving for Arica, I read a local Antofagasta newspaper article that described the *Tompkins Foundation's* donation of 4.5 million hectares to become national parkland in Patagonia as the largest by a private individual in the world.

Hugging the coast northwards, we passed a sizable, skyscrapered-city called Iquique nestled in the gap between the mountains and the sea. According to Eddie, it was the centre of saltpetre mining and Charles Darwin had passed through a little while before us, in 1835!

Arriving at Arica, *ATC* confirmed the opening hours of Tacna in Peru and informed us that we would gain two hours due to the time difference. They arranged our flight plan and general declaration for Sunday. Coming up, we had planned visits with *Inkaterra* in the very north of Peru and then *STC* in Columbia.

Our hotel had a nice view of the huge beach and Arica Bay; we dealt expeditiously with our administration and chores and researched tours for our rest day. It would have been nice to see the incredible landscapes, local flora and fauna, geoglyphs and more lakes and volcanoes climbing right up to the Altiplano region. However, the shortest tours available were 11 hours! So, we settled for beach walks and a trip to the local malls.

I expected the next two weeks to just fly by and I wanted to stay right on top of my administration and planning to enjoy flying the final legs. I was now conscious of reaching the end of the third physical journey of my *Three Journeys Round* project.

It was a pleasant 25°C with a clear-blue sky in Arica. It was dry but we could see that storms in the Andes had washed tonnes of debris down the rivers and onto the beach where it was a hazard, so a big clean-up operation was in progress.

We filed our flight plan at Arica Airport, taking pictures of the sunrise, and lifted at 8:30am to fly 25 nautical miles north into Peru. We gained two hours with the time difference on our side, but it transpired that we were going to need all of it to get to Pisco before dark. We arrived in Tacna at 7am local.

Tacna *ATC* were helpful, providing us with cold drinks and trying to explain to Customs that our papers were good for our flight to Pisco via Nazca. However, we struggled in Google Spanish. Eventually, after a delay of five whole hours, Customs conceded that the same documents employed to get DIGA into Puerto Maldonado would suffice. I was really pleased that I had scanned all those documents. At one point, I thought we might not be moving at all! All this time, Immigration was nowhere to be seen but I didn't really care by that point.

We took off in the heat of the day to fly northwest up the coast of the Sechura Desert. This was also an epic, isolated, hazy coastline, similar to Chile. We saw big, dark patches of shoaling fish and birds diving into them and three more whales. It was a desert mountain landscape with the mountains punching up into the clouds, cliffs and sandy-coloured ravines heading to the shore and more verdant, cultivated valleys issuing brown, muddy water into the sea. We cut across the shore of an extensive beach and over proper desert towards the low hills hiding Nazca. It was gusty, dusty and beautiful.

Tacna *ATC* had paved the way for our quick turnaround, and we relaunched directly across the desert to Pisco on the coast. We were controlled clear of all the sightseeing traffic but could see the threatening, rain-laden skies over the Andes inland, the verdant valleys and the wonderful, crescent-shaped Barkhan dunes. There was definitely 'weather' in the Andes, which we were avoiding this close to the coast. We were met by administrative shenanigans at Pisco, finally securing DIGA after dark. We had been with her for 14 hours and it had been a long, exhausting day with the coastal humidity and desert heat thrown into the stressful mix of adrenalin-fuelled excitement.

We gratefully accepted the bread and jam with black coffee for breakfast and found the three-wheeler ride to the airport during daylight much more illuminating. The forecast was rain over the Andes on the 13,000 feet plus mountains but dry on the coast. After delays, we were airborne at 9:30am.

We maintained 1,600 feet under a sky overcast at 4,000 feet. We were heading up the coast to Chiclayo for fuel before flying on to Talara to meet *Inkaterra* again. The desert coastal views were similar to the previous day, perhaps more populated, but once again, conurbations with desolate desert sections in between and very different to the Amazon side of Peru.

We passed Lima (population 11 million), Chimbote with its two natural harbours and then Trujillo, where the area of flat land between the coast and the Andes started to increase considerably. There were dark CBs over the mountains. We made landfall over a massive, green, cultivated valley. It was a delta with alternate desert and river sections, running east to west as we flew north northwest. Chiclayo was a big town and we landed on the civilian side of the newish-looking airport next to the fuel and only 50 metres from *ATC*.

We were on time and in contact with Romulo of *Inkaterra* who would be waiting for us in Talara. We lifted low-level over Chiclayo, taking pictures of the dusty roofs. It was bizarre to be flying one moment over desert, wadies and dunes, then over a cultivated valley floor, and then back to the desert. We did have the briefest moment of raindrops on DIGA. The last little section of valley that we crossed consisted of green, wet fields like rice paddies but with palm trees. It was amazing what life was produced by the waters from the Andes.

Piura control passed us to Talara tower and we landed at this small airport to a friendly welcome from airport staff, all wanting photographs with DIGA. We would be back the day after next, to fly north to Guayaquil in Ecuador, using Piura as our point of exit.

Romulo drove us 45 minutes to Cabo Blanco. We were here to take a snapshot of *Inkaterra's* journey developing a world-class eco-product out of the desert, with wonderful surfing beaches and a special fishing spot with a glorious history made famous by Ernest Hemingway. The development would open in a couple of years. Right now, it was hot and humid in the tropics on this desert coast. We reached the *Inkaterra* property as the sun was setting and dumped our bags to get a few pictures of the sunset. We had good Wi-Fi and amazing views plus the fabulous, soporific sound of the waves, which worked for me every time.

The *Inkaterra* crew looked after us well, even though I am sure they had other work. We sailed out on Miss Texas, the boat that Hemingway fished from in the 1970's, and trawled without luck, photographing the development project from the sea. Romulo described the project and proudly showed us around the site, including the private house platforms and the sample chalets. For scale, we were talking 109 dwellings, two hotels, with the restaurants, coffee shops and stores, plus the *Inkaterra Asociación* scientific research station facilities.

Turning the desert into green, planted and grassed landscapes would be impressive and the sample chalets were to *Inkaterra's* incredibly high standard. It was a massive construction project and the earthworks looked like they had moved mountains to make the terraces, which had an Inca feel to them. From my porch, I watched one surfer walking home, Robin coming out of the sea, pelicans resting between fishing dives and a handsome orange sunset developing. It was beautiful on so many levels. Soon my reality would become a rush to eat, wash and dry my clothes and complete administrative chores.

We thanked Romulo at Talara Airport and went through all the formalities, only to be denied our start up at 9:30am. Sheepish officials asked us to wait and finally, by lunchtime, they acknowledged that Piura didn't have Immigration available today and wouldn't even park us there. This was very frustrating, bearing in mind that I had confirmed my intentions two days ago.

We had planned to make it to Guayaquil because it positioned us for a long flight complicated by weather and terrain into Cali in Colombia on Thursday, where on Friday we were meeting *STC* staff for organised visits. Ecuador and Colombia both had tropical weather, which according to *Windy*, looked to be still reasonable for Guayaquil but mixed for Cali. Damn!

We dismounted and took a tuk tuk to a hotel, which Eddie had organised. It was a clean, new hotel situated in scruffy Talara, made worse by the inevitable desert dust. Carolina of *STC* was very understanding but I knew that it would be inconvenient for them to conduct our visits on a Saturday. After Cali, we had flexibility in either Panama, Costa Rica or Belize, where I had planned two-night stops in order to hold our West Palm Beach (WPB) arrival, which was now agreed for Sunday 2nd March.

Back at Talara Airport, the administration was streamlined, our fees waived and off we went to Piura. There, fuelling and flight planning was quick, but five Immigration officials signed and stamped forms to death because we hadn't passed through Immigration at Tacna: Robin and I smiled innocently! Paying the 25 USD fee consumed time as we queued for the bank to open. This seemed an unproductive, demoralising and energy-sapping way to run a country.

Our flight from Piura to Guayaquil was from desert over a range of forested hills right back into tropical weather. We crossed the border into Ecuador at the Rio Zarumilla, flew over the Canal Pinacho and crossed the Grande Estuary, with Punta Island on our left (west) flying over the Gulf of Guayaquil and its rice paddies. It was an amazing transformation, all within a space of 200 miles.

Flavio welcomed us to the GA apron and handled formalities seamlessly. It was hot and humid again but we were soon enjoying the air-conditioning of our third-floor hotel rooms. We attended to our chores and watched another beautiful sunset. I received a nice message from Jennifer Murray to say that she was following our journey and wished us well.

20

Earthquake alarm call

Our alarm call was an earthquake! The five-storey hotel swayed violently for about 20 seconds. Looking outside, the pylons were also swaying, alarms sounding and people running from the building. It started at about 5:17am (magnitude 7.5/centred 148 kilometres away) but it was over before we could really process it and everything calmed down, including us. Now wide awake, I was examining the forecast when BANG! There was a much stronger, single shock wave. I bloodied my shin, bashing it on the furniture as I jumped with fright. On the way to the airport, Flavio shrugged his shoulders saying that this was a normal occurrence!

Everything was lined up, including a Customs sniffer dog for DIGA. We had a long, tricky flight to Cali, our point of entry into Colombia. The Guyaquil city views quickly turned to rice paddies glinting in the sun, reminding me of Langkawi. We picked our way north over the sweating, forest hills through very challenging marginal VFR flying conditions, avoiding CBs and manoeuvring lower to follow the coast northwest. We crossed into the northern hemisphere, having spent 71 days below the equator.

We flew the low-lying Pacific Coast below the 2,000 feet cloud base and as the estuarine coast wiggled, we saw variously forest, winding rivers or seashore below. People eked out a living from small, stilted houses and canoes.

At Buenaventura, I was planning to either cross the Andes via a valley flying route under the clouds or by flying right over the top of the clouds and descending into the next valley. I had prepared both routes. Cali was clear according to another pilot and I judged that the mountains were completely covered with cloud. I decided to climb through the broken cover at the coast, then turn east southeast before crossing the last 40 miles VFR on top at 7,500 feet.

Cali was situated in a long, wide, flat, green cultivated valley between two mountain ranges, both wearing thick cloud blankets. My second antipode, Neiva, was 'just' across the next bigger range. On the apron, it was 34°C and we were swamped by good-natured officials with enough English to assist us and all wanting selfies! Our Uber took 45 minutes in the busy traffic on bumpy roads and tree-lined streets, playing infectious, Colombian music loudly. Soon we were on the fifteenth floor with good views but the forecast wasn't looking too clever for our planned day of departure.

I had now experienced an earth tremor or quake on each *TJR* journey. After my 'earthquake alarm' and a long, stressful flight in the increasing humidity, I was ready for bed early.

In the morning, Carolina met us at our hotel and described her dream job with *Save the Children*. She safety-briefed us, explaining that *STC* worked in the poorest areas and was 'protected' by the guerrillas because they valued its work. Nonetheless, we would keep a low profile, wear our *STC* bibs and not stay anywhere too long.

Having set the scene, Carolina continued with the story. Colombia was an upper income country with natural resources but was recovering from 50 years of armed struggle. The Pacific coastal regions we'd flown over the previous day were the most deprived because of poor access and armed groups. There was a huge 'out of school population', combined with a large displacement of people who often ended up living side by side with ex-guerrillas in basic, government-provided apartments. Differences of opinion and poor job prospects were a continuing source of drug-fuelled 'business', criminality, violence and domestic violence, and women and children suffered the most.

With Carolina, a driver and her colleagues, we visited the work of two *STC* programmes on four sites in the poorer areas of Cali. We were shown their friendly and safe place programmes, which offered disadvantaged children living in tough, urban environments a chance to form healthy habits and build peace. It was moving to witness how the teaching staff, social workers and psychologists related to the kids, giving them back their right to dream of a better future.

STC Columbia was doing an incredible job fundraising locally, organising, improving infrastructure and transferring skills to tackle the almost intractable challenge of drug and gang-related urban life against a backdrop of conflict. We had nothing but admiration for Carolina and her colleagues and we thanked them sincerely for accommodating us on a Saturday.

Save the Children was the first global movement to support children and the charity commemorated its 100th anniversary over the course of 2019. It was a magnificent record to achieve 100 years of helping the world's most marginalised and deprived children to have a healthy start in life, access to a basic education and protection from harm.

At 6am on Sunday, *Windy* still forecast poor conditions over the mountains and north of Buenaventura, with weather cells delivering a low cloud base, poor visibility and rain. The following day's weather looked much safer. So, I delayed our flight to Panama and messaged Eddie. If we only spent two nights in Belize, we would still be on schedule. We both cleared all of our actions and went for an early dinner. From the viewing platform on the hotel's 42nd floor, we had a 360° view of the city, valley and mountains.

Once at the airport, we located its free handling service, *CECOA*, who were friendly English speakers. It transpired that our one-day weather delay in Cali had unwittingly pushed us beyond our 48-hour grace period as 'pilots in transit'. We therefore relied on *CECOA* to get us out of Colombia, which included a retrospective authorisation from the Colombia *CAA* in Bogotá and a thumbs-up from Customs who luckily remembered our fun arrival and waved us through. This consumed the whole morning and made for an anxious wait.

We were now tight for time to activate our flight plan when the *CECOA* boss beckoned us to his truck airside and wanted to show us some helicopters for sale. Really?! I looked at my watch but we humoured him and made use of the hangar toilets! After preparing DIGA and entertaining the Customs sniffer dog, I finally called for clearance with just two minutes to spare as Robin made final checks and climbed in. It was very hot and DIGA climbed slowly to 6,500 feet (about 10,500 density altitude) heading west on the VFR route over the mountains.

We talked to Buenaventura and then only Eddie, as we headed across virgin forest with isolated signs of life along the rivers winding their way to the Pacific. We travelled north northwest to the sea, crossing some higher ground with its own murky, local weather. We passed the remnants of the dissipating weather cell and Utria National Park, which boasts one of the highest rainfalls in the world at 10 metres per year. We continued up the coast past the Darién Gap, which is a break across the North and South American continents within Central America. The Pan-American Highway also has a corresponding gap of 106 kilometres in length.

Panama control vectored us across the hazy Gulf of Panama and into the small city airport where we were greeted by Operations with DIGA's folder and my business card from 2017! In the flight planning office, the *ATC* controller who had just landed us made sure that we sorted our documents before leaving the airport, then we grabbed a taxi to our hotel ready for another early night.

The following day, our airport taxi drove us past the bleak-looking Curundu slum area, with no intention of stopping. The weather was behaving but crosswinds would be very strong. We breezed through Panama Airport formalities (in contrast to my 2017 nightmare) and routed round the Pacific side of Panama and Costa Rica, with all the weather on the windward side of the Central American mountains wearing their thick, cloud blankets. We mostly flew over lowland, close to the coast or on it, cutting across protruding land features. The crosswinds were indeed fierce, as was the turbulence.

Panama and San Jose controls were excellent. Tin-roofed housing was prevalent and must have been unpleasantly hot in these stifling conditions. As we crossed the wetland and farmed fields, part of the Palo Verde National Park, Liberia approach warned us of their gusty airport conditions. We were experiencing the Guanacaste Papagayo winds, which blow all year.

We could fly DIGA in windy conditions if we had to but it required skill when manoeuvring on the apron and caution when flying with ground features causing nasty turbulence effects over great distances, including funnelling and rotors. We tied DIGA down securely and recovered to the airport hotel.

UNESCO said that Costa Rica had many exemplary policies in place to promote sustainable development, spanning the protection of biodiversity, the promotion of multiculturalism and the advancement of quality education and global citizenship. There was a cosmopolitan mix of guests using the hotel as their launching point for longer tours into the various national parks.

We'd had good, albeit bumpy, flying with proportionate administration; I expected the same, heading to San Salvador the next day. In fact, the weather was looking bright all the way to Key West. We both had fun making short videos for Carolina, for *STC's* 100-year celebrations in Colombia.

In the morning, DIGA was sharing the apron with a US military Chinook, with the stiff wind providing air-conditioning against the heat, while the mountains still sported their cloud blankets. The conditions turned out to be incredibly bumpy and flying manual, it was hard to even read the *iPad* or message Eddie.

My flight plan had been accepted as Liberia to San Salvador direct, but Nicaragua wanted my routing since I didn't have an overflight clearance for flying their coast. Almost out of radio range, I was trying to understand

Liberia, message Ahmed and write down a suggested route 12 miles offshore that didn't need a permit. We managed with only a few more minutes' reception left. The shame of it was, this made it difficult for Robin to see the best of the coastline and volcanoes through the haze, but my heart rate dropped back to normal.

Landing at San Salvador was easy and the wind had now died down completely. We were taken care of by the organised and efficient airport administration who remembered DIGA from 2017. Watching the forecast, it remained good enough to fly across the mountains of El Salvador, Guatemala and Honduras to Belize City, sightseeing some more volcanoes and new countries.

On Thursday, we climbed directly to 5,500 feet up over the western side of San Salvador city, passing Volcán de San Salvador. There was an inversion layer, smoky fires and not much wind, making the views of other volcanoes terribly hazy and smoggy.

We flew northwest to Santa Ana, then north into Guatemala, where I elected to stay underneath the cloud layers ahead. It was hilly below and could have been Africa, with dirt roads on the watersheds and tin-roofed houses along them on either side. The trees mainly followed the water courses. We dog-legged down into a valley with Honduras to our right of track (east) under the last remnants of dissipating low cloud, and then northeast across Lago Izabal, the largest lake in Guatemala, famous for its manatees.

We entered Belize over the Sartoon-Teresh National Park which, according to Eddie's message, supported several threatened species, including the black howler monkey, hickatee turtle and Morelet's crocodile. It was lush forest below and looked wet underfoot. On reaching the coast, we followed it less than 30 minutes north to Belize City. Belize is home to the world's second largest barrier reef, which was a bit too far offshore for us to make out.

Landing was really easy with busy Caravan traffic moving people about locally and bigger jets arriving intermittently. We were handled by the characterful Rudy who was clearly well-known and was on top of everything we needed. Our taxi driver chatted all the way to the hotel and we agreed our pickup for 6:30am on the Saturday. For the first time since Guyana 85 days ago, we were back into Caribbean English. As night fell, the starlings were deafeningly noisy outside our room, hiding in the palms just a few feet away. We ate outside on the deck with everybody else, who were apparently mostly holiday-makers; there weren't many people doing what we were doing!

At 9am the next day, Robin set off to see a Mayan temple, go wet caving and try her hand at a zip line. For me, Friday was spent worrying about getting all the permissions, handling and paperwork in place to make our double hop into America work. I just needed exercise to keep me happy since I had holidayed in Belize before, meeting Rene Chamorro.

I had planned routing to Key West via Cancun for Saturday but Ahmed didn't have a permit, nor had he selected a handler for Mexico yet. I needed the permit for filing my flight plan and then my eAPIS into America, in that order, but I felt sure that there would be many iterations before I could go to bed.

Finally, Ahmed's chosen Cancun handler said we must use Cozumel. Ahmed adjusted the permit request and researched a handler there, while I adjusted my PLOGs and

RunwayHD routes and waited.

Robin returned late and had enjoyed herself; I went to get something to eat downstairs. It was a lively Friday night and whilst I ate, I chatted to a prosecutor from Breckenridge who was there on holiday. At 8pm, Ahmed messaged me the permit number and the handler details and I scampered upstairs to file it, using *Rocket Route* and to wrestle with the eAPIS, copying everyone in. It was getting late. Then Tomasz Wojtowicz (who owned the Cessna 152 we flew with part way on *RTW*) messaged me and said he would like to rendezvous for a combination flight to WPB on Sunday, and so I corresponded happily. Finally, I was done for the night.

At the airport, Rudy had sorted out absolutely everything: he was good! We found DIGA covered in dust and the light rain had just moved it around her paint work.

We set off north northeast at 1,000 feet. It was hot and humid, with scattered cloud giving some shade in the cockpit. To our left was mangrove forest with lagoons and squiggly waterways. Below, we saw a very shallow, turquoise-coloured water lagoon with dark ink on blotting paper-type coral marks and little, white sand banks and tiny islands. It looked as beautiful as Nature could be at sea.

We crossed into Mexico with Eddie monitoring our *InReach* track over the short mangrove scrubland. We could see water glinting through the greenery below. The horizon was hazy and flat, either green or blue, depending on the direction of view. We crossed a single, elevated road and continued over the San Ka'an Nature Reserve, a World Heritage Site. We were converging with the coast for our water hop to Cozumel, 60 nautical miles direct.

We crossed the southern reef of Cozumel and then its

coastline, with all the tourist fishing boats. With the town of Cozumel ahead and the leeward coast inhabited, we approached the airport apron directly to help the chirpy controller who was also parking a jet.

We were met by 10 people with a dog and guns. Luckily, Daniel, our handler, was there to help and DIGA was searched in good humour. Within an hour, we were flying over the north of Cozumel island, electing to climb to 5,500 feet with Cancun control. It was 15°C in the cockpit as we cruised at the top of the inversion layer, routing around Cuba's airspace and talking to Havana control. Cuba itself was 50 nautical miles to the right of track but very hard to distinguish through the haze. Lines of Sargasso weed, blown by the wind, stretched for miles below. We received a discretionary descent to 800 feet from Miami control and scooted directly to Key West down the taxi way to the Customs square, before air taxi-ing back over to *Signature Flight* who once again looked after us.

Later, I finalised timings with Tomasz, then Robin and I had a meal, celebrating that Robin, at least, was back on home soil and the final journey was nearly complete. Only 30 days ago, we had been at the tip of South America! We could relax and enjoy the next day with Tomasz.

Our last day was a beautiful day for flying and we were comfortable for our take-off at 9am. I started DIGA while Robin captured video before she got in. We flew low, following the Florida Keys to Marathon, before we headed north across the shallow water to fly up the western coast of the Everglades National Park and into Everglade Airport, elevation five feet!

Tomasz was there already and it was fabulous to catch up with him and his Cessna 152. Our next combination flight and some air-to-air photographs would make a fitting end to my journeys. I would chase Tomasz with DIGA's better speed and we took off on time to make West Palm Beach by midday.

More by luck than judgement, Tomasz landed on the runway simultaneously with us, directly on the apron at *RotorTech*. I touched DIGA down in front of the hangar, acting as a beacon for Tomasz to taxi towards.

Robin and I dismounted from the *Three Journeys Round* configuration for the last time. My wife, Lavinia, was there to meet us and there was a lot of congratulatory hugging and hand shaking. It was a proud moment for me. We pushed the little Cessna 152 and DIGA nose to nose for the obligatory photographs and selfies. Then I said farewell to Tomasz, with every intention of meeting him again in the future, before he set off to fly back to Fort Myers.

RotorTech kindly helped Lavinia and I clean DIGA, giving her a thorough washing using their ladders, hoses and cleaning materials, while Robin dealt with the final day's photographs in the office. I was feeling both jubilant and despondent: the end of a big, long mission was always so brutally short in my experience. I was of course very happy that we were all back safely, but I was always sad to stop and to part company with friends, and of course DIGA. It would take time to assimilate the scale of our achievement.

Robin and I separated our personal gear from DIGA and were reunited with our suitcases. We packed the hire car and took Robin round to friends of her mum's where she was going to stay. Before we knew it, Frank and Janet had kindly plied us with a couple of beers and snacks but it was getting dark and it was time to say goodbye to Robin and find our hotel. The rest could wait until the following day: I was ready for my bed!

My next steps were clearly laid out: get DIGA home and back working for *Helicopter Services*; escape the 'mission bubble' blues which I knew I would sink into; thank people; process the beautiful pictures; and tell the story. People were already asking me what I would do next but I was going to leave any announcement of an encore until I knew what it was myself!

On the Monday, I supported Paul at *RotorTech*, and we worked hard all day to disassemble DIGA back into her major parts and prepare them for homebound shipping. In fact, we only had a few items to tidy up on Tuesday morning and the job was complete. I visited *ATC* where Dana Bunch, the *FAA* officer, was happy to see me back safely and duly stamped all my *FAI* paperwork. I also found time to attend to my final administrative chores and close my journey diary. Eddie of *G.A.S.E.* put out his final Facebook post and social media messages went back and forth.

John and Sasha Pattinson of *Aircovers* had encouraged me to visit them at their stand at the *Helicopter Association International Heli-Expo* being held in Atlanta. So, on Wednesday, Lavinia and I flew from warm West Palm Beach to freezing Atlanta for the day to go and look around the huge celebration and exhibition of all things vertical flight. We bumped into Raphael Audi of *HBR*, and the ebullient Sergio Nuño with Sandra of *Arrayán Aeromar Helicópteros* and generally had a good social day. I was also able to personally thank both Tim Tucker and Kurt Robinson, CEO of *Robinson Helicopter Company*, for all their assistance.

On Thursday morning, I went to check with Art and Paul that everything was in order for DIGA's shipping back to *HQ Aviation*, settle up and thank *RotorTech*, before Lavinia and I drove to Miami Airport for our flight to the UK.

Back home, I visited *Helicopter Services* in their new hangar at White Waltham and returned Thingy to Leon for safe keeping. Leon finally explained the origins of Thingy who was made for him by a young boy, who had later died of cancer at the age of six. He had been a courageous young person who had carried a bowl around with him as his chemotherapy kept making him sick. He had wanted to be a pilot when he grew up, so Leon used to take him flying. Leon told me that he had promised that boy that Thingy would always fly and look after anyone with whom he flew. Thingy had become a very special inspiration to Leon and taught him to never, ever give up. He confided in me that he had never shared this story with anyone before, but I knew why he had given me Thingy, and I felt truly humbled to be considered a special friend. Thingy had certainly done his job for *Three Journeys Round.*

I had travelled with Robin for 91 days, landing in 23 countries to complete our journey of about 17,500 nautical miles around Latin America. The scenery had been absolutely breathtaking throughout. South America was a beautiful continent of big contrasts: forests and deserts, flat and mountainous, wet and dry, windy and calm. The constant had been the incredible generosity and hospitality of everyone we were privileged to encounter.

I started to wrap up the third journey website celebration materials, plan a photographic coffee table book and start structuring a book of my travels. I was in contact with James Ketchell too as he made final preparations for his solo gyrocopter expedition departure and I joined hundreds of supporters to send him off on Sunday 31st March when he took off from Popham airfield to fly around the world. Once

DIGA had been reassembled by David and his crew, on 15th May, I flew her into White Waltham for the first time.

The main purpose of my three journeys was to raise the profile of 'a better planet through sustainable development'. I was gratified by the number of people I did meet around the world who understood the issues and I felt that the momentum for applying the *UN Sustainable Development Goals* was growing.

I believe that humanity can cope with the complexity of the change but the developed countries need much bolder leaders to inspire and motivate. Meaningful action by governments is required now. Greta Thunberg, a young Swedish environmental activist on climate change, hit the nail on the head when she said that the time for talking was over.

With every act, purchase and vote, we individually choose what kind of world we want to live in. Capitalism needs to understand that Nature is not free and we need to act accordingly to live sustainably.

My objective was also to have an adventure. I was privileged to have completed three amazing journeys by helicopter, flying a total of 122,500 kilometres in 684 hours, over 285 journey days, landing in 86 countries. It was the stuff of dreams really.

I had the good fortune to witness much of the world's geography at first hand, visiting locations by helicopter that very few people ever do. I cannot believe I have flown across the Sahara twice, Arabia once, up the Amazon River, over the Greenland ice cap, low-level across the Okavango, Moxos Plains and Pantanal, past Torres del Paine, around volcanoes, and so much more. I felt earthquakes, caught Dengue fever, have been up close and personal with the gorillas of Virunga National Park, the cheetahs of Otjiwarongo and have met literally thousands of wonderful people.

On 16th May 2019, I was extremely proud to be awarded the Britannia Trophy for my *Three Journeys Round* project by the *Royal Aero Club of Great Britain*, witnessed by my flying mentor, Leon Smith and my wife, Lavinia. I honestly couldn't have done any of this without either of them. The award was really also a dedication to all my supporters and sponsors who made the project possible: to my sustainable development mentor, Nigel Winser; my crew members; our families and friends; and to so many other incredible people for their understanding, encouragement, help and kindness along the way.

Peter Wilson

Fellow of the Royal Geographical Society,
International Member of The Explorers Club NY,
Fellow of the Institution of Mechanical Engineers,
Helicopter Pilot

I learned to fly in 1998 and have been a weekend instructor for much of that time. Flying round the UK in 2004 and rubbing shoulders with friends doing crazy things like climbing Mount Everest or cycling round the world gave me an idea to do something epic. I wanted an adventure by helicopter with a purpose.

A serendipitous meeting while flying in Scotland led to the development of a working relationship with Nigel Winser who became my mentor for sustainable development. I was struck by the arguments for living within Earth's means and doing something to raise awareness of the United Nation's Sustainable Development Goals. It also made a lot of sense to fundraise for two charities that champion the rights and choices of children, women and the incapacitated.

www.threejourneysround.com